IMAGINING OTHERWISE

Imagining Otherwise

HOW READERS HELP TO WRITE NINETEENTH-CENTURY NOVELS

DEBRA GETTELMAN

PRINCETON UNIVERSITY PRESS

PRINCETON & OXFORD

Published by Princeton University Press
41 William Street, Princeton, New Jersey 08540
99 Banbury Road, Oxford OX2 6JX

press.princeton.edu

All Rights Reserved

ISBN 9780691260419
ISBN (pbk.) 9780691260426
ISBN (e-book) 9780691260457

British Library Cataloging-in-Publication Data is available

Editorial: Anne Savarese and James Collier
Production Editorial: Sara Lerner
Cover Design: Katie Osborne
Production: Lauren Reese
Publicity: William Pagdatoon
Copyeditor: Cathryn Slovensky

Cover Credit: Vincent van Gogh, *L'Arlésienne: Madame Joseph-Michel Ginoux (Marie Julien, 1848–1911)*, oil on canvas. Bequest of Sam A. Lewisohn, 1951 / The Metropolitan Museum of Art

This book has been composed in Arno

10 9 8 7 6 5 4 3 2 1

For my family

CONTENTS

ACKNOWLEDGMENTS

THIS BOOK exists because of generous readers who imagined it otherwise.

The book was born under a lucky star: the direction of Elaine Scarry, Philip Fisher, and Leah Price, whose wisdom is hopefully still evident in its pages. I would *still* be imagining its sentences otherwise were it not for my extraordinary writing group, Anna Henchman, Maia McAleavey, and Aeron Hunt, whose years of insight and encouragement are incalculably diffused throughout the book's pages. Thanks also to Sophie Gee for making brilliant cameos at the right moment.

My colleagues at Holy Cross believed in me and this book far beyond my deserts: Shawn Maurer, ideal mentor, friend, and everything else; Jonathan Mulrooney and Paige Reynolds, who have kept me sane, honest, laughing, and loving literature; and Melissa Schoenberger, who makes me optimistic. Thanks to Christine Coch for many shared adventures. I am grateful to my students, particularly those whose theses I advised or were in seminars and upper-level classes I taught. They pushed me to think harder and made doing so a thrill.

My fellow readers of Victorian novels are the real reason I write. John Plotz, as mentor, editor, and enthusiast, has made both my writing and being a Victorianist better. I am grateful for memorable conversations with and generous writing feedback from too many other Victorianists to name, but among them are Rachel Ablow, Elaine Auyong, Rosemarie Bodenheimer, Aviva Briefel, Jim Buzard, Nicholas Dames, Erik Gray, Michele Martinez, Andrew Miller, Adela Pinch, Ann Rowland, Matt Rubery, Talia Schaffer, the members of the Northeast Victorian Studies Association, the regulars at the Mahindra Center's Victorian Literature and Culture seminar, and Boston Writing Group members, especially Carolyn Betensky, Laura Green, Martha Vicinus, and Jade Werner. Audrey Jaffe and Mary Ann O'Farrell have made me proud to be a close reader with them. My thanks go also to the numerous audiences who listened and asked formative questions.

Especially at this moment in the humanities, I am grateful to have had so much institutional support. Generous grants from Harvard University, the

Whiting Foundation, and especially the College of the Holy Cross gave me time to write. Tamar Brown, Alicia Hansen, and Rebecca Mead shared their research expertise with me. Anne Savarese patiently supported this project and, with her expert team, brought it to fruition. Three generous readers for Princeton University Press proved how much readers can improve what an author imagines. Cathy Slovensky made the manuscript so much better.

Friends, colleagues, and their children made the years of writing joy-filled. In addition to those named above are Tamar Brown, Amy Kidd, Anne Leonard, Maile Meloy, Meryl Perlman, Jason Puskar and Erin O'Donnell, Alison Syme, and many fellow Radcliffe, Graham & Parks, and Fayerweather parents, especially Angela Chang, Johanna Lahdenranta, and Melissa Feuerstein. Stephanie Smith deserves more thanks than I ever let her know.

This book is dedicated to my family, from my inspiring grandparents to my inspiriting children, who have given me the gift of their unconditional support. Judy and Gary Pasquinelli, Betsy and Bob Koelzer, and all my cousins, in-laws, and their children have made family meaningful and joyful. Andrew, Francesca, Fiona, and Natalie Gettelman have brightened our lives with their Colorado sunshine. My profoundest debt is to Nancy Gettelman and Alan Gettelman, my indefatigable parents, whose never-ending belief and support made it possible for me to build a whole life out of loving to read long books. If I have words for Sophie Koelzer and Beatrice Koelzer, they are Elizabeth Barrett Browning's (though they wouldn't let me name our cocker spaniel Flush). I love you "to the depth and breadth and height / my soul can reach, when feeling out of sight / for the ends of being and ideal grace." And from the first moment of graduate school to the last copyedit, I have been buoyed by Rob Koelzer, to whom (to paraphrase from *Middlemarch*) I am bound by a love stronger than anything I could have imagined.

Robert Buss's *Dickens's Dream* is reproduced courtesy of the Charles Dickens Museum, London. Parts of the introduction are drawn from "The Victorian Novel and Its Readers," in *The Oxford Handbook of the Victorian Novel*, edited by Lisa Rodensky (Oxford: Oxford University Press, 2013), 111–28; and "'Those Who Idle Over Novels': Victorian Critics and Post-Romantic Readers," in *A Return to the Common Reader: Print Culture and the Novel, 1850–1900*, edited by Beth Palmer and Adelene Buckland (Farnham, Surrey, England: Ashgate, 2011), 55–68. An earlier version of chapter 3 appeared as "Reading Ahead in George Eliot" in *Novel: A Forum on Fiction* 39, no. 1 (Fall 2005): 25–47. Copyright 2005, *Novel*, Inc. All rights reserved. Used by permission of the publisher, Duke University Press.

IMAGINING OTHERWISE

Imagining Readers

(Another open secret that everyone knows and no one wants to: the immense
amount of daydreaming that accompanies the ordinary reading of a novel.)

—D. A. MILLER, *THE NOVEL AND THE POLICE*

It may seem strange, but it is the fact, that the ordinary vulgar vision of which
Mr Casaubon suspected him—namely, that Dorothea might become a widow,
and that the interest he had established in her mind might turn into acceptance
of him as a husband—had no tempting, arresting power over him; he did not
live in the scenery of such an event, and follow it out, as we all do with that
imagined "otherwise" which is our practical heaven.

—GEORGE ELIOT, *MIDDLEMARCH*

ANYONE WHO has ever read a novel knows that the images that form in a
reader's mind in the course of reading contain more than the fictional characters and events as they are described by the author. In *The Novel and the Police*
(1988), D. A. Miller suggests that literary critics are reluctant to admit this
"open secret," which he embeds in a footnote, in parentheses: "(Another open
secret that everyone knows and no one wants to: the immense amount of
daydreaming that accompanies the ordinary reading of a novel.)"[1] Both writers and readers recognize that such "daydreaming" can take innumerable
forms, from "stopping as you read . . . because of a flow of ideas, stimuli, associations," as Roland Barthes describes, to "plung[ing] into the tale in our
own person," in Robert Louis Stevenson's words.[2] Sometimes an author directs readers to visualize on their own: to "make up from bare hints dropped
here and there," as Virginia Woolf puts it,[3] or to picture a real-life beloved in

the place of a fictional character, as numerous novelists from Laurence Sterne to Wilkie Collins do. In these varied ways, readers imagine things other than the words on the page while reading a novel. Novelists, critics, and readers know how "ordinary" such imagining is (a word both Miller and George Eliot use in the epigraphs above), but as Miller implies, literary criticism as a discipline lacks productive ways of talking about this unscripted imagining. Such acts of imagining otherwise—imagining initiated in the reader's mind, of things *other* than the words on the page—are the subject of this book.

Like Miller, Eliot acknowledges how continually imaginative we are as beings, no less while we read novels. In *Middlemarch* (1871–72), referring to Will Ladislaw's unusual *lack* of such fantasies, Eliot expresses her characteristic mix of sympathy and critique for what "we all do" in inventing our own more desirable alternatives to what is. She suggests we live in thrall to the "tempting, arresting" "scenery" of our own imaginings, to a point that can comprise an entire "imagined 'otherwise' which is our practical heaven."[4] Unfortunately for Eliot, she found her own readers engaged in imagining her novels "otherwise," wishing for the realist worlds she portrays to be more idealized. She satirizes this readerly desire for the fictional world to be "just what we like" within the realist manifesto that interrupts her novel *Adam Bede* (1859).[5] In fact, Eliot belongs to a host of nineteenth-century British novelists who engage with how readers bring their own continuations, speculations, and substitutions to bear on fictional worlds an author has created.[6] As the numbers of both novels and readers—and with them, the novel's cultural presence—grew exponentially during the nineteenth century, authors like Charles Dickens, Anthony Trollope, Thomas Hardy, and others were characterizing novel readers in letters, prefaces, and within their novels as engaged in an "immense amount" of their own imagining.

Densely imagined, with highly directive narrators, Victorian realist novels have long been thought to depict self-contained worlds that were brought into being solely by their authors. We have missed how many of these writers engage reader-initiated imagining in constructing their novel-worlds.[7] At times, these directive writers attempt to limit independent invention. In *Little Dorrit* (1857), Dickens instructs "patience" as he fends off readers of his serially published novels, who formed their own versions of the narrative between installments. He writes about Mr. Merdle's strange behavior, "Had he that deep-seated recondite complaint, and did any doctor find it out? Patience."[8] At other times, however, these writers openly appeal to the universal tendency to fill out the "scenery" of imagined alternatives as a potentially enriching part of novel reading. In *Adam Bede*, Eliot enlists the reader's private store of images to personalize a scene of Adam and Dinah falling in love: "That is a simple scene, reader. But it is almost certain that you, too, have been in love" (537). Though known for their intrusive or didactic narrative voices, these novelists were fully alive to the aesthetic possibilities generated by independent minds.

Novel readers always have and always will form images of their own while reading novels, while the discipline of literary criticism has relegated and continues to relegate readers' independent imaginations. In the nineteenth century, novelists sought to incorporate and make use of imaginative acts that occur within readers' minds, outside of a novel's pages, to an unprecedented extent. Despite long-standing critical efforts to exclude readers' imaginations from both criticism and the classroom, identifying an appreciation for the reader's imagination within the very novels that literary studies has made canonical underscores how inextricable readers' free-floating imaginations are from literary history. I concentrate on the period from the 1850s through the 1870s, when the triple-decker novel increasingly codified into formulas of plot, character, and description. Novelists like Dickens and Eliot were concerned with how ubiquitous novel reading was forcing readers' imaginations into conventional paths. As the novel began to gain literary prestige, a host of novelists and critics began to recognize that the mixed activity of reading, inventing, and daydreaming could be engaged in aesthetically constructing a novel's world in a more capacious way.[9] Although they are known for meticulous efforts to manage readers' affects and expectations, nineteenth-century realist authors ceded authorial control for the sake of capturing authentic readerly experience in their novels. In fact, over the course of the nineteenth century the novel became an aesthetically elevated form not by eschewing the common reader's tendency to imagine alternatives but by increasingly using syntax and prose style to engage that tendency all the more.

The Critical Problem of Readers' Minds

The novel reader's imagination has long gotten a bad rap. We lack productive models to account for the creative, unscripted work the novel reader's imagination does when it is not strictly envisioning the described fictional world.

From the novel's early history and continuing subtly into recent literary criticism, readers' creative imaginations—especially those of female readers—have regularly been dismissed as either too weak or too powerful. The eighteenth-century rhetoric about novel readers' minds is well known: on the one hand, overly weak imaginations lead to passive absorption or clichéd and imitative action. Writing in 1817, Coleridge chides "the devotees of the circulating libraries" for their supposed indulgence in a weak form of imagining: "I dare not compliment their pass-time, or rather kill-time, with the name of reading. Call it rather a sort of beggarly Day-dreaming, during which the mind of the dreamer furnishes for itself nothing but laziness, and a little mawkish sensibility."[10] On the other hand, eighteenth-century antinovel critics worried about powerful imaginations, which were supposed to be dangerously erotic and potentially subversive. It is striking that early critics of the novel assumed that readerly imagining would be stimulated in one of these two directions and spill over beyond the fictional world as it is described in the text. As my first chapter examines, recent critics have been belying these myths of a naive, uncritical, eroticized female novel reader by portraying women's novel reading as an intellectually rigorous exercise.[11] Recasting novel reading as actively interpretive and critical, however, has had the effect of denying, rather than reclaiming, the ways that novel reading can stimulate a productively creative play of mind.

Two hundred-plus years on, the modern discipline of literary criticism has subtly continued to characterize the reader's imagination as, on the one hand, too powerful. With New Criticism, English developed into an academic discipline in the early twentieth century by suppressing the reader's personal associations, affects, and imaginative excursions—by characterizing these subjective additions as disruptive, anti-academic forces that needed to be reined in. Q. D. Leavis reacted against the practices of ordinary Victorian readers and dismissed their reading as motivated by affect and imagination rather than aesthetic analysis, by "the voluptuous day-dream instead of the dispassionate narration of a complicated plot."[12] As impersonalizing protocols took over literary criticism, I. A. Richards even coined a technical-sounding term ("mnemonic irrelevances") for the "irrelevant personal associations" that interfere with the proper practice of criticism. What followed was a long history, from New Criticism to surface reading, of critical approaches devoted to minimizing the free associations that "common" readers bring to bear on a text.[13] Even today, after Deidre Lynch has shown how foundational affective labor is to literary study, lively debate about "surface," "distant," and other critical modes of reading has continued to devalue and minimize the unscientific subjectivity inherent in professional methods of literary interpretation. For instance, Sharon Marcus and Stephen Best, in their 2009 introduction to the practice they call "surface reading," describe how a critic should try "to correct for her critical subjectivity" and seek "to occupy a paradoxical space of minimal critical agency."[14]

By contrast, within Victorian and novel studies, readers' imaginations have been portrayed as almost too compliant with a text, another form of weak imagination. As reader-response criticism gained prominence in the 1970s with the work of Wolfgang Iser, literary texts were seen as constructing and addressing an "implied" reader who passively thinks as a directive author wills. Under the influence of Michel Foucault in the 1980s and 1990s, Victorian novels especially appeared to envision the reader's unresisting submission to the text. Garrett Stewart's *Dear Reader: The Conscripted Audience in Nineteenth-Century British Fiction* (1996) epitomizes this view of authors from Jane Austen to Oscar Wilde directing the reader's sympathies, schooling the reader's morals, and training the reader's cognitive processes through "the relentless micromanagement of reaction" enacted in direct address and analogous scenes of reading.[15] The joint legacies of reader-response criticism and a "hermeneutics of suspicion" have arguably prevented us from seeing a Victorian novel's addressed "reader" constructed as an independent figure, one who is capable of imagining as freely as some of the real readers these novelists encountered. Most recently, a wealth of interdisciplinary studies has argued that readers follow instructions in showing how novelists draw on a scientific understanding of cognitive processes in order to evoke discrete effects.[16] In *Dreaming by the Book* (1999), Elaine Scarry uses contemporary research about perception in order to identify ways that literary authors instruct their readers in the act of imagining so that the reader's visualized images have the solidity of actual perception. While this approach identifies how space is made within fiction for the reader's faculties, we have not yet accounted for ways readers' imaginations act independently: how they add to and replace what an author describes, and participate in ways that are unscripted or even directly contradict what is happening in the novel. In fact, recent studies of the shifting levels of consciousness that operate in reading fiction has further helped us understand—and see that Victorian writers understood—how readers pay partial or discontinuous attention to their books.[17] We need a theoretical model to account for a "reader" implied in the text whose imagination is independent of the author's control, whose reader-initiated additions, such as daydreaming, identifying, conjecturing, and making comparisons with real life, are neither dictated nor included but left room for in works of fiction.

Whether it is even possible to find evidence of readers' imaginations—and, if so, which readers' imaginations—has long been a topic of debate among historians of reading who, until recently, largely sought out reading as a material and social, rather than psychological, phenomenon. The mental experience of the individual reader has long been "the ever-elusive holy grail of the historian of reading," as Heather Jackson puts it.[18] Victorian material culture is filled with artifacts, narratives, and dramas spun off of freshly published fiction that give some indication of how readers added imaginatively to authored fictional worlds.[19] What we have yet to recover fully is how authors at the time *responded* to the historical reading habits we have been able to map. At times with the market in mind, novelists tried to anticipate the tastes and tendencies of readers in aggregate, even if only by recognizing the unpredictability of readers' minds. "'Tis an incalculable animal the general Reader!," George Henry Lewes wrote to Eliot's publishing house about sales of the early books of *Middlemarch*, which he hoped would "in time haul in the general public."[20]

That the novel genre prompts readers to imagine possibilities for alternative *plots* has been repeatedly discussed as one of the defining features of the genre. John Plotz describes how the novel as a form generates an extraordinary number of possible outcomes, keeps the reader in a state of "ongoing uncertainty," and ultimately, in a kind of letdown, realizes only one of many possible paths.[21] More recently, counterfactual acts of imagining that are explicitly carried out in literary texts have gained broad currency as constructions that raise moral, philosophic, and epistemological questions.[22] In Andrew H. Miller's work on unled lives, a character's "optative" mode of thinking about how else his or her own life might have turned out functions to highlight consequential moral choices.[23] Other critics of nineteenth-century literature have identified a variety of ways in which the period's writers use counterfactual propositions, seeing them as a marker of the provisionality, contingency, and interest in probability that pervade Victorian thinking, particularly scientific thinking.[24]

Literary studies has had fewer concrete ways of describing how readers independently imagine what Eliot calls "the *scenery* of . . . an event," by which she means the images readers generate, not only narrative outcomes they project. Initially in the nineteenth century, alternative plotting preoccupied writers, because they knew plotting preoccupied readers: my first chapter focuses on the alternative possible endings that Austen includes within half of her finished novels; my second chapter shows Dickens leaning in to his readers' confusion about how his multiplot novels fit together and, counterintuitively, seeking to prolong this uncomfortable uncertainty in constructing *Little Dorrit*. Yet a subtle trajectory emerges over the nineteenth century, as psychological theories develop in depth and the novel gains prestige as an art form, in which authors increasingly prompt readers to the capacious imagining of alternative images rather than the formulaic prediction of events; moreover, these authors increasingly do so through syntactic means. The particular novels I examine stand out for how visibly they show authors grappling with the challenge of engaging readers' independent minds by using the formal elements that make up the novel, both structurally and stylistically. Eliot, whose career-long frustrations with plot-obsessed readers are well known, makes direct appeals to readers to use their power of memory in *Adam Bede* before embedding the imagining of alternative images in the grammar of her last two novels. In *Middlemarch*, it is syntax—the frequent use of negation—that stimulates the reader to imagine more than one possibility for the fictional world nearly at the same time. As I show, reading such a novel consequently feels layered, three-dimensional, and what we tend to call "literary."

The discipline of literary studies continues to lack a term or terms to define those moments in a novel when an author acknowledges the unscripted, independent imagination that "accompanies the ordinary reading of a novel." Robyn Warhol's concept of "disnarration" applies to what the *author* describes as not happening, something not belonging to the realized fictional world.[25] Ellipsis describes a moment in a text when a narrator claims to leave something to the reader's imagination. But critical discussion of ellipsis tends to stop with the vague phrase that a reader "fills in" those narrative gaps. (With what? I think, when I read that phrase.) We have no technical way of referring to what readers meaningfully invent, envision, and integrate into their experience of the fictional world—which is, after all, infinitely variable and unknowable.

I focus on moments we *can* identify concretely: when novelists render or address readers as independent imaginers who mentally add, associate, and conjure alternatives to the author-created world. Using an array of rhetorical moves, the writers I examine refer to what a reader might imagine other than what is described on the page. They use direct address to invite a reader to summon private memories, use negation to describe what a character does not look like, or depict characters engaged in specific forms of imagining they observed in their readers, like speculation. Alternative imagining is thus recognized in the text and becomes one of the narrator's tools. Like free indirect discourse, description, summarizing a character's thoughts, or using perceptual cues, making space for the many individual acts of imagination in a reader's mind constitutes a valued technique for getting the reader invested in a three-dimensional, realistic imagined world.[26]

What I identify are narrative techniques that can be seen developing along with, and conveying, authors' changing attitudes toward readerly imagining. When Austen's narrator explicitly proposes how else the novel could have ended, or Eliot's narrator directly invites readers to daydream about their own past loves, these novelists anticipate and parry their readers' characteristic imaginative thrusts and pull these external images into the novel's orbit. As case studies, these novels can suggest a more collaborative way of viewing the author-reader relationship than has been typical in literary studies. Henry Jenkins, foundational critic of fan studies, emphasizes the contentious aspect of Michel de Certeau's analogy of reading as a kind of poaching, "an ongoing struggle for possession of the text and for control over its meanings."[27] Nineteenth-century British fiction in particular has been described as exerting a high level of control over the reader's imagination. But control is too simple a formulation. I show how these authors stage both struggle *and* collusion with their readers about the illusion the author has set up, which the reader is participating in creating. They allow us to further develop a dialectical model of novel writing and reading, one that highlights authors' engagement with and dependence on the separate and ongoing imaginative lives of real readers.

Nineteenth-Century Readers, Authors, and Critics

Literary studies is overdue for seeing *nineteenth-century* readers' imaginations in a different light.[28] Victorian studies of reading have repeatedly featured dramatic rhetoric from conservative skeptics of the novel about the "vice" or "disease" of novel reading.[29] We have yet to reconcile these negative images with what we know about publication practices like serialization, which gave readers ample time in which to generate narrative possibilities between installments.[30] In other words, we have yet to understand how present and determining the active imaginations of readers were for nineteenth-century British authors, for a variety of material, cultural, and intellectual reasons—sometimes present as an irritating reality but also as a desirable aid in reading fiction.

Nineteenth-century anxieties about the freedom with which the public could read novels have been well traversed.[31] What the commercial growth of the fiction market also heightened was a sense of imaginative entitlement toward the fictional worlds readers encountered. As Ian Duncan has suggested in writing about the popularity of the Waverley Novels in the early nineteenth century, the novel as a genre came into existence not because of patronage but because there was an increasingly large audience who would in some form or another pay to read it. Thus, he says, "a novel *belongs* to the market and the reading public convened there" and "lays itself open to imaginative appropriation by different communities and interests and for divergent intentions."[32]

While we cannot reconstruct what any individual reader, at any time, pictures while reading *Jane Eyre* (1847), as Duncan suggests, we can trace some subjective attitudes toward novels and speculate about why these attitudes are particularly present in a given historical moment. Across a range of both material and imaginative experiences that the nineteenth-century reading public commonly had with novels—from borrowing circulating library books to resisting unhappy endings—we find an attitude repeated in the way that readers encountered fiction and in how authors and critics thought they ought to approach it. Concerns about quixotic readers simply imitating what they read gave way to depictions of readers having their own subjectivities. Those subjectivities were interdependent with the fiction they read, resulting in a complex, imaginative intermingling.

The intermingling of novels with daily life began on a physical level, with innovations in publishing and book distribution, which fostered a dynamic in which novels moved physically and psychically in and out of the flow of readers' daily lives. For example, the high cost of books meant that from the eighteenth century onward, an increasing number of readers paid an annual fee to borrow, rather than buy, their books from subscription libraries. Mudie's Select Library provided more middle-class readers with the books they read than any other venue did between its founding in 1842 and the end of the century.[33] Mudie's encouraged what was, for them, a profitable dynamic of fiction cycling in and out of the Victorian household. Typical references to Mudie's in print took forms that emphasized the sense of books in constant motion—the "box from Mudie's," the vans coming and going to and from New Oxford Street—while Mudie's itself advertised that it offered "a constant succession of the principal books of the season."[34] The period's other commercially successful innovation in book distribution, W. H. Smith's bookstalls in railway terminals, marketed novels as something one read in the temporal and physical space between destinations. W. H. Smith's bookstalls similarly, if more subtly, conveyed a sense of fiction as something that traveled physically as well as psychologically throughout Victorian life.

Publication in parts, one of the most recognized publishing trends that made fiction more accessible in the nineteenth century, meant that novels intermingled creatively in readers' lives as well. Periodicals and serials literally circulated in and out of a reader's daily, weekly, or monthly experience; during the temporal gaps between installments, readers could think, talk, and read about a number of fictional worlds even as they were going about their own lives.[35] In a lecture published in 1870, Trollope claims to speak for "everyone from the Prime Minister down to the last appointed scullery maid" in describing how novels of all kinds have become integrated into readers' minds until, "Our memories are laden with the stories which we read, with the plots which are unravelled *for us*, and with the characters which are drawn *for us*."[36] As Trollope intimates, a sense that fiction was available for imaginative appropriation drew strength from numbers, from the very wealth of fiction that was being published for all kinds and classes of readers. According to Trollope, readers infused everyday experience with the contents of novels and projected their real experiences into those works of fiction.

This participatory way of viewing literary reading was not new, but did gain strength with the expansion of novel reading in the nineteenth century. Deidre Lynch has shown meticulously how literature became "something to be taken personally by definition" beginning in the late eighteenth century.[37] Lynch shows how, in the early nineteenth century, worshipped authors and grateful readers had clearly defined, hierarchical roles to play. By the mid-nineteenth century, however, the personalization of literary reading had developed, along with the growth of novel readership, to the point that authors regularly grappled with readers, like the one who wrote to ask Eliot "not [to] be angry with me for having ventured to finish the novel in my own way."[38] Novelists can be seen guiding readers within their novels in ways that strikingly accord with the tendencies— especially the irksome tendencies—of real nineteenth-century readers. Eliot complained in a letter to her publisher about "that infinite stupidity of readers who are always substituting their crammed notions of what ought to have been felt for any attempt to recall truly what they themselves have felt under like circumstances."[39] Within her novels, she models wrongheaded imagining through characters who daydream egoistically about their own futures, while the narrator invites the novel's addressed reader to compare a fictional scene with his or her own poignant, real-life experiences. Such alignments between the tendencies of real and constructed readers may be found in many periods. In using formalist strategies, we can recover a historicized understanding of the "reader" whom novels address, which would otherwise remain unimaginable.

Thus, nineteenth-century British novelists offer a guide to recasting novel reading as a shared imaginative exercise, in which the allegedly separate functions of author and reader overlap, sometimes collaboratively and sometimes in a thorny way. Even within the same essay, nineteenth-century authors can alternately idealize and express frustration with novel reading as "the exercise of a generous imaginativeness," in Hardy's words. Hardy was especially aware of readers' capacity to shape a work of fiction to their own specifications, for good and ill. In "The Profitable Reading of Fiction," he rails against "mentally and morally warped" readers for misinterpreting his frank critiques of conventional morality—a reception that eventually caused him to give up writing fiction. Yet in the same essay, he describes a quite different and desirable outcome that can result from the reader's absorbing, interpreting, and mentally adding to the novel's pages. The aim of reading for pleasure, he says,

> should be the exercise of a generous imaginativeness, which shall find in a tale not only all that was put there by the author, put he it never so awkwardly, but which shall find there what was never inserted by him, never foreseen, never contemplated. Sometimes these additions which are woven around a work of fiction by the intensive [sic] power of the reader's own imagination are the finest parts of the scenery.[40]

Hardy describes the process of reading as completing the novel: the fictional world is cocreated, albeit sometimes "awkwardly," by the author and by mental images the work sparks in the reader's mind. The sense of a reader's determining agency is similarly present for Stevenson, who writes in "A Gossip on Romance," "Something happens as we desire it to happen to ourselves; some situation that we have long dallied with in fancy, is realized in the story with enticing and appropriate details. Then we push the hero aside; then we plunge into the tale in our own person . . . and then, and then only, do we say we have been reading a romance."[41] For Stevenson the figurative waywardness that the story encourages in the reader's mind ("we push the hero *aside*") is crucial to transforming a simple story into a particular aesthetic form, romance. What Hardy and Stevenson describe is how absorption in a book is a stimulus to creativity.

The visualizing that Hardy and Stevenson describe, however, differs from a form of readerly creativity, anticipating plot, which became a nuisance for nineteenth-century authors of long and often serialized novels. Hardy describes the reader's imagination adding to the novel's "scenery" and images "woven around" the original tale adding to its artistry; Stevenson refers to "enticing and appropriate details" fleshing out a situation the reader has more casually "dallied with" in fantasy. Novelists and critics from the time repeatedly extol the pleasures of engaging deeply in a novel by fleshing out its images, not its sequence of events. One Victorian reviewer criticizes Dickens for not offering this means of engagement: "Mr Dickens never trusts to a vigorous sketch, or a few characteristic touches; he accomplishes his purpose by minute description and copious dialogue, and leaves no work to the imagination of the reader."[42] Mid-Victorian critics repeatedly judge novels based on how hospitably they invite the reader's separate imagination to add to the fictional world. A critic finding fault with the newest sensational fiction in 1860 uses similar terms to praise earlier novelists like Austen:

> Nothing indeed is ever felt in the highest spirit of art, which is altogether real. Something must always be left for the reader's imagination to supply; and imitation ceases to please when it assumes reality and rejects the aid of that imagination which is the surest way of obtaining sympathy. [. . .] The imagination does the work to which it is invited, and it does it best when most left to itself.[43]

Repeatedly, nineteenth-century novelists and critics describe an author's imagined world as incomplete, as requiring the "aid" or "additions" (in Hardy's term) of a reader's imagination, which emphatically acts "best when most left to itself." Some of these critics were also expressing concerns about the mind-lessness of reading sensation novels and an increasing body of less educated readers who, as Collins put it, have yet to become attentive to "the delicacies and subtleties of literary art."[44] Thus, critics at the time can be found distinguishing literary quality (novels that attain "the highest spirit of art") from those that do not on the basis of the aesthetic invention that a novel stimulates in the reader's mind. "For the full enjoyment of fiction," another critic outlined in 1853, "the imagination must be in a productive mood; the figures then start into life, and the various aspects of nature flit through the mind, forming a background to the living scene."[45] Even before the sensation novel heightened the perceived need to shield "literary" fiction from the encroachment of mindless, "popular" reading, Victorian critics were making such distinctions based not on a work's intrinsic qualities but on the nature of the reading experiences the work induced. In doing so, these critics were also articulating in detail numerous ways the creative, "productive" exercise of the reader's autonomous imagination enhances novel reading.[46]

For some of the period's most influential and seemingly controlling novelists and critics, then, the reader's fertile imagination was an important resource, full of potential, that could add literary, aesthetic layers to the novel-world. Victorian authors who were concerned about reading narrowly for *the* plot encourage readers in various ways within their novels to read capaciously for the plots or the scenery. These novelists use formal structures that invite readers to construct a multiplicity of mental images that both are and are not part of the realized novel-world. They do so pedagogically, trying to engender a more rigorous, analytical use of imagination than narrativizing or wish-fulfilling fantasies. They figure the reader who imagines otherwise as hyperliterate and hyperaware, able to navigate among layers and weigh the feasibility of different options. Having the mental flexibility and patience to discern probabilities and make choices are laid out as vital skills for, as well as effects of, reading complex realist fiction. Eliot in particular was well versed in current theories about the independent, unconscious, and uncontrollable nature of imagination. She and other novelists reacted with concern to how ubiquitous novel reading seemed to be schooling readers' imaginations to take prescribed, linear forms—forms that did not reflect what either imagination or real life is like, and thinned out a novel's imaginative world. Moreover, realist authors knew that reading their novels was not always a pleasurable experience. Serial publication has largely been seen as creating pleasurable opportunities to exercise imagination, but Victorian novelists were aware of readers' dissatisfaction with a novel's slow progress, prosaic outcome, or "repulsive" characters, as they worked to direct readers away from purely comfortable forms of imagining. The discomfort inherent in reading a realistic novel is one we will see in numerous forms throughout nineteenth-century fiction.

For these reasons the book takes a deep dive into Eliot, who has long been seen as an extreme case of the bossy, didactic Victorian narrative voice that intrudes on the reader's imagining in order to control it. Deeply aware of and anxious about her audience, Eliot often prompts readers' personal imagining, for the professed aim of realist fiction to capture truthful experience is at stake when these authors seek to enlist some portion of the reader's private fantasy life within the realm of the novel itself.[47] Many definitions of "realism" or realist art include a sense of representational depth: what is depicted on the surface, and known to be fictional, is a means of accessing further layers of experience that are not fictional.[48] In prompting readers to form a continuous multiplicity of images, rather than a single, static image, Eliot develops the lifelike, three-dimensional depth of the fictional world. In her essay "The Natural History of German Life," Eliot contrasts the effect of one-dimensional "generalization" with the expansive effect of "a picture of human life":

> The greatest benefit we owe to the artist, whether painter, poet, or novelist, is the extension of our sympathies. Appeals founded on generalizations and statistics require a sympathy ready-made, a moral sentiment already in activity; but a picture of human life such as a great artist can give, surprises even the trivial and the selfish into that attention to what is a part from themselves, which may be called the raw material of moral sentiment.[49]

Eliot's preoccupation with expanding an audience's imaginative capacities beyond the "ready-made" informs her entire novelistic career. For Victorian realist novelists generally, as we know, moral good and aesthetic appreciation are in-terdependent. In Eliot's description of *how* aesthetic feeling results in moral sentiment, art causes one to "attend to what is apart from themselves," or makes a recipient's gaze more panoramic or multidimensional, as opposed to the one-note, narrow view of the "trivial" or "selfish" person. In other words, carrying out the social and moral values of Victorian fiction depends on expanding the reader's capacity for imagining several alternatives at the same time.

In tracing how, as the nineteenth century progresses, novels increasingly seek to incorporate the reader's independent imagining into their formal con-struction, *Imagining Otherwise* ultimately offers an alternative literary-historical narrative, and one that may be counterintuitive. Novelists writing in the early twentieth century are usually associated with expecting readers to envision more than what is directly represented by the words on a novel's pages, to do what Virginia Woolf calls "the reader's part in making up from bare hints dropped here and there."[50] I show how nineteenth-century novelists use direct address, verb tense, negation, and other rhetorical gestures to encourage the formation of multiple, alternate images that go beyond plot alternatives. They engage aesthetically with their readers' imagining for its capacious resistance to teleological and formulaic narratives, a capaciousness that increasingly marked the novel as an elevated art form. Well before modernism, novelists were treating the reader's capacity for creative projection as having the poten-tial to be a real and intricate part of the increasingly cultivated art of fiction.

This particular historic preoccupation with readerly imagination constitutes a specific dynamic in the history of the novel but also helps to unlock the com-plexity of similar dynamics when they appear in other literary periods. In the social and material revolution taking place now, online accessibility has brought heightened attention to readerly independence, and it has become increasingly difficult to separate institutionally recognized truths from unauthorized con-tributions, as the growing field of fan studies has shown. These questions have become pressing in our classrooms as today's readers and viewers increasingly assess works of art based on their own ease in imagining the represented experi-ences: in other words, how "relatable" the work is.[51] Our twenty-first-century grappling with audience participation, welcome or not, gives insight as well as urgency to understanding how earlier novelists responded to the ways readers insinuated their own imaginations into authored texts.

Imagining Otherwise began as a book about Victorian authors. In teaching Aus-ten's novels, however, I was struck by her elaborating other possible endings and *not* leaving them to the reader to imagine independently. At the time Austen was writing, novel-inspired imagining was seen as frivolous and dangerous, a defining trait of women's reading. Beginning with eighteenth-century commentaries on novel reading, I show a striking shift in how various literary readers describe the realistic pleasures of novel reading in the first quarter of the nineteenth century. In *Sense and Sensibility* (1811), *Mansfield Park* (1814), and *Persuasion* (1818)—all novels in which a heroine suffers intensely from unreciprocated love and is not rewarded with an overly romanticized marriage—Austen uses alternate endings to chide her reader into more rigorous imagining. Austen's appropriation of "serious possibilities" into a component of realism offers a glimpse of a broader trend toward novelists enlisting readers' independent imaginations in aesthetically complex ways.

By midcentury, however, reader-directed imagining—particularly about plots—had become a source of frustration for Victorian novelists. Dickens's own creative process was filled with anxiety and strain, so he sympathized when Victorian readers who engaged in open-ended imagining between serial installments were eager to be done with uncertainty and confusion about the innumerable ways his novels' convoluted plots might come together. However, in *Little Dorrit* Dickens designs an extreme experiment in drawing out the not always pleasurable imaginative process by which a multiplot novel comes together as a whole in the reader's mind. Dickens's awareness of being dependent on readers whose imaginations were subject to the constraints of living in an industrialized, mid-nineteenth-century world reveals a more vulnerable, less controlling side to what is still seen as his "Inimitable" authorship.

Chapter 3 is devoted to Eliot, who was both optimistic about readers' capacity for imagining as an aesthetic resource and frustrated when she saw how this capacity was being used. Within her well-known directive, narratorial presence, Eliot uses a range of strategies at various formal scales to preserve what she knew was the fluid, capacious nature of imagination. From early in her career, Eliot was keenly aware of the conflict between her realist aims and the fantasies of readers who wished for particular plot outcomes. In *Adam Bede*, she tries to direct this fertile readerly invention away from wish fulfillment and enlist it in developing sympathy. Eliot at once chides readers for forecasting their favorite characters' futures and lyrically invites readers to import their own memories into fictional scenes, to imbue her realist fiction with authentic affect. Our ingrained perception of Eliot's controlling narratorial presence, like Dickens's, has concealed her tenuous dependence on readers to imagine her novels as *she* wished.

Eliot's later novels reveal how even at the level of prose style, she was concerned that novelistic conventions were narrowing her readers' imaginative reception of fiction. In *Middlemarch* Eliot experiments with how syntax influences a reader's creative engagement with a novel. Chapter 4 focuses on her incessant use of negation, of referring to things only to identify them as not being part of the novel's realized world. Within Eliot's sentences, what a character does not know, or what a character does not look like, becomes entangled with what does exist within the contours of the fictional world. These habitual negations call upon readers to continually practice developing two or more contradictory images at once. Over the lengthy experience of reading Eliot's prose, the imagining of alternatives becomes a nearly unconscious habit in reader's minds and results in a more capacious, multidimensional, realistic reading practice.

What happens when readers do not *want* to imagine a novel's world is the subject of chapter 5. Eliot expected reflexively that anti-Semitic Victorian readers would feel repulsion toward the Jewish elements of her last novel, *Daniel Deronda* (1876), and within the novel, characters repeatedly repulse others with whom they could identify. This repulsion, rejection, and exclusion both within and toward *Daniel Deronda* puts Eliot's characteristic use of the first-person plural pronoun "we" in an unusual predicament. "We" is an imaginative projection of beings outside the novel who share emotions, behaviors, and experiences, a communitarian ideal threatened by readers unwilling to envision Jewish people as part of "all of us." Eliot's career-long concern with imaginative limitation overlaps with an increasing awareness, in the latter part of the nineteenth century, that novel reading did not necessarily lead to inclusive compassion. Rather, Eliot recognized that novel reading could stimulate virulently negative affective experiences—including discomfiting, though potentially productive, self-reflection.

Nineteenth-century writers imagined the reader's daydreams and distracting thoughts as part of reading an artistic novel, making them part of the history of the novel as an art form. The afterword follows this unscripted imagining forward into twentieth-century literary criticism and the twenty-first-century classroom. Focusing first on Virginia Woolf, the afterword recasts the imperative to envision more than what is directly represented by a novel's words as underwritten by a longer arc of recognition than modernist writers admit. The book ends in the classroom, where recognizing the prehistory of readerly imagining may help us to stimulate more nuanced ways of talking about the readerly imagination and subjectivity that undergirds both students' engagement with literature and, though critics have long sought to deny it, our criticism. Readers today are embracing the increasingly sophisticated creative opportunities that new participatory media affords. Whether in the form of fan fiction or "relatability," the individual, common reader's imagination has become a determining part of our current literary environment. Its checkered and overlooked history deserves a closer look.

1

Jane Austen's Other Endings

READER, SHE could have married him. Or so Jane Austen suggests a few paragraphs before the end of *Sense and Sensibility* (1811), when she describes a way the thwarted marriage plot between Willoughby and Marianne could have worked out, although both are now married to others. Willoughby's elderly cousin, who throws him off as an heir after learning of his improprieties, reinstates him as her heir because he has since married "a woman of character."[1] This gives Willoughby "reason for believing that had he behaved with honor towards Marianne, he might at once have been happy and rich" (379). Though brief, this moment of imagining an alternative plot outcome is part of a pattern in Austen's fiction. Three of Austen's six novels end by including accounts of how the central courtship could have ended differently. Some brief, some prolonged, all three hypothetical endings are placed conspicuously after such an alternative is no longer possible. In *Mansfield Park* (1814), after Henry Crawford has absconded with Maria Rushworth, the narrator spends almost a page describing step-by-step how, eventually, he might have married Fanny Price. In the final moments of *Sense and Sensibility, Mansfield Park,* and *Persuasion* (1818), the novel's course of events becomes a fictional reality that the reader first accepts and then is belatedly asked to imagine as only one possible outcome.

Cultivating possibilities for alternative plots and leaving them *unstated* is one of the novel form's defining features and a keen point of recent interest in Victorian fiction.[2] Gary Saul Morson has described how this "plurality of possibilities" is present within narrative as a phenomenon he calls "sideshadowing": not explicitly spelled out by the author but rather a "ghostly presence of might-have-beens or might-bes" that has "its own shadowy kind of existence in the text."[3] Austen's page-long narration of the road to Everingham that Henry Crawford does *not* take—literally and figuratively—is hardly shadowy. Austen is known for being elliptical about the details of the actual love scenes between her most beloved couples like Elizabeth and Darcy, Emma and Mr. Knightley. ("What did she say?—Just what she ought, of course. A lady always does," she writes archly of Emma's reply to Mr. Knightley's proposal.[4]) The unrealized, hypothetical plots that, in contrast, Austen spells out in detail are evocative of popular, formulaic romance plots that she knew, and knew her readers might expect: poor, Cinderella-like Fanny Price marrying a wealthy reformed rake; poetic Marianne Dashwood marrying dashing Willoughby rather than Colonel Brandon, "who still sought the constitutional safeguard of a flannel waistcoat" (378).[5] One result of addressing "what if?" fantasies a reader might reasonably have is to create a contrast with the potentially disappointing, complex nature of the fictional world Austen portrays with the more romanticized, simplified, or formulaic way readers might desire it to be. Saying explicitly, "It's *not* that—it's this," underscores the realistic choices Austen as the author has made and writes this potentially frictional dynamic between realist author and imagining reader into her novels.

What Austen's elaboration of other possible endings also illuminates is a subtle shift in the way a variety of authors and readers can be seen thinking about the imaginative and creative pleasures of novel reading in the early nineteenth century. The eighteenth-century discourse on novel reading that preceded Austen's writing denounces the daydreaming and fantasizing that novels allegedly stimulated. Striking new images of readerly imagining characterize Austen's encounters with readers of her own novels, who were preoccupied with how readily they could imagine her novels themselves. Writing at a time when the "probable" and "natural" were increasingly the terms in which fiction was being judged, Austen joined other literary writers in exploring how such realistic representation reshapes the common novel reader's experience. Her fiction offers a bridge to new, realistic ways of imagining on one's own. In other words, readers now who value novels for their "relatability" are carrying on a practice that gained popularity two hundred years before we think it did.

A New Kind of Daydreaming

Scholarship about eighteenth-century and Romantic reading history has been remarkably consistent in focusing on the troublesome nature of novel-inspired imagining. A novel reader—usually a young female reader—projecting romanticized images onto the surrounding world remains a dominant figure in scholarship about eighteenth-century reading culture. No discussion of how the novel reader's imagination has figured in British literature could be complete without this figure, however familiar she is by now. Multiple critics have shown the supposed dangers of reading freely. With the ever-increasing availability of books, solitary reading became newly possible on a wide scale, as did fears of the passion that might be aroused during this unsupervised reading. Patricia Spacks has traced pervasive eighteenth-century anxieties about "the unruliness of unleashed imaginations, imaginations that might be stimulated by solitary reading."[6] David Richter has argued that the craze for Gothic fiction in particular between 1770 and 1820 heightened fear that novel reading would only make readers more imaginative and inward. Examining periodical rhetoric around 1795, he finds "with increasing frequency a new cause of disapproval—distrust of the power of fiction to seduce the reader into an inward world."[7]

The danger lay in the potential content of the reader's creative imaginings, which in antinovel rhetoric was assumed to be erotic. Concerns about how novel reading "inflamed the imagination," as William St Clair puts it, tended to coalesce around particular authors, such as repeated claims that reading Byron would lead to erotic fantasy, which would lead to masturbation and physical decline.[8] Concern lay less with readers using their own imaginations *during* the act of reading than with what imagining might lead to: the lasting, loosening effect that such unsupervised freedom of mind might have on moral behavior *afterward*. As Jacques Du Bosc writes in *The Accomplish'd Woman* (1753), "nothing is more common than to see Persons wholly changed after reading certain books; they assume new passions, they lead quite another life."[9] St Clair suggests the whole category of "the 'imagination,' a key concept of later constructions of romanticism, was seldom approved of by those who believed that reading had lasting effects."[10] Several recent works of criticism have shown how women readers in this period were more active and critical than the figure of the passive female reader in the antinovel press. Yet they emphasize how actual women readers at the time, as well as novels written in both the eighteenth and nineteenth centuries, portray novel reading as a rational, self-conscious, and intellectually *critical* activity.[11] We have left what Austen calls the "play of mind" to continue to be seen as potentially mischievous.

In response to the looming, "anarchic potential of reading" (in William Warner's term), readers' imaginations were frequently portrayed in a different way as weak and one-dimensional, lacking in complexity and depth.[12] Women readers were frequently cast as Arabella, the heroine of *The Female Quixote* (1752): as literal, gullible misreaders, or what Warner calls "pleasure-seeking automaton[s], liable to an imitative acting out of novelistic plots."[13] Imitative-ness was common to discussions of readers' weak imaginations. Samuel John-son, in a 1750 *Rambler* essay about modern and ancient romances, assumes that copying from example is the natural reaction of the fiction reader's imagi-nation. He writes, "If the power of example is so great, as to take possession of the memory by a kind of violence, and produce effects almost without the intervention of the will, care ought to be taken that, when the choice is unre-strained, the best examples only should be exhibited; and that which is likely to operate so strongly, should not be mischievous or uncertain in its effects."[14] For Johnson the reader's imagination is almost forcefully stripped of auton-omy; a work of fiction hijacks the imagination, "take[s] possession" with a kind of violence, and compels the reader to imitation almost against the reader's will. While these repeated claims are obviously polemical, Jon Klancher sug-gests that hearing novel reading described in a particular way again and again has an effect on potential readers, arguing that, "Readers are *made*, created as a public through a network of circulatory channels and the writer who con-sciously directs the reader's 'habitual energy of reasoning.'"[15]

A shift to a more natural novelistic aesthetic in the early nineteenth century has also been seen as merely shifting old concerns about overactive imagina-tions to how readers' daydreams might become too realistic. Lynch has shown how an aesthetic shift in Romantic-period fiction from "earlier fiction's strange, surprising adventures, to . . . more modest happenings" went hand in hand with readers imagining a personal, steady, and ever-changing relationship as a way to "think of their intensely felt transactions with their reading matter as something other than enthrallment to empty fictions."[16] What readers wanted to imagine appears to have shifted too. William Galperin has shown how Austen's first reviewers and readers invariably discussed and evidently found interest in the details of everyday life in her books, more than in the novels' didactic, virtue-rewarded plots; he suggests that the very "microscopic" atten-tion Austen pays to the quotidian "open[ed] the probable to a greater range and possibility."[17] At the same time, familiar worries about overactive imagina-tions reappeared with a new focus on the dangers of the possible. An 1821 re-view describes daydreams inspired by unrealistic romances—"the lucky inci-dents and opportune coincidences of which he has been so much accustomed to read"—as fantastic and harmless, whereas fiction that occurs in a real-world setting is said to be more dangerous because it blurs the line between fiction and reality.[18] Antinovel critics particularly worried that novels depicting more probable events would obscure the ability of readers with still-overactive imaginations to separate actual and fantasy worlds. Johnson writes in the *Rambler*, no. 4:

> In the romances formerly written, every transaction and sentiment was so remote from all that passes among men, that the reader was in very little danger of making any application to himself; . . . But when an adventurer is levelled with the rest of the world, and acts in such scenes of the universal drama, as may be the lot of any other man; young spectators fix their eyes upon him with closer attention, and hope, by observing his behaviour and success to regulate their own practices, when they shall be engaged in the like part.[19]

Johnson has inverted the usual hierarchy, so that outlandish invention here is preferable to close attention, regulation, and observation; obvious imaginativeness is a safeguard against imitation.

There are few widely circulated, direct images from the later eighteenth century of how else creative, imaginative capacities might be enlisted while reading other than in these dangerous, "mischievous" ways. However, a number of other indicators suggest that by the turn of the nineteenth century, the literary environment was ripe for understanding the imaginative and creative pleasures of novel reading in a new way. For instance, recent criticism on eighteenth-century literature has emphasized a broader sense of intimacy and interchange between readers and novels at the time, which enables us to identify ways readerly imagination was beginning to be seen as consonant with fiction. The eighteenth-century novel's depiction of realistic fictional worlds first paved the way for readers to integrate novels imaginatively into their own lives, J. Paul Hunter has argued. Hunter describes that while we do not have any more of an advanced sense of how readers "relate to imaginary worlds" than Aristotle did, we do know that "eighteenth-century readers could see a lot of themselves in English novels, more than they could locate in earlier fiction that described more extraordinary circumstances and was set in more remote places."[20] Without having to "identify" with a hero or heroine, readers could recognize situations, words, and places like their own experience in novels. Recently some critics have discussed how eighteenth-century novels encourage reveries and offer spaces for readers' subjectivities to operate freely, as Natalie Phillips shows.[21] Christina Lupton argues that Sterne and Fielding, as well as Austen, were drawn to the tension inherent in the bound book with its pages open to the contingencies of reading, which serves as a model for "formally closed narrative ventilated to readerly agency."[22]

The proliferation of physical books heightened a sense of intimacy and continuity between readers and what they read. People not only wanted to possess books but to be possessed *by* them, Andrew Piper has argued. Piper traces the emergence of what he calls "the bibliographic imagination," in which the physical forms that books took could determine the form of imagining in the reader's mind. For example, the popularity of miscellanies went hand in hand with minds becoming accustomed to exercising imagination in fragmentary forms.[23] Likewise, Lynch, in her two book-length studies focused on "the turn of the century's reading revolution," finds abounding evidence of literary readers learning to use their minds to develop individuated, layered relationships with their books. For Lynch the shift is most evident in how "'good' books" became "no longer those proclaiming standards of conduct but instead those supplying readers with practice in feeling."[24] What we find are readers who increasingly define novel reading as an activity that depends on their own imaginative and affective capacities being stimulated to participate in constructing a fictional world. Through meticulously examining the marginalia of two thousand physical books, annotated by Romantic-era readers, Heather Jackson identifies a "repeated theme" of readers describing a sense (as she says of one reader) "that in reading she could entertain two trains of ideas at once, her own and the author's."[25] Among Austen's readers we will see what I call "imaginability," or how much a reader's own imagining accords with the author's depiction, become a determining part of the novel-reading process.

As scholarship has increasingly been showing, then, a literary culture that had been striving to keep readers' imaginations in check for moral reasons was, in the early nineteenth century, becoming one that encouraged readers to use their minds creatively for literary benefit. Romantic poetry factors in this shift toward a more reciprocal model of the imaginative relationship between author and reader, a subject that deserves deeper study than I can undertake here. As Piper notes, the Romantic period is frequently identified with dreaming while reading and is the first time, historically, that this connection is frequently made.[26] Poetry was praised for stimulating the reader's imagination in simulation of the Romantic poet's state of creative reverie. The Romantic reader's creative role is described near the end of Wordsworth's "Simon Lee":

O reader! Had you in your mind
Such stores as silent thought can bring,
O gentle reader! You would find
A tale in everything.

What more I have to say is short,
I hope you'll kindly take it;
It is no tale; but should you think,
Perhaps a tale you'll make it. (11.73–80)[27]

David Perkins has identified specific ways that poems in the early nineteenth century divert the reader's attention from the poem to imaginative associations. "Romantic readers interpreted the course or sequence of 'ideas' in a poem as a product of association," he writes, "moreover, as they read, they departed on associative excursions of their own." For Perkins, however, in Romantic literature, association was often synonymous with allusion. Mental digressions were often directed toward other texts, and thereby "less personally than culturally produced."[28]

One new set of issues arose around the novel at the time: a worry that the new, more realistic representation might not spark readers' imaginations enough. As fiction like Austen's was beginning to be praised for its "accurate and unexaggerated delineation of events and character" (as Richard Whately describes Austen's novels in a review article in 1821), reviewers and novelists began asking whether and how realistic novels could captivate the imaginations of readers.[29] In Walter Scott's review of *Emma* (1816), he marvels that Austen's "correct and striking representation" of the everyday and domestic can excite as much interest as the Gothic once did through its many improbabilities. He also underscores the realist novelist's *problem* of interesting readers in "that which is daily taking place around them." In fact, whether and how a novel captivates a reader's imagination is a repeated focus of novel reviews at a time when, as Scott writes:

A style of novel has arisen, within the last fifteen or twenty years, differing from the former in the points upon which the interest hinges; neither alarming our credulity, nor amusing our imagination by wild variety of incident, or by those pictures of romantic affection and sensibility, which were formerly as certain attributes of fictitious characters as they are of rare occurrence among those who actually live and die. The substitute for these excitements, which had lost much of their poignancy by the repeated and injudicious use of them, was the art of copying from nature as she really exists in the common walks of life, and presenting to the reader, instead of the splendid scenes of an imaginary world, a correct and striking representation of that which is daily taking place around him.[30]

Scott claims that at this moment in the novel's history, not only novels but readers have changed: they seek more comparative and sophisticated mental stimulation rather than being primitively "alarmed" or "amus[ed]." At a time when the literary marketplace was flooded with similar novels and people were (as Piper says) "adapting to a world saturated by printed books," Scott imagines a hyperliterate reader, "familiar with the land of fiction, the adventures of which he assimilated not with those of real life, but with each other."[31] The kind of hyperliterate reader Scott portrays has developed what Peter Brooks calls "literary competence," or the ability to recognize "structures, functions, sequences, plot, the possibility of following a narrative and making sense of it," and, Brooks says, has become "himself virtually a text, a composite of all that he has read, or heard read, or imagined as written."[32] Scott and others were beginning to rethink the nature, purpose, and potential of imaginative play in the reader's mind. At the same time, Scott also perceives that these new readers who are interested by depictions of ordinary life pose a new challenge for a writer who "places his composition within that extensive range of criticism which general experience offers to every reader."[33] It is this specific act of comparing novelistic representation with their own experiences that Austen's fiction inspired in her first readers.

Austen's Delicious Play of Mind

The term "pleasure reading" first came into frequent use in the first quarter of the twentieth century—a shift that can be glimpsed quantitatively in a Google Ngram.[34] An earlier shift in how readers en masse refer to the pleasures of novel reading can be found in the first quarter of the nineteenth century by examining the discourse about reading Jane Austen's fiction. Austen's novels are a rich place to look at the history of pleasure reading for several reasons. First, readers' experiences of Austen's novels are well documented and have long been a robust subject of criticism in their own right.[35] At the same time, though Patricia Spacks argues that Austen "explores in her fictions the actual processes of reading,"[36] we have recovered relatively little evidence of Austen's own views on novel reading. Critics have repeatedly relied on a few explicit comments in her letters or the single passage in Northanger Abbey (1818) that defends novel reading against imagined slights. At best, as Adela Pinch has modeled, critics have identified "oblique and phenomenological ways" Austen addresses the effects of reading in novels like Persuasion.[37]

Austen herself collected family and friends' responses to the last two novels she published in her lifetime, comments that reveal the habits of mind that Austen observed, responded to, and shared with her readers. As Katie Halsey suggests, Austen "was extremely interested in the novels' effects on the readership of her own time."[38] While I only focus on a small group of Austen's documented, contemporary readers, an important new category of aesthetic response becomes visible in their case. We know that Austen herself defended the mental exercise of novel reading from its many virulent critics, but we have tended to see her doing so by reinventing novel reading as a rational and intellectual activity. In contrast to negative images of women's mindless or fanciful reading in the antinovel press, Anne Elliot has been seen as bookish and learned; *Northanger Abbey* is thought to train its reader to be more critical and less naive than its novel-reading heroine, Catherine Morland. In Catherine's character, Austen does parody the starring figure of the eighteenth-century antinovel debate: the quixotic female reader who projects imitative fantasies onto the world around her. But we have taken little notice of how Austen's responses to what she read, both literature and letters, suggest she also valued what she called the "*play* of mind": in responding in a letter to her niece Fanny, she describes Fanny's previous letter as showing her "delicious play of Mind" in "such a lovely display of what Imagination does."[39]

Critics have indeed characterized Austen's own responses to reading literature in terms of pleasure and personal affect, rather than what Lynch calls "the ethos of critical reading."[40] Austen even responded in this playful way to her own novels. *A Memoir of Jane Austen*, by Austen's nephew, suggests she would offer "many little particulars about the subsequent career of some of her people"—invent impromptu sequels—when family members asked her.[41] Scholars have long noted that, in her writing, Austen's playfulness often takes the form of rewriting what she has read in an alternative way. Halsey describes Austen's borrowings and rewritings from other authors as "pleasurably resistant"; she claims that "intertextual parody," a comic imaginative form, is one of Austen's most powerful artistic impulses.[42] As Judy Simons has suggested, one reason Austen's novels may inspire so many variations and continuations is Austen's own delight in playful, derivative imaginative forms, "burlesque, pastiche, and excess."[43] Thus, a sense of imagining an alternative or addition, something that builds on what is expected or given, underlies Austen's experience of creatively responding to books as both a reader and writer.

Austen playfully refers to novelistic conventions both within and outside her fiction, specifically what Gillian Beer describes as the circulating libraries' "plentiful flow of wish-fulfillment literature in the late eighteenth and nineteenth centuries."[44] Brian Southam describes how Austen "expressed her amused contempt for popular fiction, with its rigid black and white characters, its melodramatic action, episodic plots, and lack of structural coherence" in the satirical "Plan of a Novel, according to Hints from Various Quarters," which she wrote in response to the prince regent's librarian "badgering" her with clichéd ideas for a new novel.[45] Within her own novels, in moments of addressing the reader, she gently satirizes formulaic elements of popular novels, a humor that depends on readers' familiarity with and shared condescension about them. These moments enact the difference between the clichéd narrative choices she does not make and her own more realistic purpose. (In a letter to her niece Anna, after the latter sent her a novel in draft, Austen warns her away from a clichéd expression, which she calls "such thorough novel slang—and so old, that I daresay Adam met with it in the first novel he opened."[46]) In *Northanger Abbey*, for example, when Catherine is abruptly sent home by General Tilney, Austen describes for several sentences "a heroine returning, at the close of her career, to her native village" in triumph, with three maids in tow, before adding "—But my affair is widely different."[47] Here the narrator forms a distinct image of an event in the reader's mind and then, afterward, speaks from an authorial position to tell us that what she has just described did not happen. Rhetorically, such moments call to mind the English poetic tradition and its use of the classical gesture of *recusatio*, a speaker's claiming to reject a grandiloquent style in favor of a plainer one. Austen uses the gesture rather cheekily to separate her plain fiction from the improbable romance novels with which it all too closely shares a plot structure.[48] She underscores her own artistic choice by invoking, and rejecting, cliché, much as she does in explicating the other possible endings to her novels' marriage plots.

Austen's unusual collection and transcription of responses to her last two novels from the circle of readers around her shows her interest in what historians of reading call her readers' "horizon of expectations"—a broad category that includes the habits of mind that readers expect to practice in reading a novel. "Opinions of Mansfield Park" and "Opinions of Emma" are booklets Austen made, "written out in a neat and even hand," that show her care in recording the colloquial remarks of family, friends, and friends of friends, about her work.[49] Laura Fairchild Brodie, in her thorough analysis of these booklets, describes Austen as "textualizing a real community of respondents through her transcription of their comments" and modeling the kind of intimate, familial response that continued to characterize Austen's reception history.[50] Most of the entries in these two booklets sound like summaries or shorthand for Austen's self, apart from a few quotations from letters. The titles of her novels are almost all abbreviated, and Austen repeats terms that broadly sum up responses, including "like," "prefer," and "not so well" as her other novels, as in these observations about *Emma*: "Cassandra—better than P. & P.—but not so well as M.P.";[51] "Mrs Lefroy—preferred it to M P—but like M P. the least of all" (438). She also repeats the terms "delighted" and "pleased" in describing readers' affective responses to specific characters in both novels, as with Cassandra, who "Delighted much in Mr Rushworth's stupidity" (432). Each response seems to calibrate how much pleasure the novel gave that particular reader, and from what specific sources. Often, though not always, it is when the opinions are not as positive that Austen includes particular, frank wording, which suggests she found the words amusing: Mrs. Digweed's opinion of *Emma*, that she "did not like it so well as the others, in fact if she had not known the author, could hardly have got through it" (437); or Mrs. Augusta Bramstone's opinion about *Mansfield Park*, who "owned that she thought S & S.—and P. & P. downright nonsense, but expected to like MP. better, & having finished the 1st vol.—flattered herself that she had got through the worst" (433).

The frankness and informal style of the entries in the "Opinions" booklets make Austen's acquaintances' approaches to reading her novels sound personal, even as they are judging the novels based on a widely valued effect at the time: how "natural" they find the author's choices and renderings. Readers of *Mansfield Park*, for instance, comment on how realistic (or not) the novel's plot is and implicitly compare its events to other novels as well as to the actual world. She records her brother Edward Austen Knight's opinion of Henry Crawford going off with Mrs. Rushworth "at such a time, when so much in love with Fanny, thought unnatural by Edward" (431); his son also "objected to Mrs Rushworth's elopement as unnatural" (432), though her brother James's wife thought the same elopement to be "very natural" (432). Though these readers are seeking verisimilitude, they are not objectively critiquing the novelist's artistic skill in rendering reality. They are expressing their pleasure in a novel and basing their personal aesthetic judgment on how much their own imaginations of an event accord with the author's depiction. Captain Austen liked *Emma* "extremely," and "on account of it's [*sic*] peculiar air of Nature throughout, preferred it" to *Pride and Prejudice* and *Mansfield Park* (436). Annabella Milbanke, in calling *Pride and Prejudice* "the *most probable* I have ever read," similarly judged that novel based on the degree to which she could picture its events.[52] Austen herself expresses personal liking through commenting on verisimilitude when she criticizes a work of fiction for having "a thousand improbabilities in the story" and some of the same novels' characters as "flat and unnatural."[53] In doing so, she is not just critiquing its artistic skill but revealing the extent to which she herself takes pleasure in reading, depending on the ease with which she can realize the work of art in her imagination. In other words, we can see readers experiencing pleasure when their own independent imaginings harmonize with an author's. I call this "imaginability": the tendency to judge a novel based on whether the reader's own imagining accords with the author's depiction, or how easy it is for the reader to imagine an event or character. A depiction that does not require *any* effort of imagination to realize, because of its extreme verisimilitude, could disappoint. One reader describes *Emma* as "too natural to be interesting" (437).

Describing a novel as "natural" or "probable" may not sound like an assertion of individual imagination, but as the century proceeds, mid-nineteenth-century accounts of reading Austen repeatedly feature an even more assertive imaginative phenomenon that her realism enables: readers describe imagining themselves physically within her fictional worlds. From the beginning some of Austen's readers praise her novels for allowing them to envision themselves moving within and feeling as if they were part of the novel's world. Catherine Gallagher identifies a generalized form of referentiality as a new feature of fiction in the mid-eighteenth century. What newly distinguished fictional characters was that novels "renounced reference to individual examples in the world" and instead "refer[red] to a whole class of people in general (as well as in private) because its proper names do not refer to persons in particular."[54] Some of Austen's early readers recorded feeling as if her characters were universally knowable. One early reader whose opinion Austen recorded ("Mrs C. Cage wrote thus to Fanny") uses concrete language to describe reading *Emma* as, "I am at Highbury all day, & I can't help feeling I have just got into a new set of acquaintances" (439). Austen's collected opinions of *Mansfield Park* includes this detailed elaboration of a similar effect, which the reader noted as new to her in reading Austen's fiction:

> Lady Gordon wrote "In most novels you are amused for the time with a set of Ideal People whom you never think of afterwards or whom you the least expect to meet in common life, whereas in Miss A-s works, & especially in MP. You actually *live* with them, you fancy yourself one of the family; & the scenes are so exactly descriptive, so perfectly natural, that there is scarcely an Incident or conversation, or a person that you are not inclined to imagine you have at one time or other in your Life been a witness to, born a part in, & been acquainted with." (435)

In other words, Austen's characters are "relatable." What Lady Gordon describes as pleasurable is not only recognition but an ease in imagining vividly—so vividly that she feels physically part of the imagined scene. A reviewer in 1823 describes a sense of being so absorbed that, without the reader realizing it, the real world has dissolved into the fictional one: "Without any wish to surprise us into attention, by strangeness of incident, or complication of adventure, etc. the stream of her tale flows on in an easy, natural but spring tide, which carries us out of ourselves and bears our feelings, affections, and deepest interest irresistibly along with it."[55] George Henry Lewes writes similarly, if more concretely, in an 1859 assessment: "The reader breakfasts, dines, walks, and gossips with the various worthies, till a process of transmutation takes place in him, and he absolutely fancies himself one of the company."[56] The detail of Lewes's account expresses his liking for the book increasing the more he is able to imagine himself within it; ending with the phrase "absolutely fancies himself" suggests even a kind of *belief* in what he imagines. He is willing to suspend disbelief until he enters the fictional picture, and then the image takes on an even greater sense of reality. Lewes's "process of transmutation," which takes place in the reader's "fanc[y]," a process of imagining oneself, as oneself, as an acting body within the fictional world of the novel, seems to be a new pleasure of reading that gets articulated with the novel's shift toward realism. (Lewes, incidentally, thought a lot about a book's "relatability" and was concerned that *Adam Bede*'s sales might depend upon it, as I discuss in chapter 3. He wrote in his journal that readers "like to fancy themselves doing and feeling what the heroes and heroines do and feel" and "no one would care to be a merely upright carpenter."[57])

Austen also weaves into her fiction her awareness of one other crucial habit of novel readers' minds: that they exercise much of their own imaginations on desiring a particular ending. Mary Russell Mitford, for example, admitting in a letter that she had not read the newly published *Mansfield Park*, praises *Pride and Prejudice*, but she finds Elizabeth too outspoken and unconventional, and suggests an ending that would better accord with the conduct novels usually rewarded: "Darcy should have married Jane."[58] Austen's novels offer ongoing opportunities to imagine alternative endings, as Deanna Kreisel shows: her novels abound with "juicy and outrageous subplots" that realize (usually offstage) some of the more dangerous narrative alternatives to the conservative, realized central courtship.[59] That Austen's actual proposal scenes are repeatedly occluded, at least in part, has long frustrated readers. Though Fanny Knight liked *Mansfield Park* "in many parts, very much indeed," Austen singles out her response to the ending: "but not satisfied with the end—wanting more Love between [Fanny] & Edmund" (431).

In fact, in the endings of her novels Austen tends to direct readerly invention toward how the story is elaborated, suggesting that the plot is a fait ac-
compli, but the reader is welcome to expend imagination on its details. Within
Austen's evasive references to the central couple finally coming together, she
marks out precisely what she is leaving the reader to imagine on her own—and
lightheartedly suggests that the reader, well versed in novels, can easily do so.
("What did she say?—Just what she ought, of course. A lady always does," as
I earlier quoted from *Emma*.) The tone is arch and playful, nowhere more so
than in the passage about Fanny and Edmund that Austen's niece may have
been objecting to:

> I purposely abstain from dates on this occasion, that every one may be at
> liberty to fix their own, aware that the cure of unconquerable passions, and
> the transfer of unchanging attachments, must vary much as to time in dif-
> ferent people. I only entreat everybody to believe that exactly at the time
> when it was quite natural that it should be so, and not a week earlier, Ed-
> mund did cease to care about Miss Crawford, and became as anxious to
> marry Fanny as Fanny herself could desire.[60]

However facetious the tone, Austen delineates a specific, minute gap—merely
"dates"—for each reader to imagine in her own individual way. She uses
another fill-in-the-blank structure that offers slightly more leeway when introducing the rest of the novel's cast in the opening sentence of the final chapter:
"Let other pens dwell on guilt and misery. I quit such odious subjects as soon
as I can, impatient to restore everybody, not greatly in fault themselves, to
tolerable comfort, and to have done with all the rest" (461). Again, though
Austen's invitation to "let other pens" fill in the didacticism is an ironic gesture,
such moments inscribe the tendency of readers to want to imagine on their
own concretely into the history of the novel. What Austen tellingly does is
delegate a specific imaginative task, and only that task, to the reader. The
reader is free to fill in romantic details; the plot outcome is hers alone to "fix."

I am not suggesting Austen is alone in recognizing the pleasure readers take in
imaginability, but she certainly appears less invested in curtailing creative fantasies than the novel culture that preceded her. Nor was Austen alone at the
time in doing so: Christina Lupton notes how, within a number of novels written slightly before and at the time Austen was writing, the narrator raises a
question of what else might have occurred.[61] As part of a larger history of
pleasure reading, then, we can see the novel reader's imagination getting described and figured in a new way with the emergence of the realist novel in the

early nineteenth century—not as making dangerous projections onto real life but as potentially applied to the novel itself in ways that make for more imaginative, less formulaic novel reading.

Nothing to Regret in *Sense and Sensibility*

Sense and Sensibility includes multiple accounts of the same hypothetical ending to Marianne's marriage plot: one account is brief, romanticized, and ironic, narrated by Austen; the other is prosaic and painfully realistic, narrated by Elinor Dashwood. Andrew Miller has shown how counterfactual narratives that take place within a character's mind are a signature feature of nineteenth-century moral psychology and fiction, signaling the value Victorians placed on an "optative" awareness of other lives one could have lived.[62] In this case, neither account focuses on Marianne's thoughts, nor on a sense of lost opportunities or consequential choices. Rather, Austen contrasts two different ways of thinking about Marianne's marriage plot that structurally mirror what it is like to read about a marriage plot. One type of witness imagines in paltry, vague, conventional terms, the other in aesthetically thick and even contradictory ways. *Sense and Sensibility*'s multiple narrations of another ending highlight the value for Austen of readers tolerating multiplicity and resisting a teleological narrative that neatly fulfills readerly wishes—wishes that cancel out the lessons of suffering.

The rosy image of Willoughby married to Marianne, with which I began this chapter, comes in one of the novel's last paragraphs, after the now-married Willoughby makes his nighttime visit to Cleveland and confesses his real affection for Marianne. Even Elinor feels at least a momentary desire for this impossible marriage: she "for a moment wished Willoughby a widower" (335). So when Austen describes Willoughby's "pang" of regret, it is one the reader may also, "for a moment," experience:

> Willoughby could not hear of her marriage without a pang; and his punishment was soon afterwards complete in the voluntary forgiveness of Mrs Smith, who, by stating his marriage with a woman of character, as the source of her clemency, gave him reason for believing that had he behaved with honor towards Marianne, he might at once have been happy and rich. That his repentance of misconduct, which thus brought its own punishment, was sincere, need not be doubted;—nor that he long thought of Colonel Brandon with envy, and of Marianne with regret. (379)

Imagining what might have been is a punitive exercise for Willoughby here, serving to complete his "punishment." Yet the passage stops short of reforming the rakish Willoughby. For the more reformed he appears, the more the reader, like Elinor, might momentarily wish for him to marry Marianne. Thus, rather than narrating his thoughts in free indirect style and inviting us sympathetically into them, Austen summarizes Willoughby's feelings as if reporting on them from the outside. We are to take the narrator's word—it "need not be doubted"—that he has developed a "sincere" ability to regret his hurtful actions; an ironic tone, and perhaps a touch of doubt, can be heard in such an assertion. Keeping the reader at a narrative distance makes it harder to sympathize with an allegedly redeemed Willoughby or to feel regret on his behalf. As the passage continues, the tone becomes lively and ribbing at both his and the reader's expense: "But that he was for ever inconsolable, that he fled from society, or contracted an habitual gloom of temper, or died of a broken heart, must not be depended on—for he did neither. He lived to exert, and frequently to enjoy himself" (379). This "gloom[y]" series of further alternatives, articulated in an arch recitation of novelistic clichés, can be read as a humorous rejection of how a predictable romance plot might end, underscoring the novel's superior realism.

In fact, several pages earlier, Elinor narrates to Marianne a lengthier, darker, realistic account of what marriage to Willoughby would actually have been like. Where Willoughby has some vague "reason for believing" that he could have been generically "happy and rich," pragmatic Elinor uses her empirical knowledge of his character to spend two pages reasoning out to Marianne how Willoughby would likely have felt given their relative poverty. "Had you married," she begins,

[h]is expensiveness is acknowledged even by himself, and his whole conduct declares that self-denial is a word hardly understood by him. His demands and your inexperience together, on a small, very small income, must have brought on distresses which would not be the *less* grievous to you, from having been entirely unknown and unthought of before. *Your* sense of honour and honesty would have led you, I know, when aware of your situation, to attempt all the economy that would appear to you possible: and, perhaps, as long as your frugality retrenched only on your own comfort, you might have been suffered to practice it, but beyond that—and how little could the utmost of your single management do to stop the ruin which had begun before your marriage?—Beyond *that*, had you endeavoured,

however reasonably, to abridge *his* enjoyments, is it not to be feared, that instead of prevailing on feelings so selfish to consent to it, you would have lessened your own influence on his heart, and made him regret the connection which had involved him in such difficulties? (350–51)

This is only the first half of Elinor's lengthy lecture arguing Marianne out of the sentimental effect Willoughby's regret has on her. In Elinor's hypothetical ending, his regretting a lack of money simply replaces his regretting the lack of an amiable wife, leaving no real alternative after all—for Marianne or the reader—to an unhappy ending between Marianne and Willoughby. Elinor dwells on a pretty miserable picture, the emotional extreme of which has an effect on her extremely emotional sister. Marianne is equally pronounced in claiming the immediate dissipation of her regret about how things turned out. "'I have not a doubt of it,' said Marianne; 'and I have nothing to regret— nothing but my own folly'" (352). Nearly a century before Freud, Austen shows Elinor performing a talking cure that gives Marianne a sense of agency, an awareness of her own excesses ("nothing but my own folly") that she did not have at the time of her interactions with Willoughby. Though envisioning a hypothetical series of events is the thought experiment of a moment, it is seen to have lasting and empowering consequences.

The mental exercise Elinor puts Marianne through of imagining realistic possibilities for her own marriage plot structurally resembles the reader's experience of the novel. As Elinor completes the narrative of Marianne's broken-off courtship, Marianne is finally able to look backward on real events, and—much as a novel reader does—give them new meaning, constructing a story caused, less painfully, by her own headstrong improprieties rather than an uncaring Willoughby. This process of understanding is what Peter Brooks describes as "reading back from the end," and for him it is fundamental to a reader's experience of narrative. "Our chief tool in making sense of narrative," Brooks writes, is knowing that when we get to the end, our retrospective imagination will "restructure the provisional meanings of the already read," or enable us to see a fuller meaning in events other than the limited meaning we experience at the time.[63] For Marianne, as for a novel reader, then, there is a crucial difference between imagining what might be while it is still possible and imagining what might have been after the full course of events is known.

Austen clearly suggests the harm in romantic, predictive visions and the restorative value of probable, conditional scenarios. Early on, Marianne starts to picture a hypothetical ending to her own marriage plot when she tells Elinor about having secretly toured Allenham, the estate Willoughby is to inherit: "There is a remarkably pleasant sitting room upstairs," she tells Elinor, describing its exact situation. "[N]othing could be more forlorn than the furniture,—but if it were newly fitted up—" (69). But Austen does not invite the reader to share in Marianne's teasing, happy spirit here: she suggests her wariness of such forecasting through the narrative perspective, which is Elinor's, and for Elinor the whole visit to Allenham is so improper that she "could hardly believe [it] to be true" (68). The narrator pokes fun at Marianne's premature decorating visions with the closing comment that, given the opportunity, "she would have described every room in the house with equal delight" (69). Elinor's belated version of what marriage with Willoughby would have been like is full of "difficulties" rather than redecorating, but it enables Marianne to envision the probable end of her story and look back on the whole in a less regret-filled light.

Austen privileges Elinor's capacity to shape possibilities in her mind even after they are no longer viable. This is especially true when she juxtaposes Elinor's response with Mrs. Dashwood's comical insistence on having only ever envisioned one possible end. Having decided that Marianne should marry Colonel Brandon, Mrs. Dashwood tells Elinor, "'There was always a something,—if you remember,—in Willoughby's eyes at times, which I did not like.' Elinor could *not* remember it" (338). In retroactively making Colonel Brandon the only real, viable suitor, Mrs. Dashwood constructs a narrative that does not have space for alternative endings or desires. Austen not only satirizes but explicitly discredits such a sanitized remembrance of the novel's events. Elinor observes that "her mother must always be carried away by her imagination on any interesting subject" and regards this version of events as "the natural embellishments of her mother's active fancy, which fashioned everything delightful to her, as it chose" (336).

Elinor and her mother epitomize two different types of thinking about marriage plots. While for Marianne "reading back from the end" weakens her residual desire for what is no longer possible, Mrs. Dashwood's retrospective account of Marianne and Willoughby's relationship does not just diminish any continuing desire for a marriage between them: she erases the desire she felt at the time. Unlike a single-minded reader or her intellectually unreliable mother, Elinor is able to hold two possible outcomes in her mind at once. Elinor tells her mother that "if Marianne can be happy with [Colonel Brandon], I shall be as ready as yourself to think our connection the greatest blessing to us in the world" (337). One page later, she "could not quite agree" with her mother's pronouncement about Willoughby that "Marianne would yet never have been so happy with him, as she will be with Colonel Brandon" (338). Elinor, whose judgment is irreproachable and who admirably sees good in both men, preserves the desire she felt for Marianne to marry Willoughby even as she desires Colonel Brandon for a brother-in-law. She derides as fanciful her mother's desire to make Marianne's marriage plot neatly teleological and erase Marianne's disappointment. Like the reader, Elinor and Mrs. Dashwood have been in the position of witnessing and developing their own wishes about another person's marriage plot. They are stand-ins for two very different types of reader, however: one who is comfortable with the multidirectional, creative play of mind that novel reading stimulates and one who wants to see nothing but a single, happy, romantic end.[64] Writing during this transitional moment in the novel's, and novel reading's, history, Austen sides with the figure who tolerates stories that stir up multiplicitous and uncomfortable feelings.

There is one moment in the novel when the reader has no choice but to read like Elinor, imagining an ending full of suffering. Very soon after Elinor has "cured" Marianne of her regret, the family's "man-servant" announces that "Mr Ferrars is married" (310). Mrs. Dashwood's subsequent cross-examination of the servant provides two pages of corroborating evidence to convince us that Lucy has married *the* Mr. Ferrars; for six pages, Austen allows the reader, along with the Dashwoods, to picture Edward married to Lucy, although she has married his brother. As she does for Marianne, Elinor's imagination spares no details in drawing the painful mental picture of an imagined marriage: "She saw them in an instant in their parsonage house: saw in Lucy, the active, contriving manager, uniting at once a desire of smart appearance, with the utmost frugality . . . pursuing her own interest in every thought" (313). Elinor's imagining seems fully endorsed by the novel, for her consciousness has provided the most truthful perspective throughout the novel. The description of her imaginings begins in the language of "certainty itself": "Elinor now found the difference between the expectation of an unpleasant event, however certain the mind may be told to consider it, and certainty itself. . . . But he was now married." More text is devoted to what Elinor imagines in "the pain of the intelligence" than to simply the "tears of joy, which at first she thought would never cease" that she feels when she learns the truth (316). As usual, Austen coyly downplays the actual denouement, in which Edward's "errand at Barton, in fact, was a simple one. It was only to ask Elinor to marry him" (316). Instead, she attaches intense emotion and devotes descriptive detail to painful imagining of what has not occurred. Austen takes the reader, and Elinor, far down a divergent imaginative path that involves, in Elinor's case, superfluous suffering.

The denouement that immediately follows between Elinor and Edward is far from conventionally romantic, when its happiness really consists of release from such pain.

Reading realistically for Austen means not reading for *the* plot, for only *one* plot, like *Persuasion*'s bereaved Captain Benwick, who reads too much poetry and reads it selectively for "the various lines which imagined a broken heart, or a mind destroyed by wretchedness."[65] From her first completed novel to her last, Austen repeats the satiric portrayal of characters who read too narrowly, from Catherine Morland, who admits to not liking any books other than novels, to Sir Walter Elliot, who "never took up any book but the Baronetage" (3) and always opens it to the page containing his family's history. Catherine Gallagher has described how alternate history narratives, which proliferated in the late twentieth century, use counterfactual thinking to imagine a more just series of events that might have occurred, fulfilling a need "to see the logic of justice triumph over the dynamics of historical determination."[66] One way of looking at Austen's other endings is that they offer a kind of reparative narrative justice. In returning attention to a courtship that does not materialize, she acknowledges and brings closure to the emotional investment the novel has had the reader make in another possibility—not erasing it but still affirming that we have nothing to regret in its loss.

Mansfield Park's Primer in Probability

The first readers of *Mansfield Park* were keen on entertaining different possible endings while reading the novel, though Austen herself was decisive about the novel's plot. As I quoted earlier, readers in Austen's own circle repeatedly discussed how "natural" or not they found the two equally sudden events that determine the ending: Henry Crawford's absconding with Maria Rushworth and Edmund Bertram deciding he loves Fanny Price. One reader whose opinion Austen recorded, John Plumptre, recognized her artistry in prolonging the uncertainty for so long: "The plot is so well contrived that I had not an idea till the end which of the two would marry Fanny, H.C. or Edmund" (434). Austen wrote to her sister Cassandra about their brother having a similar response while reading the novel's proofs: "Henry has this moment said he likes my M.P. better & better; he is in the 3d volume. I believe *now* he has changed his mind as to foreseeing the end; he said yesterday at least, that he defied anybody to say whether H.C. would be reformed or would forget Fanny in a fortnight."[67] In this, one of the few examples we have of Austen responding directly to a reader, there is a slight triumph in her italicizing "*now*," acknowledging that the novelist has written a plot he cannot so easily predict. Henry's liking the novel "better and better" as he was increasingly uncertain about its direction also suggests the pleasure he felt as a reader in being kept guessing.

Austen herself does not appear to have vacillated about the novel's outcome. One of her nieces, Louisa Knight, wrote that Cassandra "urged her to 'let Mr Crawford marry Fanny Price,'" but Aunt Jane "stood firmly and would not allow a change."[68] Austen's certainty is not surprising given that no heroine in any of Austen's novels marries a rake, nor do her rakish characters fully reform. The closest Henry Crawford comes to reform, as the narrator describes in damning terms, is that his "cold-blooded vanity" had once "by an opening undesigned and unmerited, led him into the way of happiness" (467). For a well-schooled reader of Austen's oeuvre, a marriage between Henry and Fanny *should* be unimaginable, as the cool, critical language she uses in hypothesizing suggests. Austen is also explicit about the finality of Fanny's refusal. The apex of Fanny's good feeling toward Henry comes in a moment when she realizes that marriage to him would enable her to offer her sister Susan a better home. Yet Austen uses the perfect conditional tense to convey that in Fanny's mind even this pleasant scenario is impossible:

> Were *she* likely to have a home to invite her to, what a blessing it would be!—And had it been possible for her to return Mr Crawford's regard, the probability of his being very far from objecting to such a measure would have been the greatest increase of all her own comforts. She thought he was really good-tempered, and could fancy his entering into a plan of that sort, most pleasantly. (419)

Austen makes Fanny appear as tempted as she could possibly be in this moment. Given Fanny's character, the "blessing" her marriage might bring to her beloved sister could more reasonably sway Fanny than anything else; she reasons out the "probability" that her marriage would result in this advantage for Susan. But there is no wavering in as explicit a statement as "had it been possible for her to return Mr Crawford's regard." In contrast, a similar moment of wistful projection occurs in *Pride and Prejudice*, in which Elizabeth Bennet, who has also rejected a wealthy suitor—irreversibly, she thinks at that point—imagines the domestic comforts that would have been hers if she had accepted Darcy. But in this case Austen uses the future tense: "At that moment she felt that to be mistress of Pemberley *might be* something!" In contrast to determined Fanny, Elizabeth's picturing such a scenario upon seeing his house figures within a process of changing her mind, as she later jokingly admits to Jane that she began to love him upon "first seeing his beautiful grounds at Pemberley."[69]

Why, then, does a feeling of uncertainty about Fanny's marital fate figure so significantly in these accounts of reading *Mansfield Park*? Why is it a commonplace in criticism of the novel to express disappointment with the ending? In *Mansfield Park* Austen continually tasks the reader's imagination with envisioning, comparing, and discerning the probability of different marriage plots. The novel's characters constantly think or talk about the likelihood of Edmund's proposing to Mary, of her accepting, and the possibility of Fanny's accepting Henry.[70] By looking closely at a long hypothetical passage near the end of the novel, we can again, as in *Sense and Sensibility*, see the shape that Austen thought novel reading could take in the mind of someone reading a realist novel. Rather than working against the alleged tendency of novel readers to extend the fictional world into their own lives, for Austen, realist novels both finely hone and depend upon the reader's independent capacity to imagine different possibilities and to compare their reality with one another and with the real world.

The explicit projections of alternative marriages I have been discussing appear at the end of Austen's novels, when both characters and reader know the outcomes they posit are no longer possible. Yet throughout Austen's novels one character can imagine a marriage that another character—and, eventually, the reader—knows to be impossible. For example, in *Emma*, while Emma imagines successive, seemingly possible marriage plots, Mr. Knightley cautions her "that Mr Elton would never marry indiscreetly" (135) and alerts her of "symptoms of attachment" between the secretly engaged Frank Churchill and Jane Fairfax (350). Emma demurs, but Austen has established a subtle dramatic irony that teaches the reader to question the heroine's willfully imaginative plotting. At the same time, aligning the novel with Emma's point of view makes the reader privy to the impossibility of another marriage plot—between Emma and Frank Churchill, whom she decides she could not love—which the Westons and Mr. Knightley continue to imagine, whether with hope or fear, is possible. Austen has her characters speculate about who will marry whom, generate a great deal of narratability, and get it wrong, while placing the reader in a privileged position from which to learn how to distinguish likely from unlikely outcomes.

Instruction about realistic and unrealistic possibilities also occurs through the narrative structure of *Mansfield Park*. Dramatic irony is created early on as the reader knows what no other characters do: that Fanny already loves Edmund. While Edmund, Sir Thomas, and Mary Crawford all consider Henry's marriage to Fanny a real possibility, the frequent narrative alignment with Fanny's perspective makes evident to the reader that Sir Thomas, Edmund, and Mary Crawford do not see real probabilities but chances for their own wishes to be fulfilled. ("Well, though I may not be able to persuade you into different feelings," Edmund says to Fanny about her refusing Henry, while he himself is besotted with Mary, "you will be persuaded into them I trust. I confess myself sincerely anxious that you may"; 351.) The closest any character comes to sharing the reader's insight into Fanny's feelings is the moment in which Sir Thomas, speaking to Fanny and puzzled about why she is so decided against Henry, rejects the one true possibility just before uttering it: "Young as you are, and having seen scarcely any one, it is hardly possible that your affections—" (316). Austen repeatedly shows the novel's characters as unable or, in this case, as refusing to imagine unwelcome possibilities. Of Mrs. Grant and Mary Crawford, Edmund says to Fanny that could she "refuse such a man as Henry Crawford seems more than they can understand" (352).

"Rational" Fanny (as Edmund calls her; 347), on the other hand, is frequently seen in moments of reverie, not wishfully daydreaming but reasoning out the most natural and probable explanations for others' feelings. From Mrs. Norris's need for self-importance to Edmund's susceptibility to Mary Crawford, other people's feelings are continually causing Fanny pain; she tries to anticipate and navigate their feelings like obstacles. As she sits "very earnestly trying to understand what Mr and Miss Crawford were at" in pushing for marriage (305), Austen shows Fanny's logical, empirical thought process:

> There was everything in the world against their being serious but his words and manner. Everything natural, probable, reasonable, was against it; all their habits and ways of thinking, and all her own demerits. How could she have excited serious attachment in a man who had seen so many, and been admired by so many, and flirted with so many, infinitely her superiors; . . . And farther, how could it be supposed that his sister, with all her high and worldly notions of matrimony, would be forwarding anything of a serious nature in such a quarter? Nothing could be more unnatural in either. Fanny was ashamed of her own doubts. Everything might be possible rather than serious attachment, or serious approbation of it toward her. She had quite convinced herself of this before Sir Thomas and Mr Crawford joined them. The difficulty was in maintaining the conviction quite so absolutely after Mr Crawford was in the room; for once or twice a look seemed forced on her which she did not know how to class among the common meaning; in any other man, at least, she

would have said that it meant something very earnest, very pointed. But she still tried to believe it no more than what he might often have expressed towards her cousins and fifty other women. (305–6)

Fanny thinks comparatively here: she compares herself to the "many, infinitely her superiors," "her cousins and fifty other women" with whom Henry has also flirted; she compares the meaning of Henry's glances with those of "any other man." She seeks out the most "natural, probable, reasonable" narrative. But Austen also highlights Fanny's capacity for imagining undesired, even "unnatural" possibilities. At first she accepts one explanation: "everything might be possible rather than serious attachment." But then, in contrast to Sir Thomas, the unwelcome possibility is grudgingly present in her mind as she "still *tried* to believe" it not possible that he actually loves her. There are several things going on in this passage. First, Fanny is a model comparative reader of her own marriage plot, in contrast with the unimaginative, willful, and mistaken other characters. Seeing Fanny go step-by-step through the process of imagining multiple possible explanations and weighing the evidence for each offers the reader a guide in how to reason out what is not known. At the same time, passages like this emphasize that there *are* multiple possible narratives. At such moments Austen cultivates that uncertainty about "whether H.C. would be reformed or would forget Fanny in a fortnight" that readers like Austen's brother Henry found so engaging.

One reason Austen's first readers may have continued to weigh the plausibility of a marriage between Fanny and Henry—and modern critics continue to debate it—is that the narrator does so at length, within the novel, after Henry's actions make it unacceptable. For more than half a page near the end of the novel, Austen describes step-by-step a chain of events beginning with Henry going to Everingham, instead of to London and the Rushworths' party, and ending with the prediction that he "must" eventually marry Fanny. The novel lays out the projected sequence of events in precise, realistic terms, in language that continually gauges its likeliness:

> *Could he have been satisfied* with the conquest of one amiable woman's affections, *could he have found* sufficient exultation in overcoming the reluctance, working himself into the esteem and tenderness of Fanny Price, *there would have been every probability* of success and felicity for him. His affection had already done something. Her influence over him had already given him some influence over her. *Would he have deserved more*, there can be no doubt that *more would have been obtained*; especially *when that marriage had*

taken place, which *would have given him* the assistance of her conscience in subduing her first inclinations, and brought them very often together. *Would he have persevered*, and uprightly, Fanny *must have been his reward*— and a reward very voluntarily bestowed—within a reasonable period from Edmund's marrying Mary.

Had he done as he intended, and as he knew he ought, by going down to Everingham after his return from Portsmouth, *he might have been* deciding his own happy destiny. (467; my emphases)

One way to read this passage is that Austen is not describing a real possibility. The passage is so overrun with conditional phrases that we are continually reminded of the unreality of Henry's reform. As in Austen's account of Willoughby's thoughts, sympathy with and a belief in Henry's reform is held at a distance, here by the formal language in which Austen describes his feeling "sufficient exultation" or experiencing "success and felicity." Again, instead of the free indirect style Austen uses to heighten the immediacy of the reader's sympathy with a character's thoughts, the closest we come to Henry's own consciousness is in the brief reference to his not having acted "as he knew he ought." Austen continues to report his subsequent feelings in the elevated rhetoric of a parallel construction: Henry is "regretting Fanny, even at the moment, but regretting her infinitely more, when all the bustle of the intrigue was over" (468). Austen does later write lyrically of his feeling regret at having "lost the woman whom he had rationally, as well as passionately loved" (469). Yet this language is, if anything, more elevated, more distant from Henry's feelings, and more like a Johnsonian maxim about human nature: he is said to be "providing for himself no small portion of vexation and regret—vexation that must rise sometimes to self-reproach, and regret to wretchedness" (468–69).

Read another way, however, the passage is equally devoted to spelling out the necessary series of events in precise, realistic terms. The premise is plausible: Why wouldn't the peripatetic Henry make one more change to his often-changing travel plans? In fact, as the passage proceeds, the possibility of Henry's acting in the requisite way, and the certainty of his marrying Fanny, both increase. Beginning with "there would have been every *probability*" of Fanny's accepting his proposal, the thought experiment in the passage ends with the inevitability that Fanny "*must* have been his reward." What enables this increasing likelihood is that the passage shifts from suggesting that Henry's flawed character would have needed to be different ("could he have been satisfied," which we know temperamentally he could not) to the emphasis falling on a single act of fulfilling his intention to go to his estate. Ruth Yeazell claims that by the end of the passage, "the 'probability' of such an ending has become a certainty"—so much so that only the author's interposition, making Henry run off with Maria, saves Fanny from him.[71] Halsey, too, reads this alternate ending as uncomfortably plausible, intended to show the real danger that exists for Fanny in following the rules and doing as others demand of her.[72] Either way, the effect is a feeling that Fanny has had a close call.

What interests me is more basic than Henry's or Fanny's character, whether he reforms or she acquiesces. Austen's belated explications of alternate endings ask the reader to perform mental work that can, like any close call, feel uncomfortable. Visualizing the now-adulterous Henry marrying Austen's most prim and proper heroine feels more like vertigo than wish fulfillment. Brooks argues that novel readers want to look backward at the end and see a novel's events as inevitable; reopening speculation and a sense of contingency at the end of a novel is cognitively unsettling. Patricia Rozema's film adaptation of *Mansfield Park* (1999) highlights the irreverence of Austen's going against readers' expectations. Rozema chooses to focus on the playfulness present in the novel's final chapter, which begins with a breezy dismissal of narrative conventions, by ending the film with a series of moving tableaux as Fanny, in a voiceover, describes the fates of minor characters. The action pauses for a moment and Fanny says, "It could have all turned out differently, I suppose," then the characters go about their business again, and Fanny adds in a lively tone, "But it didn't."[73] While capturing Austen's irreverence, the film does not capture the somber tone of Austen's writing when she describes an imagined marriage in which Fanny is made into a "reward" and sacrificed to Henry.

Mansfield Park's prolonged, realistic recounting of hypotheticals is hardly romantic, or even playfully ironic, in tone. It is cautionary, full of references to Fanny's "conscience" and Henry doing "as he knew he ought," a textbook (or rather conduct book) moral narrative in which self-denying behavior has its "reward" and self-indulgence is punished. It is also notable that Austen stops short of describing Fanny as married to Henry, even hypothetically, but only goes so far as to say she "must" marry him after an unspecified, "reasonable period"—only after another hypothetical marriage, between Mary and Edmund, occurs. Like Sir Thomas cutting off his thought before allowing himself to imagine that Fanny might love Edmund, Austen's focusing on the run-up to, rather than marriage between, Fanny and Henry suggests that some possibilities might simply be too unwelcome to entertain. With every conditional verb, Austen underscores what she as novelist chose *not* to have happen; this unfulfilled possibility is included only to be marked as not possible in the novel's *realized* fictional world. As Gallagher notes, counterfactual speculation does not challenge the difference between what has and has not happened, "is not trying to convince you otherwise," but depends on the "admittedly false" nature of the statement to incite speculation.[74] Alternative imagining for Austen is at once a lively play of mind and a serious pedagogical exercise, from which a moral lesson "ought" to be learned.

What is the lesson? Austen's commitment to the readerly work of imagining other possibilities is part of her realist project—a project to depict a world in which women's social options were painfully limited. William Galperin has described *Mansfield Park* as hyperrealist: "relatively uncontained and continuous with life, rather than a world circumscribed by narrative deliberation and closure."[75] There are real consequences to learning to distinguish the most likely contingency in novels that so closely mimic the real world. Two of *Mansfield Park*'s most often-quoted lines focus on female powerlessness. When Maria Bertram says "I cannot get out" (99), as she and Henry Crawford are waiting for the key to open a garden gate at her fiancé's estate, the reader understands she is referring to both her immediate predicament and her imminent marriage. Fanny's insistence when pressed by the others to join in their theatricals, "I really cannot act" (146), is often seen as referring, in part, to her constrained situation as a poor, dependent female relation. Including another ending subtly highlights how constrained Austen's narrative options were as a female novelist who eschews the clichés of romance and focuses on realistically representing the everyday female world. Austen's hypotheticals focus on the marital choices male characters make—what *they* could have done differently and how they felt in consequence. The passage in *Mansfield Park* dwells on Henry's freedom of movement and agency, in contrast to Fanny's limited choice (had Henry asked Fanny, the narrator pronounces, she "*must* have been his reward"). Fanny can only refuse, as Henry Tilney says in *Northanger Abbey* about courtship: a man "has the advantage of choice, woman only the power of refusal."[76]

But even the power of refusal requires a young woman to imagine possible futures for herself, compare them with one another, and decide which is the most natural choice. How else, other than through reading novels, might a young girl learn to reason about possibilities so that she can decide whom to marry in real life? Trollope defends novel reading in similar terms more than half a century later, as the means by which "girls learn what is expected from them, and what they are to expect when lovers come."[77] Learning to compare possible marriage plots, to weigh the evidence and imagine likely outcomes, is a way of reading a realist novel that enlists creative fantasy yet has real-world consequences. In continuing to offer hypothetical alternatives after the central marriage plot has been decided—to make the reading experience *feel* narratable, when the narrative itself is actually not—Austen exercises one last time the reader's capacity to compare the probability of vastly different outcomes. The abilities to tolerate multiplicity and complex possibilities: these are the productive and realist uses of imagination that Austen models in her characters and invites readers to exercise further.

As Mary Favret, Emily Rohrbach, and others have shown, Austen was living in a politically unsettled time and was herself keenly sensitive to uncertainty and dependence on circumstance.[78] Where critics of her novels have traditionally focused on how Austen returns this unsettled social world to certainty, what has emerged recently is Austen's appreciation for the possibilities afforded by provisional situations. Her "provisional logic" is evident in a series of letters she wrote to her niece Fanny Knight, who was deciding whether or not to marry a suitor.[79] Austen assures Fanny that her "mistake has been one that thousands of women fall into"—thinking herself in love with "the *first* young man who attached himself to you."[80] Austen goes on to offer her niece detailed descriptions of how she might feel upon either accepting or rejecting him, writing, "And now, my dear Fanny, having written so much on one side of the question, I shall turn round & entreat you not to commit yourself farther."[81] Fanny Knight happily married someone else, after having been helpfully instructed—like the reader of another Fanny's marriage plot—in how to envision the most natural ending.

Persuasion's Serious Possibilities

Edmund Bertram fears the effect on Fanny of hearing her own unrealized marriage plot when he repeats what Mary Crawford says about Henry: "[Fanny] would have fixed him; she would have made him happy for ever." Edward goes on, "My dearest Fanny, I am giving you, I hope, more pleasure than pain by this retrospect of what might have been—but what never can be now" (455). Fanny, who is as certain as Austen was that she would never marry Henry, only feels relief at being "safe from Mr Crawford" (461). But elsewhere in Austen's novels, imagining "what might have been—but what never can be now" results in a mingling of painful and restorative affects. In particular, as we are seeing, Austen complicates the enjoyment of a happy ending even to a novel (or three) in which her heroine has suffered for most of it. *Persuasion's* happy ending comes with the often-quoted caveat that Anne Elliot has married into the navy, with "the dread of a future war all that could dim her sunshine" (252). Austen's realist novels also subtly "dim" the romance plot's conventional "happily ever after" by including a subsidiary, but still painful, imaginative exercise that casts a healthy shadow over the ending. In closing this chapter, I examine *Persuasion* as Austen's own ending to her career-long exploration of the salutary pain of realistic imagining.

Persuasion's entire plot reads as an alternative ending to a marriage plot that ended badly seven years before the novel begins. It is "in effect a second novel," as Tony Tanner calls it.[82] The reader is immersed in Anne Elliot's consciousness through Austen's extensive use of free indirect discourse, and Anne has thought enough in the past conditional tense for eight years for Austen to state emphatically: "She was persuaded that under every disadvantage of disapprobation at home, and every anxiety attending his profession, all their probable fears, delays, and disappointments, *she should yet have been* a happier woman in maintaining the engagement, than she had been in the sacrifice of it" (29; my emphasis). As events happen in the novel, Anne experiences them as having less meaning than if they were part of a different, unrealized narrative.[83] "'These would have been all my friends,' was her thought" when meeting Captains Harville and Benwick at Lyme, "and she had to struggle against a great tendency to lowness" (98). Anne's regret suffuses the novel even when she is not directly thinking of what might have been. D. A. Miller calls the novel "extravagantly rueful"; William Deresiewicz describes it as a "meditation" on grief.[84] Marriage between Anne Elliot and Captain Wentworth is never technically impossible, unlike in Austen's other postscript-like elaborations of alternative marriages. But it is not until three-quarters of the way through the novel that Anne first has hope and considers Wentworth "unshackled and free" (167). Until then, and even after, her old feelings revive "agitation" (85), resulting in what Mary Favret refers to as Anne's "repeated bouts of vertigo and dislocation" when Wentworth is present and Anne's "intensely felt but thwarted desire to find 'peace.'"[85]

Reading Austen's prose is often a rational, smooth, pleasing experience. But in addition to steeping the reader in Anne's melancholy, *Persuasion* repeatedly refers to the pain of thinking about imagined things; at least, that is how the word "pain" appears often in the novel. Recalled or anticipated events bring pain in a variety of minds and situations. Backward thinking for Anne is, of course, painful: the memory of former meetings with Wentworth in Bath "would be brought too painfully before her" (93). "*Too* painfully": Anne repeatedly evaluates her own and others' different degrees of pain. Early in the novel Anne imagines that Wentworth is not hurting from memory as much as she is: "She was very far from conceiving it to be of equal pain" (63). Anne specifically uses imaginative projection to determine which course of events would involve *more* suffering. At the end of the novel, she reasons in retrospect that she made the right choice in breaking her original engagement. She tells Wentworth, "I was right in submitting to [Lady Russell], and that if I had done otherwise, I should have suffered more in continuing the engagement than I did even in giving it up, because I should have suffered in my conscience" (246). A similar projection into the past, which I discuss below, brings Wentworth "a sort of pain, too, which is *new* to me" (247; my emphasis). As we know, painful imaginings are gendered, and women have a greater share. (Twice Anne anticipates that Lady Russell will feel pained in situations that have not yet happened; 141, 218.) At the same time, for female characters like Anne or Marianne, following out fully the fantasy of having done otherwise at least frees them from the pain of regret. In a realist novel like *Persuasion*, imagining all of the possibilities shows that there is no imagined alternative in which "suffering might have been spared" (247) entirely; it can just be lessened.

More than once, hypothetical scenarios that occur to Anne provoke a particular, uncomfortable, even physical response: shuddering. Austen uses a physiological language in the novel that does not seem to belong to her usual palette, often to describe visceral, impulsive responses the characters have in moments of heightened feeling. In a letter, Maria Edgeworth describes the images in the novel as vivid to the point of almost physical sensation, as she writes of an early scene between Anne and Wentworth: "Don't you see Captain Wentworth, or rather don't you in her place feel him taking the boisterous child off her back as she kneels by the sick boy on the sofa?"[86] Claudia Johnson, noting that in *Persuasion* "the body is foregrounded as never before"—especially its susceptibility to being damaged—describes how "unguardedness and involuntary losses of self-control are prized as reliable indicators of deep feeling."[87] Anne even has impulsive physical responses to things she only imagines. Early on, when Wentworth recounts his history and his having had the good luck to arrive in Plymouth in his old ship, the *Asp*, six hours before a massive storm "which would have done for poor old *Asp*," Anne "shudder[s]" at his projecting:

"Four-and-twenty hours later, and I should only have been a gallant Captain Wentworth, in a small paragraph at one corner of the newspapers; and being lost in only a sloop, nobody would have thought about me."

Anne's shudderings were to herself alone. (66)

Anne's imagination of what might have been—even though the possibility is past—is so vivid that Austen uses a highly physical metaphor, "shudderings," to convey an intense feeling. In another moment, Anne's envisioning how she might have married Mr. Elliot also makes her "shudder." As Mrs. Smith explains why she assumed Anne was to marry Mr. Elliot, the step-by-step consideration of how such a marriage might have come about occupies much more of the text than any description of Anne's feeling. Anne's affective state is conveyed by a single word, which in this case could describe a physical response, not just a metaphor: "Anne could just acknowledge within herself such a possibility of having been induced to marry him, as made her shudder at the idea of the misery which must have followed. It was just possible that she might have been persuaded by Lady Russell!" (211). As in the emphasis Austen puts on the plausibility of an alternate marriage between Henry Crawford and Fanny Price, Austen's realist technique in *Persuasion* involves repeatedly making plausibility, the "just possible," do the work of stirring feeling.

As in *Mansfield Park*, possibilities have a didactic effect, but in *Persuasion* this occurs through stirring heightened emotion rather than the rational language of probability. Lady Russell says that just picturing the same image of Anne married to Mr. Elliot, "if I might be allowed to fancy you such as she was," would give her "more delight than is often felt at my time of life!" Anne has to physically walk away to "try to subdue the feelings this picture excited," because "[f]or a few moments her imagination and her heart were bewitched." "Bewitched" is a strong feeling for a character to have in an Austen novel: Austen uses it to describe Darcy's attraction to Elizabeth in *Pride and Prejudice*. But in the melancholic *Persuasion*, bewitchment does not lead to marriage, and is followed by a second and ultimately more powerful response: "The same image of Mr Elliot speaking for himself brought Anne to composure again. The charm of Kellynch and of 'Lady Elliot' all faded away; . . . her judgement, on a serious consideration of the possibilities of such a case, was against Mr Elliot" (159–60). What Austen juxtaposes in this moment are two contrasting ways one can use imagination to envision alternate plots. The first is the kind of wish-fulfilling daydreaming that novel readers were accused of engaging in. But Anne here is a model of another "serious" way of imagining: she does not stop with picturing a bewitching, charming romance plot but reviews the imagined narrative and considers the possibilities from multiple perspectives. For Wentworth, too, his one pained outburst about Louisa's fall, when he imagines how else he might have acted, is serious: the thought experiment both renews his own suffering and increases his just sense of moral failure. In the carriage driving back from Lyme to

Uppercross, he imagines aloud: "Oh God! That I had not given way to her at the fatal moment! Had I done as I ought!" (116). Imagining a plausible series of alternate events after they are no longer possible is a serious moral exercise, a punishment for his overall behavior to Louisa.

One hypothetical in the novel brings pain without a seeming lesson. Captain Wentworth does what the narrator does in the endings of other novels: even after they have become reengaged to each other, he imagines aloud an ending for himself and Anne that is no longer possible. In Marianne Dashwood's case, a conversation in which Elinor imagines a different, now-impossible marital ending lays Marianne's wishes to rest. Here a similar conversation puts the heroine through seemingly superfluous pain. As Anne and Wentworth are talking over the past, Wentworth asks if she would have accepted him a year after his first proposal had he not been "too proud to ask again." He asks Anne,

> "Tell me if, when I returned to England in the year eight, with a few thousand pounds, and was posted into the *Laconia*, if I had then written to you, would you have answered my letter? Would you, in short, have renewed the engagement then?"
>
> "Would I!" was all her answer; but the accent was decisive enough. (247)

Whereas the narrator describes how Marianne or Fanny could have married someone else, Wentworth himself imagines a no-longer-possible alternate ending to his own marriage plot. He virtually enacts the belated proposal in asking Anne, "Would you . . . would you . . . ?" The happy narrative actuality that Anne and Wentworth have finally renewed their engagement pales in comparison to an even happier, unrealized narrative in which "six years of separation and suffering might have been spared" (247). Lynch describes how typically in an Austen novel's penultimate chapter the newly engaged couple discuss their history together in a "vaguely giggly conversation."[88] Wentworth's plausible imagining momentarily deflates the happiness of Anne's renewed engagement, for Anne's "Would I!" and Austen's elaboration of her "accent" as simply "decisive" suggests multiple strong feelings: emphatic assent, pained longing, frustrated regret. The reader knows that Anne had already thought of this scenario long ago, as she thinks when he first returns, "Had he wished ever to see her again, he need not have waited till this time; he would have done what she could not but believe that in his place she should have done long ago, when events had been early giving him the independence which alone had been wanting" (58). Austen here emphasizes how powerless Anne is, as a woman, to do anything more than think or wish; later in the novel Anne claims this as a "privilege" for women: of "loving longest, when existence or when hope is gone" (235). Wentworth's hypothetical question raises the specter of something many women have to endure, beyond the happy conclusion of Anne's marriage plot.

A hypothetical scenario in which she did not suffer for so long is an unspeakably painful thought experiment for Anne; two words is "all" she can respond. Wentworth and Anne repeatedly communicate without speaking, as numerous critics have noted.[89] *Persuasion*—a novel whose hero captained the *Laconia*—communicates intimately with the reader without speaking, in a sense, too. The novel's extensive use of free indirect discourse has so immersed the reader in Anne's consciousness that it takes only two words ("Would I!") to conjure Anne's painful, complex feeling. Austen's last novel is suggestive of the ways that the syntax or, in this case, lacunae in a novelist's prose style shapes imagining, as becomes increasingly evident in George Eliot's fiction.

Throughout the novel Austen appears to be pondering how painful it might be for a reader to imagine a novel in which imagining brings so much pain to the characters. Adela Pinch argues that there are parallels between Anne's experiences and the reader's experience of *Persuasion*. Anne's sense of experiencing painful but transient feelings, which mingle with pleasurable feelings, could describe the reader's experience of reading a novel steeped in Anne's consciousness.[90] When Anne is not overwhelmed by feeling, Austen uses her thinking about past experiences to theorize about how painful experience can be tempered with some kind of pleasure in a way that sounds Wordsworthian— especially within a novel that explicitly refers to Romantic poetry. Deresiewicz has argued for the "strikingly Wordsworthian characteristics of the mature novels," in particular, a "Wordsworthian redemption of painful experiences through the harmonizing power of memory," which he describes as the "affective ground bass" of *Persuasion*.[91] For instance, on leaving Uppercross, Anne thinks, "It stood the record of many sensations of pain, once severe, but now softened" (123). Remembering their time at Lyme, Anne's response to Wentworth sounds well considered, almost theoretical: "When pain is over, the remembrance of it often becomes a pleasure. One does not love a place the less for having suffered in it, unless it has been all suffering, nothing but suffering" (184). In the preface to *Lyrical Ballads*, Wordsworth claims the poet has a special capacity "to produce an infinite complexity of pain and pleasure."[92] It can be painful and uncomfortable to exercise one's imagination in realistic ways while reading literature, Austen seems to suggest, but the pain is fleeting, while such an exercise of imagining can have long-lasting, instructive, and pleasing effects.

Finally, such mingled affect poignantly characterizes Anne and Wentworth's interactions during their returning feelings for each other, an intimate, precious state of dawning love that Austen also leaves notably unexplicated. Early on, at Uppercross, after Wentworth hands her into the carriage with the Crofts, Anne analyzes not only his act but its effect on her: "It was a remainder of former sentiment; it was an impulse of pure, though unacknowledged friendship; it was a proof of his own warm and amiable heart, which she could not contemplate without emotions so compounded of pleasure and pain, that she knew not which prevailed" (91). Shrewdly as she analyzes Wentworth, Anne's powers of analysis fail when it comes to feeling her own mixed feelings—"she knew not which prevailed." Amid the busy, happy chaos of the Musgrove family making demands on her at Bath, Anne "was deep in the happiness of such misery, or the misery of such happiness, instantly" (229). The striking interchangeability of phrases here suggests a flustered state of mind, and one Anne is thrown into so "instantly" that Austen cannot stop to describe it. When she and Wentworth first reencounter each other in Bath, in the shop while it is raining, Anne's state of feeling is even harder for her to define: "Still, however, she had enough to feel! It was agitation, pain, pleasure, a something between delight and misery" (175). The English language has words that mean "a something between delight and misery": in this moment of free indirect discourse, when Anne is so overwhelmed by the very mix of her feelings that she is unable to put her feelings into words in her head, the narrator also can't stop to think of such a word. Strong feeling, so central in *Persuasion* to Austen's recurring interest in "what might have been—but what never can be now," gains strength by being left for the reader to fill in, wordlessly.

Nearly half a century after Austen, Eliot similarly reflects, within a novel's pages, on readers' unrealistic expectations for how her realist novel will end. In *The Mill on the Floss* (1860), Eliot includes a satiric narration of an alternative, romanticized ending to Maggie Tulliver's marriage plot—an ending Eliot insisted was never possible for her to write.[93] After Maggie Tulliver returns to St. Ogg's alone from her river journey with Stephen Guest, the narrator uses a comically exaggerated voice to mimic what the town gossips would have said if she had married Stephen:

If Miss Tulliver, after a few months of well-chosen travel, had returned as Mrs Stephen Guest—with a post-marital trousseau and all the advantages possessed even by the most unwelcome wife of an only son, public opinion, which at St Ogg's, as elsewhere, always knew what to think, would have judged in strict consistency with those results. . . . —"and a deformed young man, you know!—and young Guest so very fascinating; and, they say, he positively worships her (to be sure, that can't last!), and he ran away with her in the boat quite against her will, and what could she do? . . . and how very well that maize-colored satinette becomes her complexion!"[94]

Eliot follows out the rejected, Cinderella-like plot in excessive, sartorial detail. Such an ending prefigures and caricatures the preferences of readers and reviewers, like the one who later objected to the novel because "there is too much that is painful in it."[95] Eliot herself was unequivocal that such an ending had no realized place in her novel, as she wrote in response to such a critique: "If I did not really know what my heroine would feel and do under the circumstances in which I deliberately placed her, I ought not to have written this book at all, but quite a different book, if any."[96] As the nineteenth century progressed, realist authors found themselves grappling all the more earnestly with that "quite a different book" they anticipated might be developing in their readers' minds.

2

Little Dorrit's Complaint

"WHAT CONNEXION can there be . . . ?," the narrator of *Bleak House* (1853) asks the reader early on in that convoluted novel, when the stories of the aristocrat and the crossing sweeper have not yet been "very curiously brought together."[1] Hints like these are usually seen as evidence of Charles Dickens's skill at building suspense and manipulating readers' emotions, particularly over the many months of his novels' serial publication. Critics have discussed his success in controlling readers' responses in every genre in which he worked, from the serial installment to the public readings.[2] But as teachers and readers of Dickens's novels, many of us are familiar with exactly the opposite experience: not feeling guided but unmoored, lost in a sea of characters and overwhelmed by imaginable options. Reading the late, big, multiplot novels set in London—*Bleak House, Little Dorrit* (1857), *Our Mutual Friend* (1865)—it seems as if anything could happen, as if any character could turn out to be connected to any other right up until the last page.

This chapter moves forward in time to the mid-nineteenth century, when open-ended creativity appears as an essential, though uncomfortable and hard to sustain, facet of novel reading in Dickens's writings. Compared to the binary choices available to Jane Austen's characters (will Marianne Dashwood marry Willoughby or Colonel Brandon?), in Dickens's multiplot novels, the possibilities for how characters have been and will be related to one another are vast. A "little bit (two inches wide) of ivory" contains the whole social world of an Austen novel, in which options can be poignantly limited. The large social canvas of Dickens's multiplot novels makes possible a new reading experience in which readers genuinely do not know and cannot foresee a clear path to the ending, even if the ultimate pairing of the central marriage plot can be predicted, for in Dickens's novels, possibilities proliferate at more than just the level of plot. Andrew Miller describes the inherently counterfactual quality of

Dickens's imagination, with its "relentlessly metaphoric habits" that "express the continual presence of alternative patterns of experience and meaning."[3]

Such an overwhelming state of imaginative excess, freedom, and license was, for Dickens himself, the ideal, creative consequence of reading literature. In a variety of writings, fiction and nonfiction, he romanticizes how a reader is stimulated to add to, transform, and export images and characters out of a book's bound pages. Dickens presents fiction as offering a rare opportunity for Victorian readers to exercise open-ended creativity, a form of thinking he thought was endangered by the "utilitarian spirit" of the time. However, his own restless, directionless experience of creativity made him familiar with how taxing and engulfing a prolonged state of free-form imagining could be. And he knew how impatient serial readers of his novels were to make up their minds about a character or direction for the plot. At one moment in *Little Dorrit*, after describing Mr. Merdle as suffering from a mysterious, undefined illness or "complaint," Dickens addresses the reader in a way that suggests his own authorial complaint against overhasty readers: "Had he that deep-seated recondite complaint, and did any doctor find it out? Patience" (250). Drawing on a variety of Dickens's writings, this chapter first reconstructs his idealized depiction of reading literature as a porous, creative exercise. In the latter parts of the chapter, I focus on *Little Dorrit*, a dystopia of closed-down imaginations in which Dickens confronts his readers on multiple levels with what he saw as an especially mid-Victorian problem: keeping readers' imaginations open-ended enough to perceive both the aesthetic complexity of his fiction and real life's mysteries.

Poring Over Dickens

Robert Buss's watercolor *Dickens's Dream* (1875; fig. 1) has become an icon of Dickens's fertile imagination. Dickens's creativity has long been characterized as a bountiful, excessive, "irrepressible flow of fancy" (in John Forster's words).[4] Buss's painting, which was begun after Dickens's death, depicts the author seated in his study, with his eyes closed, surrounded by the abundance of characters he created. That Buss's portrait is unfinished has become part of its mythology: the illustrator died before completing it, so that its partly completed appearance seems to depict and pay homage to the process of artistic creation in the "Inimitable" author. Studies of Dickens and novel reading have tended to reproduce the image Dickens himself fostered of a celebrity, genius author with a mass following. His prefaces express a single author's affection for readers in aggregate, the "many thousands of people of both sexes, and of

FIGURE 1. Robert Buss, *Dickens's Dream* (1875; reproduced courtesy of the Charles Dickens Museum, London)

FIGURE 2. S[amuel] Luke Fildes, "The Empty Chair, Gad's Hill—Ninth of June 1870" (1870; Beinecke Rare Book & Manuscript Library, Yale University)

all ages and conditions, on whose faces we may never look," whose numbers grew (he specifically noted) with each serialized novel.[5] Forster's biography refers to the "crowds of people" whose minds Dickens was enriching, emphasizing the collective nature of reading Dickens, which Sarah Winter has astutely examined.[6] Dickens's nearly five hundred public readings of his work have further contributed to a critical bias toward discussing the reading of his novels as an author-centered and public act rather than a private, individual one.[7] Indeed, we know a great deal about Dickens's relationship with the Victorian reading public en masse; there is more to examine about how he perceived the psychological process of reading on an individual level, informed by his perceptions of his own mind and his readers' minds.[8]

Dickens's Dream can also be viewed in light of a more collaborative type of creativity that novel reading—and particularly reading Dickens's novels—engendered. Buss's image revises a different engraving, which places even more emphasis on Dickens as a sole creative figure: *The Empty Chair* (1870; fig. 2), an engraving made by Sir Samuel Luke Fildes (who was illustrating *The Mystery of Edwin Drood* at the time of Dickens's death) depicting Dickens's study as it looked on June 9, 1870, the day after his death. Widely reproduced at the time, *The Empty Chair* elegizes Dickens the author. The vacant chair is central in the composition and the dark rows of books appear as if in mourning, tight, rigid, and closed. Buss's image follows Fildes's composition closely, but in a spirit of riotous joy rather than melancholy. He pushes the author's chair to the side, out of reach of the desk, so that the scene is focused not on the creator who is gone but on the crowd of familiar characters who remain available to the reader after his death—who have indeed burst out of their books and fill the scene (so Buss seems to have planned) in rich color. Forster, Dickens's friend and biographer, similarly describes this unique sense that Dickens's novels were available for appropriation by readers at all levels of society: "There were crowds of people at this time who could not tell you what imagination meant, who were adding month by month to their limited stores the boundless gains of imagination."[9] Indeed, the tableaux that Buss added to Fildes's rendering of Dickens's study may have been inspired by a recent series of engravings about an imaginative reader: Gustave Doré's engravings for a French edition of *The History of Don Quixote* (1863).[10]

Critics who extol Dickens's creativity as a writer echo Dickens's own idealization of fiction as Don Quixote–like, imaginatively stimulating. That fiction could, as David Copperfield puts it, "ke[ep] alive my fancy," has become familiar as an abstract value Dickens articulates for his art.[11] Dickens's nuanced

understanding of the *difficulty* of bringing about this effect has not been examined. For Dickens reading is ideally porous: readers take characters out of the
bounds of a static book and into their mobile imaginations, and independently
export them into the world. Dickens's lifelong sensitivity to feeling confined
inflects his portrayal of the reading process as an act of breaking free of authorial
control. The fertility, freedom, and mental independence of novel reading figure
for Dickens as an antidote to the particular mental confinements and rigidities
that characterized Victorian life and theories of mind. At the same time, the
license and abundance of the reader's individual imagination in his writings also
characterize his own creative process, which could be excessive, uncomfortable,
and—Dickens knew—not a state serial readers wanted to prolong.

Dickens's fundamental interest in how the mind works has been shown
across his writings, from ghost stories to essays to novels.[12] The critical view that
Dickens was not well read in the intellectual currents of his day dates at least back
to George Henry Lewes's damning portrayal in "Dickens and Criticism" (1872)
of Dickens as "completely outside philosophy, science and the higher literature."[13] While Dickens was not deeply versed in any one coherent psychological
theory, his curiosity about the mind's functioning was also not limited by one
school of thought. The psychological explanations that interested him ranged
from the inquiries of mainstream physiological psychology, which were appearing in journals and academic treatises and written by men in his social circle, to
popular forms of interest in the mind, such as mesmerism, which Dickens encountered in the contexts of medicine and commercialized entertainment, and
briefly trained in himself. Dickens did display an abiding interest in the unconscious workings of the mind, but even this took the form of a variegated knowledge of dream theory, mesmeric trance, and traumatic memory lapse.[14]

Although the theories of mind that interested Dickens differ in many ways,
they share and reinforce in one another a language of fixity and freedom to
describe mental processes. Athena Vrettos has shown how Dickens's sense of
mental rigidity appears in his work on multiple levels—psychological, social,
and narrative—in his reliance on habit "as a mode of characterization."[15] Likewise, multiple causes account for Dickens's portrayal of mental experience as
confining by nature. His father's imprisonment for debt when he was a child
has long been suggested as a deeply personal reason for his preoccupation with
mental confinement. So has associationist psychology, which by the mid-
nineteenth century was diffuse throughout Victorian intellectual culture.[16]
First put forth by John Locke and developed by such late eighteenth- and
nineteenth-century proponents as Dugald Stewart and James Mill, the

associationist model of the mind was based in crude terms on an idea that each individual's experience and environment, not innate nature, organize and determine mental activity. Early experience imprints certain sensations or perceptions on the mind; connections between such sensations then create a foundation for ordering subsequent mental experience. Nicholas Dames has argued that the subtle but continual presence of associationist ideas in Dickens's work mirrors how these ideas were ingrained in educated Victorian culture, "a generally understood cultural idea," throughout the period of Dickens's adult life.[17] This empiricist model provided a widely applied basis for social practices and institutions, which appeared to Dickens increasingly mechanized in character.

Other writers, too, were protesting that living in an increasingly mechanized culture precluded imagining. In his *Autobiography* (1873), John Stuart Mill relates how his own education, according to the utilitarian principles that grew out of associationism, ignored what Mill calls "the internal culture of the individual" and recognized "little good in any cultivation of the feelings, and none at all in cultivating them through the imagination."[18] Rick Rylance suggests that Dickens carries associationism's theories to an extreme in ridiculing its "heartless, soulless, joyless, mechanical reductions of human behavior."[19] Most obviously in *Hard Times* (1854), but also in *Little Dorrit*, Dickens was especially concerned with the ways in which socialization in Victorian culture takes the form of an "iron binding of the mind to grim realities." In his preface to the first issue of *Household Words*, Dickens sets imaginative literature against the "utilitarian" mindset of the time:

> No mere utilitarian spirit, no iron binding of the mind to grim realities, will give a harsh tone to our Household Words. In the bosoms of the young and old, of the well-to-do and of the poor, we would tenderly cherish that light of Fancy which is inherent in the human breast; which, according to its nurture, burns with an inspiring flame, or sinks into a sullen glare, but which (or woe betide that day!) can never be extinguished. To show to all, that in all familiar things, even in those which are repellant on the surface, there is Romance enough, if we will find it out:—to teach the hardest workers at this whirling wheel of toil, that their lot is not necessarily a moody, brutal fact, excluded from the sympathies and graces of imagination.[20]

The "grim realities" of Victorian life are so "moody," "brutal," and "repellant" that escaping into an imaginative world is not a given: there is escape into fantasy "*if* we will find it out." Dickens politicizes imagination here, claiming that it is a birthright that transcends a person's social condition.[21] He repeatedly portrays the ordinary exercise of imagination as an endangered act, focusing attention on the factors that would hem it in and making the exercise of imagination into a form of rebellion, not guaranteed to succeed.

Hard Times, written immediately before *Little Dorrit*, dramatizes the struggle to maintain and experience "the sympathies and graces of imagination," which Dickens encapsulates in the novel's use of the term "wonder." The satiric "keynote" of this utilitarian culture, "Never wonder," suggests that open-ended speculation is a natural inclination of the mind, which the Gradgrindian educational system, with its "utilitarian spirit," must suppress:

> "Louisa, never wonder!" Herein lay the spring of the mechanical art and mystery of educating the reason without stooping to the cultivation of the sentiments and affections. Never wonder. By means of addition, subtraction, multiplication, and division, settle everything somehow, and never wonder.[22]

Dickens here sets curiosity and the free play of the mind opposite to the mechanical, mathematical, rational form of thought that associationist theory emphasized. Wonder is also a capacity Dickens connects with reading. In *Hard Times* it is "wonder" that the satiric narrator reiterates in describing the few readers who continue to use the Coketown library: "It was a disheartening circumstance, but a melancholy fact, that even these readers persisted in wondering. They wondered about human nature, human passions, human hopes and fears, the struggles, triumphs, and defeats, the cares, and joys and sorrows, the lives and deaths, of common men and women!"[23] "Wonder" refers to the curiosity or sense of awe that draws readers to books as well as characterizes their experience of reading them—a free, imaginative outlet present almost nowhere else in the utilitarian dystopia of Coketown. In *Little Dorrit*, Dickens continues to depict the extreme emotional confinement of the central characters' lives as in part a consequence of living in a society that operates on the principle that (as the social paragon Mrs. General puts it) "it is better not to wonder" (457).

Getting out of bounds even in one's thoughts is difficult for some of Dickens's characters, though not because of the culture they live in but because of how personal experiences have shaped their minds. Dickens's belief in mental development as a kind of "iron binding" manifests in his repeated portrayals of minds that have become fixed after a traumatic loss.[24] Mr. Dick in *David Copperfield* and Flora Finching in *Little Dorrit* associate every unrelated thing to a loss experienced in youth.[25] Mr. Dick is transfixed by King Charles, who despite his irrelevance to the subject of the memorial Mr. Dick is writing, "always strayed into it sooner or later" (226). (In Aunt Betsey's protopsychoanalytic explanation, Charles serves as Mr. Dick's "allegorical way of expressing . . . great disturbance and agitation" over the source of his loss: long ago, his favorite sister's ill treatment by her husband and his own subsequent, debilitating illness; 215.) In Mr. Dick and Flora Finching, Dickens depicts minds that appear open-ended, to range freely and illogically, but in fact are always straying back to the same, deeply painful subject. Dickens himself, in the autobiographical fragment that led to his writing *David Copperfield*, describes his own repeated straying to one thought as an effect of his traumatic childhood experiences: "Even now, famous and caressed and happy, I often forget in my dreams that I have a dear wife and children; even that I am a man; and wander desolately back to that time of my life."[26] Though Dickens protested against the cultural repression of free-ranging thought, he also explores how personal experience can have a similarly constraining effect that makes freedom of mind hard to achieve.

Dickens was so sensitive to any sense of mental confinement that he portrays reading imaginative literature in terms of feeling constricted, but also as an opportunity to "get out of bounds." In "Discovery of a Treasure Near Cheapside," an article Dickens wrote for *Household Words* in 1852, he recounts how his early experience of reading imaginative literature stirred within him a creative desire to add literal quantity to a fiction first imagined by someone else. The article relates the story of his being shown an unpoetic gold refinery in Cheapside, where the boxes of gold, "lying, like any common merchandise, quite familiarly in a big uncomfortable counting house," nonetheless call to mind the treasures in all the romantic fables he encountered as a child. He remembers about the fable of Ali Baba and other tales:

> In all these golden fables there was never gold enough for me. I always wanted more. I saw no reason why there should not be mountains and rivers of gold, instead of paltry little caverns and olive pots; why Jason and his men should not have sailed in search of flocks of golden fleeces rather than one. For, when imagination does begin to deal with what is so hard of attainment in reality, it might at least get out of bounds for once in a way, and let us have enough.[27]

Elsewhere in his writings, Dickens suggests that reading novels and stories was the most profound and almost sole pleasure of his childhood. But according to the above account, that pleasure is not provided by the tales themselves, which are "paltry" and unsatisfying. The fables alone leave him like Oliver Twist, "want[ing] more"; the real satisfaction of reading comes through his own recreation of the stories as even more fanciful, less realistic narratives.

This description of how reading imaginative stories causes the reader's imagination to overflow resonates with how a reviewer late in the novelist's career described reading Dickens's novels. Dickens, he writes, has "the power of creating characters which have, so to speak, an overplus of vitality, passing beyond the limits of the tale, and making itself felt like an actual, external fact."[28]

That a story can and should spill out of a book means Dickens imagines fluid, porous boundaries between the reader and the author, the story and the world. Dickens significantly at times refers to the act of reading with the highly physical term "poring." "Poring" over a book appears to describe a reader's absorption in an author's words, but for Dickens the verb also captures how a reader deeply absorbed in a fictional work passes freely between his own and the author's imaginations, as well as between the author's fabricated world and the reader's own physical world. The often-discussed passage in *David Copperfield* in which David recalls, as a child, "reading as if for life" (67), contains Dickens's most explicit articulation in his writings of the effect reading has on the reader's imagination. The passage first sounds as if he is responding to the moralistic terms that had often been applied to novel reading. He emphasizes the innocence of David's reading, denies that any "harm" comes from novels, and imagines himself as "a child's Tom Jones, a harmless creature":

> My father had left in a little room up-stairs, to which I had access (for it adjoined my own) a small collection of books which nobody in our house ever troubled. From that blessed little room, Roderick Random, Peregrine Pickle, Humphrey Clinker, Tom Jones, the Vicar of Wakefield, Don Quixote, Gil Blas, and Robin Crusoe came out, a glorious host, to keep me company. They kept alive my fancy, and my hope of something beyond that place and time,—they, and the Arabian Nights, and the Tales of the Genii,—and did me no harm; for whatever harm was in some of them was not there for me; *I* knew nothing of it. It is astonishing to me now, how I found time, in the midst of my porings and blunderings over heavier themes, to read those books as I did. It is curious to me how I could ever have consoled myself under my small troubles (which were great troubles to me), by impersonating my favorite characters in them—as I did—and by putting Mr. and Miss Murdstone into all the bad ones—which I did too. I have been Tom Jones (a child's Tom Jones, a harmless creature) for a week together. (66)

Reading fiction is characterized by literal, physical porousness: the books are in a separate room that "adjoins [David's] own," into which he passes freely and out of which the "glorious host" of characters spill out. Porousness is joyful, offering

David—imprisoned as he is in the Murdstones' proto-Gradgrindian plan of education—the flexibility and freedom of being able to mingle his creativity with that of the author. While reading, he transforms the villains that Fielding created into the villains of his life, the Murdstones. Between and after reading, he acts out the events of the novels he reads, "impersonating" or taking its characters into himself by embodying them outwardly in the world. While Dickens sought, in the abstract, for his readers to make the world more imaginative—the first issue of *Household Words* appeared the same year—David models step-by-step how to do that: by exporting characters from the fictional world into the actual world. Dickens's reference to the scene of actual reading is brief ("I sitting on my bed, reading as if for life"), but what he describes remembering, in great detail, is the landscape he transformed through his own imaginative play of mind: "Every barn in the neighbourhood, every stone in the church, and every foot of the churchyard, had some association of its own, in my mind, connected with these books, and stood for some locality made famous in them. I have seen Tom Pipes go climbing up the church-steeple; I have watched Strap, with the knapsack on his back, stopping to rest himself upon the wicket-gate; and I know that Commodore Trunnion held that club with Mr. Pickle, in the parlour of our little village alehouse." Within the passage, the most affectionate, nostalgic, eulogistic language is evoked by the village he infused with his childhood imagination, not used to describe the "small collection of books which nobody in our house ever troubled" themselves.

In the same passage, however, Dickens hints at how the permeability and mobility of an absorbed, creative mind is not only joyful. David pores over lessons as much as novels: he is "astonished," even as an adult, that he was able to release himself "in the midst of my porings and blunderings over heavier themes" (66). The expression "to pore one's eyes out" means that one alters his or her physical state by poring; one can "blind oneself, ruin one's eyesight, or tire one's eyes by close reading or overstudy" (*Oxford English Dictionary*; hereafter *OED*). This happens to David just before he describes release through reading eighteenth-century novels. He recalls a scene of his stepfather and step-aunt torturing him with a math problem involving a large number of Gloucester cheeses:

> I pore over these cheeses without any result or enlightenment until dinnertime; when, having made a Mulatto of myself by getting the dirt of the slate into the pores of my skin, I have a slice of bread to help me out with the cheeses, and am considered in disgrace for the rest of the evening. (65)

Dickens links the two meanings of the word "pore": the first use refers to intense intellectual absorption; the second, to the porousness of the skin. David's mentally poring over Gloucester cheeses results in his physically mingling with the math problem's material form. His pores let in the debris of his slate, which, as the metaphor takes off, changes who he is: he becomes a "Mulatto." David here is absorbed in an unsolvable problem to the point of losing his identity, much as he becomes absorbed in the fantasy of being a fictional character to the point of losing his identity. But in the case of the slate, Dickens describes this metaphorical transformation in a way that Victorian readers would have regarded as undesirable: the slate darkens his skin to the point of a racial slur.

Thus, even though Dickens romanticizes the mental freedom that characterizes absorption in an imagined world, he also explores the consequences and excesses of such a state. As Forster tells it, Dickens experienced his own characters as exporting themselves where they will: "Imagination has its own laws; and where characters are so real as to be treated as existences, their creator himself cannot help them having their own wills and ways," Forster writes.[29] For while Dickens models the pleasure of imagining exportable characters in *David Copperfield*, the same novel features stories and writing as refusing to stay where they belong or originate, but getting (or trying to get) where they are not supposed to: Mr. Dick cannot keep Charles I out of his memorial; David the author reminds the reader that he is attempting to keep his works of fiction out of the narrative; David is kept awake reciting stories to Steerforth and the boys at school when he longs to sleep; and the scraps of paper on which Dr. Strong makes notes for his dictionary are coming out of his pockets, "sticking out of him in all directions" (529).

In letters Dickens describes his experience of literary production as much like Dr. Strong's and the distressing effect that invention had on Dickens in terms similar to Mr. Dick's struggles. Victorian reviewers and later biographers repeatedly comment on how difficult he found it to impose order on his creativity. Forster turns this into a merit, framing Dickens's imagination in the Romantic terms of genius beyond Dickens's control. He was "a man of genius, who never knows where any given conception may lead him"; he describes Dickens beginning *Martin Chuzzlewit* and "seeing little as yet of the main track of his design."[30] But Forster also repeatedly refers to the strain of imagining, to "the difficult terms, physical as well as mental," on which "Dickens held the tenure of his imaginative life" and "the sensitive conditions under which . . . he carried on these exertions of his brain."[31] Dickens's readers and reviewers complained about *Little Dorrit* that, "The entire story does not hold together with sufficient closeness"; "the wilderness of *Little Dorrit*," one Victorian reviewer called it; "it abounds in jolts and odd turns; it is full of singular twists and needless complexities," wrote another.[32] Forster's response is that making an orderly plot from such fertile imagining could be exhausting. Appealing to the reader's sympathy, he describes Dickens, after *Nicholas Nickleby* (1838), seeking relief in crafting a series of shorter tales, worn out by "the writing of a long story with all its strain on his fancy."[33]

According to both Dickens's own account and to observers, the open-ended stage of constructing a new fictional world proved especially disordering for him. The initial phase of conceiving of a novel in its entirety—as opposed to writing an installment in the middle—was the most taxing, chaotic period of writing for him, and especially so when he was beginning *Little Dorrit*. "I am now . . . in the wandering—unsettled—restless—uncontroullable [*sic*] state of being about to begin a new book," Dickens writes to Leigh Hunt.[34] Based in part on such letters, biographer Fred Kaplan describes how, in starting *Little Dorrit*, "his orderly pattern of anticipating one novel at a time gave way to explosive fragments of alternate possibility, which might or might not be connected, which might or might not become literary realities."[35] Kaplan suggests that experiencing such an out-of-control proliferation of options— "explosive fragments of alternate possibility"—could feel violently disordering even to Dickens. Indeed, Forster affirms that, in this moment of the creative process, Dickens had difficulty separating out relevant possibilities from other, intruding thoughts: "The first conceiving of a new book was always a restless time, and other subjects besides the characters that were growing in his mind would persistently intrude themselves into his night wanderings."[36] Working out the plot of a new book for Dickens involved wandering both around his study and around London on "night walks." Yet he describes his motion while he was writing *Little Dorrit* as frenetic, "Prowling about the rooms, sitting down, getting up, stirring the fire, looking out of the window, tearing my hair, sitting down to write, writing nothing, writing something and tearing it up, going out, coming in, a Monster to my family, a dread Phaenomenon to myself."[37] Indeed, Forster says, "it was during the composition of *Little Dorrit* that I think he first felt a certain strain upon his invention."[38] As the novel begins to progress and Dickens sounds more at ease, he writes that, "The story lies before me, I hope, strong and clear."[39] The interpolated "I hope," however, is telling of how tentatively Dickens felt his grasp of the whole, future story.

While reader and author experience imagination's disordering effects to different degrees, Dickens describes both reading and writing as states in which imagination abounds to the point of displacing the self. Thus, Dickens knew that creatively engaged readers might experience some of the "wandering—unsettled—restless—uncontroullable" state of mind that comes with not knowing how a story will proceed and speculating about (as Kaplan says) "alternate possibilit[ies] which might or might not be connected, which might or might not become literary realities." Moreover, Dickens suggests that his own initial, disordered state of mind left its stamp within his novels, as the fluid, loose mold for his narrative structures. As he writes while conceiving of *Dombey and Son* (1848), "So I mean to carry the story on, through all the branches and off-shoots and meanderings that come up."[40] Similarly, describing how he develops individual characters, he writes in a letter, "As to the way . . . in which these characters have opened out, that is to me one of the most surprising processes of the mind in this sort of invention. . . . Given what one knows, what one does not know springs up; and I am as absolutely certain of its being true as I am of the law of gravitation—If such a thing be possible, more so."[41] Creative absorption in an imagined world is an organic and growing experience in Dickens's accounts: branching, opening, shooting, and springing up in a somewhat out-of-control, delightful, but disordering way. Given the toll this imaginative state of mind took on Dickens over the course of a "long story," as Forster says, it makes sense that reading his novels in serial installments taxed readers too.

The Hazard of Writing in Parts

Writing to Forster about the literary critic and judge Francis Jeffrey making up his mind about the characters after only a few installments of *Dombey and Son* (1848), Dickens comments, "Is it not a strange example of the hazard of writing in parts, that a man like Jeffrey should form his notion of Dombey and Miss Tox on three months' knowledge? I have asked him the same question, and advised him to keep his eye on both of them as time rolls on."[42] It is noteworthy, "strange," to Dickens that a literary reader—"a man like Jeffrey"—would not tolerate ambiguity and allow for innumerable possibilities to emerge but rather succumb to the less sophisticated, popular desire for immediate certainty and clarity. "As time rolls on": Dickens identifies drawn-out time as required for the complexity and literariness of his novels to emerge, for he discovered that when readers were imaginatively "get[ting] out of bounds" of his stories, it was to escape uncertainty and hastily put together the novel's pieces. We have seen how Dickens portrays reading fiction as ideally stimulating the reader to further invention beyond the bound pages. In dialogue with and about his own actual readers, he focuses on specific ways their imaginations rush through and fail to perceive fully what he hopes to portray.

While the pleasures and benefits of serial reading have been well documented, we have paid less attention to how reading a long multiplot novel in parts over time also posed a unique imaginative challenge, and potential strain, for Victorian readers who sought immediate clarity and closure. Victorian serial readers were known for fantasizing about what they wanted to happen in the next installment, a suspenseful, imaginative experience of waiting that Caroline Levine characterizes as "a vital, vibrant pleasure."[43] But serialization, the publishing format that helped to make Dickens the most widely read British author writing in the nineteenth century, also lengthened the period of time in which perplexed readers struggled to piece a novel's disparate strands together. Dickens's personal writing in his prefaces and letters shows that he was keenly aware of readers' impatience with narrative uncertainty and frustration with having limited knowledge, inherent conditions of reading a novel that the serial publication of a long multiplot novel amplified. To Dickens, readers who were impatient to put the pieces of a novel together were not reveling in novel reading as a means of imagining freely, the state of mind he saw as under siege in Victorian life. They were eager to escape from what George Eliot calls "that unstrung condition which belongs to suspense."[44] Reading a multiplot novel immerses the reader not just in the positive effects of "inclusiveness" and "expansive[ness]" but also in the discomfort of "division," "breach," and the "immediate and fundamental problem of coherence," according to Peter Garrett in his foundational work on the Victorian multiplot novel.[45] Dickens found readers wanting to be released from the uncomfortable but creative state of speculation.

From early in his career, Dickens's prefaces show a striking awareness of how the serial mode of publication inhibits a reader's artistic perception. In multiple prefaces to *The Pickwick Papers* (1837), written in 1837, 1847, and 1867, Dickens describes how he anticipated that its "desultory" serial form would make it difficult for readers to absorb too complex a plot. He explains that "no ingenuity of plot was attempted, or even at that time considered very feasible by the author in connexion with the desultory mode of publication adopted." He claims to have aspired merely for every installment to be "complete in itself" so that "when collected, [it] should form one tolerably harmonious whole."[46]

Later he articulates in detail to Forster his awareness that readers' engagement in an immediate installment blinded them to indications of the "whole": "Of the tendency of composing a story piecemeal to induce greater concern for the part than for the whole, he had always been conscious; but I remember a remark also made by him to the effect that to read a story in parts had no less a tendency *to prevent the reader's noticing how thoroughly a work so presented might be calculated for perusal as a whole.*"[47] Critics have long agreed that comprehending one of Dickens's novels in its entirety can be a confusing, uncomfortable, and mentally strenuous experience, especially in contrast to how readily readers' imaginations conjure mobile scenes or characters.[48] When discussing readers of his own fiction, Dickens repeatedly performs a striking act of imaginative sympathy in adopting the reader's point of view and recognizing its contours and limitations. As a result, he also recognizes an irreconcilable gap between the author's and reader's perspectives. In the preface to *David Copperfield*, he laments that "no one can ever believe this Narrative, in the reading, more than I have believed it in the writing" (11).

"Peculiarly susceptible to the influence of his readers" and "obviously concerned with the reception of his books," Dickens comments repeatedly on how his readers engage in the process of constructing a united narrative as they read the initially disjointed parts of a novel.[49] In prefaces written after a novel's serial publication, he chides readers for their attempts to occupy the author's imaginative position and prematurely think they understand the work as a whole when they only grasp parts. In the preface to *Little Dorrit*, Dickens essentially tallies the hours he has spent with the novel compared with the reader as a way of asserting his authority over readers who judged the novel too soon as lacking structure: "As it is not unreasonable to suppose that I have held its [this story's] various threads with a more continuous attention than any one else can have given to them during its desultory publication, it is not unreasonable to ask that the weaving may be looked at in its completest state, and with the pattern finished" (5). Dickens repeats this figurative language of weaving, apparently in response to frequent complaints about the lack of unity in his work.[50] In the postscript to *Our Mutual Friend*, he again invokes authorial prerogative by dwelling on it being (again) "unreasonable" to expect that readers, reading the novel in serial form, "will, until they have it before them complete, perceive the relations of its finer threads to the whole pattern which is always before the eyes of the story-weaver at his loom."[51] Emphasizing his own mastery of the "finer threads," Dickens insists that any deficiency in the form is due to the reader's impatience rather than the author's lack of design.

Reviews of Dickens's fiction throughout his career reiterate the point that his novels lack unity, whether the whole is judged prematurely or not. The organic, fluid, loose structure that resulted from Dickens's "restless" creative periods simply did not match the form that Victorian critics thought creativity should take in a long novel. "The want of art is apparent, if we look only at the entire work," one reviewer of *Bleak House* wrote, acknowledging the "wonderful art" of some episodes or details within the novel.[52] (The same reviewer even imagined an alternative version of *Bleak House* that would be more unified: "If the whole of such a work as *Bleak House* were equal to its parts, what a book it would be!"[53]) The particular fecundity of Dickens's imagination made some reviewers express an even greater need to perceive a structure that could contain the overwhelming abundance. As one reviewer wrote of *Bleak House*, "Mr Dickens discards plot, while he persists in adopting a form for his thoughts to which plot is essential, and where the absence of a coherent story is fatal to continuous interest."[54] Using words like "continuous" and "coherent," as well as (in other reviews) "consistent" and "connected," to describe what Dickens's novels lack, these reviewers imply the kind of steadily coming together narrative they—and the potential readers whom they are addressing—expected and valued. Linda Hughes and Michael Lund claim that the serial form resonated for Victorian readers because they valued the kind of gradual change by which a complicated plot "work[s] itself clear by a slow and natural process."[55] Instead of offering unifying reassurance, Dickens's late novels deliberately extend the jumbled, open-ended, disconcerting period in which the reader can imagine connections between characters, with the resolution belated or "often hurried." In *Our Mutual Friend*, one reviewer wrote, "the complication of events *does not work itself clear by a slow and natural process*, but is, so to speak, roughly torn open."[56]

As his career progressed, Dickens responded to this Victorian preoccupation with steady unification in varying ways: with defensiveness, annoyance, and, most interestingly, efforts to influence his readers' ongoing mental construction of a connected narrative. The postscript to *Our Mutual Friend* conveys Dickens's pride and pleasure, late in his career, in having mastered the art of stringing the reader along with the gradual emergence of plot connections. Nicola Bradbury describes the "more assured" tone in which Dickens describes the challenge of carrying the reader along through a complex "design." He writes, "To keep for a long time unsuspected, yet always working itself out, another purpose originating in that leading incident, and turning it to a pleasant and useful account at last, was at once the most interesting and the most difficult part of my design."[57] Dickens sounds conscious of crafting the reading experience he knew readers desired, in which unity slowly comes into the reader's consciousness. In the same postscript, however, he again contrasts his own mastery with readers' mistaken judgments when they attempt to perceive the whole design. He anticipated that critics and readers would mistake his hints about how two supposedly different characters fit together; he says, "I foresaw the likelihood that a class of readers and commentators would suppose that I was at great pains to conceal exactly what I was at great pains to suggest: namely, that Mr John Harmon was not slain, and that Mr John Rokesmith was he." While he claims he "was at great pains" to orchestrate his audience's making the connection between Harmon and Rokesmith, he imagines he will be criticized for hiding the connection. In an irritated, patronizing tone, Dickens "hint[s] to an audience that an artist (of whatever denomination) may perhaps be trusted to know what he is about in his vocation, if they will concede him a little patience."[58] Dickens found it difficult to turn his readers' fantasies of a connected narrative to "pleasant and useful account" because, in his view, readers jump to conclusions too quickly; they cut short a period of speculation that can enrich his storytelling and make it more layered and complex. They want structure immediately; artistic structure, Dickens retorts, takes time and patience to perceive.

What both readers and critics failed to perceive, in Dickens's portrayal, was how the process of not understanding relations between characters and having to put a complex social world together was crucial to the realist artistry and ethical aims he sought to achieve. John Plotz has argued that the "interweaving of stories within the Victorian novel," including the interpolation of shorter stories that turn out to be relevant to a particular character, mirrors in a realistic way "a social world that is also itself constructed upon interlocking worlds of characters and stories." That a story's relevance is indefinite or opaque only further reflects "the way in which the novel succeeds at representing life itself."[59] Dickens blames the whole literary industry—critics and readers of criticism and novels—for closing down individual, open-minded "thinking." In a note to Forster, Dickens protests how critics create a certain reading of a book that readers then reflexively adopt; without such critical pronouncement, readers would be forced to allow a novel to develop its organic shape in their own minds, forestalling judgment about its lack of design. As he writes of his need to travel after the poor reception of *Martin Chuzzlewit*:

I *know*, if I have health, I could sustain my place in the minds of thinking men, though fifty writers started up to-morrow. How many readers do *not* think! How many take it upon trust from knaves and idiots, that one writes too fast, or runs a thing to death! . . . If I wrote for forty thousand Forsters, or for forty thousand people who know I write because I can't help it, I should have no need to leave the scene.[60]

As Dickens lashes back at critics who panned the novel, he describes wanting a readership of "thinking men": not a mass public of uncritical readers but informed literary men patient enough to wait for artistic complexity to emerge, comfortable enough with open-ended creativity to tolerate Dickens's wildly out-of-control imaginative process. Carolyn W. de la L. Oulton argues that in his disappointment with actual readers, Dickens became "his own ideal reader."[61] "Forty thousand Forsters" or "forty thousand people who know I write because I can't help it" does suggest Dickens's desire for an adulatory, appreciative audience. But this is a wish expressed in the conditional tense, by an author expressing frustration that such an audience did not exist.

Little Dorrit: Waiting for the Connection

In his working notes for the first installment of *Little Dorrit*, Dickens writes of his desire to structure the novel so that the reader is left in heightened doubt about the relations between the characters. "People to part and meet as travelers do, and the future connexion between them in the story, not to be now shown to the reader but to be worked out as in life. Try this uncertainty and this not-putting of them together, as a new means of interest. Indicate and carry through this intention" (792). In striving to make the characters' possible connections appear neither predictable nor predetermined, Dickens imagines drawing readers in with a lifelike, artistic effect. This "new means of interest" depends on the intricate working out of connections off the page, in the reader's mind. At the same time, Dickens knew that experimenting with how long it takes for the novel's plot to come together in the reader's mind could try the patience of Victorian serial readers. The novel itself dwells on how bewildering and oppressive that drawn-out process can feel. Dickens pairs not knowing in the novel with having a mysterious physical "complaint": the doctor who examines whether Mr. Merdle has "some deep-seated recondite complaint" determines that, "I can only say, that at present I have not found it out." It is the reader who suffers from suspense until the "complaint," forgery, is revealed four hundred pages later (250).

Throughout the novel Dickens depicts characters thinking about what will happen to them and how they might already be or will become connected, as he knew readers would also be doing. Jonathan Grossman argues persuasively that the historical rise of a networked system of international mobility helps to account for the "density and extensivity of people's interconnections" in the novel, which "exceeds their capacity to grasp them."[62] The characters' sense of "bewildering incompleteness" about their own position in the network has causes and resonates beyond the limited act of reading a serialized novel. Yet, speculating about possible connections between characters *was* on Dickens's mind as a distinctive form of imagining his fiction stimulated in readers, a form of imagining that could either heighten readers' interest or prevent them from seeing the development of literary complexity. In *Little Dorrit*, he brings readers into his thinking through the subject. Dickens dramatizes a range of negative affects that accompany speculating in a state of uncertainty, from confusion, to fear, exasperation, or feeling assaulted. Unbounded, free-form imagining, which Dickens elsewhere portrays as a joyous, ideal mindset to bring to literature, turns out not to be a helpful imaginative model to readers preoccupied with processing a disorderly plot and mentally constructing a united narrative. What these latter forms of imagining are suited to, Dickens implies, is something more significant than fictional plotting: using fiction to ponder life's real mysteries, outside of the novel's pages.

Little Dorrit begins with its characters in a state much like the readerly condition Dickens discusses in his prefaces: being uncomfortably confined to present circumstances and limited knowledge. In the opening two chapters, separate groups of characters are physically and mentally ill at ease as they await release from confinement with others who were previously strangers. The prisoner Rigaud appears "impatient" while "waiting to be fed" when we first see him (16); Mr. Meagles, in quarantine for a month, feels "like a sane man shut up in a madhouse" (29). The reader, too, is stuck in the present with barely known characters, unable to figure out the characters' histories, futures, and who or what "Little Dorrit" is. Dickens exacerbates the anxiety and uneasiness that inheres in beginning a novel and not being able to detect its design. As Miss Wade describes herself and the other characters, they appear to be helpless pawns within a larger, unknowable design, one that sounds "jar[ring]" and "evil" to innocent Pet Meagles. Miss Wade says ominously, when leaving quarantine in Marseilles,

> "[i]n our course through life we shall meet the people who are coming to meet us, from many strange places and by many strange roads . . . and what it is set to us to do to them, and what it is set to them to do to us, will all be done."

There was something in the manner of these words that jarred upon Pet's ear. It implied that what was to be done was necessarily evil. . . .

"You may be sure that there are men and women already on their road, who have their business to do with you, and who will do it. Of a certainty they will do it. They may be coming hundreds, thousands, of miles over the sea there; they may be close at hand now; they may be coming, for anything you know or anything you can do to prevent it, from the vilest sweepings of this very town." (37)

While Dickens uses spatial imagery to create unity throughout his multiplot novels, in *Little Dorrit* he literalizes the metaphor of travelers brought together "from many strange places and by many strange roads," "hundreds, thousands, of miles over the sea."[63] As Miss Wade lays the groundwork for the inevitable connections readers had come to expect in Dickens's novels by 1857, the sense of connection has a foreboding, rather than reassuring, aura. The passage emphasizes how helpless any one individual is to alter, or even know, an already "set" fate, a dynamic that particularly characterizes reading a novel. The one connection the passage begins to establish is through the phrase "the vilest sweepings of this very town," which appears to allude to the already-seen, villainous figure of Rigaud in Marseilles' jail. The repeated descriptions of people "coming" makes looking forward sound ominous and oppressive, as one might feel when setting out on a long, uncertain, potentially dangerous journey.

Through *Little Dorrit*'s characters, Dickens invites reflection on how attempting to understand preexisting, hidden connections between people can be a source of anxiety, if not a futile bewilderment. Clennam is repeatedly seen in page-long "serious speculation[s]" about "the secret reasons which had induced his mother to take Little Dorrit by the hand" (311). These speculations can be "like nightmares" (96); they cause him "much uneasiness" (311) and bring little resolution, as Dickens writes, "[l]aboring in this sea, as all barks labor in cross seas, he tossed about, and came to no haven" (312). Once again, Dickens uses metaphors of traveling to evoke an ominous state of mental suffering. Wondering how Clennam and Henry Gowan might become intertwined in the future through Pet Meagles, whom both would like to marry, Arthur thinks, "Where are we driving, he and I, I wonder, on the darker road of life? How will it be with us, and with her, in the obscure distance?" (310). "Wonder" here is hardly the free expression of imagination that the term refers to in *Hard Times*. In *Little Dorrit*, whose plot hinges on financial speculation, to "speculate" also accrues a host of negative meanings. Mr. Pancks, who brings about

Clennam's financial ruin, cannot bring himself to use the word "speculation," as Dickens notes of his using the term "investment" instead: "(Mr Pancks still clung to that word, and never said speculation)" (730). Wondering and speculating about one's own and other peoples' fortunes—sometimes literally speculating with their fortunes—is shown to be an acutely painful, as well as consequential, state of mind in *Little Dorrit*.

Thus, it is not surprising that another character, Affery Flintwinch, avoids speculative inquiry, habitually putting her apron over her head as if not to see each new, bewildering piece of the Clennam family puzzle she accidentally encounters. She appears "with her head going round and round" (53) after her first obfuscation (being told she has merely dreamed that she found her husband sitting across from his likeness, an identical twin brother unknown to her) and, when she does try to understand, "staggering herself with this enigma" (335), exclaims, "'Lord forgive me!' cried Affery, driven into a frantic dance by these accumulated considerations 'if I ain't a-going headlong out of my mind!'" (336). Affery is an exaggerated, comic character who expresses exasperation that the reader might also feel with the novel's enigmas. ("A heap of confusion," she gets called, and calls herself, when she tries to make sense of how the novel's characters are connected (732).) She is also a sympathetic victim, forced to marry her fellow servant, who gaslights her throughout the novel in telling her she has dreamed what she witnesses. Her experience of being helplessly subject to Jeremiah parallels the aggressive way that Dickens sought to keep his readers confused for as long as possible in writing the novel. In *David Copperfield*, as we have seen, Dickens projects exaggerated aspects of his own writerly experience into the kindly characters of Dr. Strong and Mr. Dick; in *Little Dorrit*, he echoes a more sinister aspect of his own authorship in the "clever one" (as Affery continually calls him), Jeremiah Flintwinch, who uses his cleverness to torment those in his power.

Being confronted with a puzzle of complicated, obscure connections is not just an energizing challenge, as Pancks approaches his unraveling of the Dorrit family finances (and everything else, for that matter), but rather, many of the novel's characters respond to mystery with intense and disabling emotion, from fear, to anxious worry, to sad pity. After Amy reads the packet from Rigaud explaining what Mrs. Clennam did that hurt her family, Mrs. Clennam asks if she knows now what she has done, and Amy replies, "I think so. I am afraid so; though my mind is so hurried, and so sorry, and has so much to pity, that it has not been able to follow all I have read" (753). Of course, Amy is still confused: the novel's secrets are "revealed in such a confused mass of exposition that they remain unclear," as Peter Garrett says (Dickens himself had to make special notes to remember the details) and turn out to be "largely irrelevant to Arthur's story."[64] Focusing on Amy's bewildered feelings instead of the ultimate explanation (which Amy burns, and Clennam never learns), Dickens emphasizes the lack of relief from confusion for either the characters or the reader.

Though the characters' responses to not understanding the plots in which they are entangled appear highly exaggerated, Dickens was seeking to mimic a lifelike effect in explicitly withholding a reassuring sense that neat connections will emerge to tie up the novel. That contrived plots have less interest and value than what happens in real life is apparent throughout Dickens's work. As Peter Brooks shows within *Great Expectations*, for Dickens fictional plots always pale in comparison to the "divine masterplot for human existence," which is "radically unknowable"; it is the "eternal orders that render human attempts to plot, and to interpret plot, not only futile but ethically unacceptable."[65] Pip, of course, jumps to an early and disastrously mistaken conclusion about the plot of his own life. For readers to be deliberately left in a state of anxious uncertainty about how the characters connect may feel like being subject to Jeremiah Flintwinch's aggressive cleverness, but Dickens's aim in "this not-putting of them together" is not only artistic but humane and didactic preparation for real life.

Writing to Forster about his plans for the novel's construction, Dickens largely repeats his working note about wanting to cultivate a realistic and artistically complex sense that uncountable possibilities could unfold in the characters' lives. "It struck me that it would be a new thing to show people coming together, in a chance way, as fellow-travellers, and being in the same place, ignorant of one another, as happens in life; and to connect them afterwards, and to make the waiting for that connection a part of the interest," he writes.[66] In both descriptions of his intention, or rather inspiration ("it struck me," he writes), Dickens links the uncertainty that dominates the beginning of a novel with the profound, "strange," awe-inspiring predicament of not knowing how human beings will come to affect one another in life. At the end of the chapter in which the travelers leave one another in Marseilles, the narrator echoes Miss Wade's ominous foreshadowing in a philosophical tone: "And thus ever, by day and night, *under the sun and under the stars, climbing the dusty hills and toiling along the weary plains, journeying by land and journeying by sea, coming and going so strangely, to meet and to act and react on one another,* move all we restless travelers through the pilgrimage of life" (40; my emphasis). Being unable to know how human fortunes will intersect feels both "strange" and "restless" to those caught in this uncertainty. Later in the novel, the narrator repeats much of this wording exactly:

> Which of the vast multitude of travellers, *under the sun and the stars, climbing the dusty hills and toiling along the weary plains, journeying by land and journeying by sea, coming and going so strangely, to meet and to act and react on one another,* which of the host may, with no suspicion of the journeys end, be travelling surely hither?
>
> Time shall show us. . . . The travelers to all are on the great high-road; but it has wonderful divergences, and only Time shall show us whither each traveler is bound. (180; my emphasis)

Though Dickens habitually repeats rhetorical structures, rarely does he repeat language so precisely and at such length. Appearing pages, and months, apart (in the first and fifth installments), the second passage has the effect of echoing the first, its question still unanswered and unanswerable; in both passages, the narrator has reclaimed the same metaphor from ominous Miss Wade and posed the question of "whither each traveler is bound" as one of perpetual fascination, for the uncertainty of human lives is not only an unsettling phenomenon but full of "wonderful divergences" and "strange," in the sense of awe-inspiring, "exceptional to a degree that excites wonder or astonishment" (*OED*). In using the first-person plural, Dickens refers to the larger human dilemma that affects "us" along with the travelers we, as readers, have now gotten to know somewhat (chapter 2 is titled "Fellow Travelers," its characters fellow to each other and to us). Thus, in reassuring the reader that there will ultimately be knowledge and closure, but "only Time" can bring it, Dickens subtly counsels the reader, much as he specifically advised Francis Jeffrey, that the story and characters will emerge more clearly "as time rolls on." Elsewhere in *Little Dorrit* Dickens offers a model of how uncertainty can be "interesting" rather than unnerving. On the night Amy and Maggy spend outside of the prison, "the sexton, or the verger, or the beadle, or whatever he was" (177), whom Amy recognizes as she and Maggy look in the church for shelter, says of the burial volume that he gives her as a pillow: "What makes these books interesting to most people is—not who's in 'em, but who isn't—who's coming, you know, and when. That's the interesting question" (178). The sexton's words could be descriptions of the two different ways of reading that Dickens wrestles with: how his readers ("most people") focused on speculating about the plot of the next installment, and how Dickens himself sought to turn readers' attention out of the book ("not who's in 'em, but who isn't") to what Brooks calls the "divine masterplot for human existence," which is "radically unknowable."

Thus, in *Little Dorrit* Dickens figures the unexplained and disconnected threads of the multiplot novel as generating "interesting question[s]" in the reader's mind, but only when the reader can tolerate not knowing more "at present." Though direct addresses to the reader are comparatively rare in his novels, in the late novels Dickens interrupts the diegesis to address the reader with a question that might, in fact, already be in the reader's mind. "But Little Dorrit?" the narrator asks, voicing Arthur Clennam's curiosity, while a reader might well be curious about a character who, at this point in the novel that bears her name, has first been mentioned fifty pages in as "a girl, surely, whom I saw near you—almost hidden in the dark corner?" (51). Another direct question in *Little Dorrit*—which I cited at the beginning of this chapter—projects an uncomfortable state of impatience onto the reader, as if the reader has expressed a grievance or "complain[ed]" about a mystery. After the doctor has examined Mr. Merdle and found nothing medically wrong, Dickens writes, "Had he that deep-seated recondite complaint, and did any doctor find it out? Patience" (250). The abrupt, terse command makes this sound like a rebuke to the impatient, imagining reader. In *Bleak House* Dickens similarly voices a direct question that might be in the reader's mind about how seemingly unrelated characters are related:

> What connexion can there be between the place in Lincolnshire, the house in town, the Mercury in powder, and the whereabout of Jo the outlaw with the broom, who had that distant ray of light upon him when he swept the churchyard-step? What connexion can there have been between many people in the innumerable histories of this world who from opposite sides of great gulfs have, nevertheless, been very curiously brought together! (256)

The passage begins with the narrator seeming to address, or express, the reader's likely state of uncertainty, confusion, and perplexity at this point in the novel. The second sentence does not offer a placating response, however, but reuses the same phrase, "What connexion can there have been" as an exclamation, an emphatic assertion of a common sense of humanity that bridges vast class boundaries. The first question, which mirrors the reader's perspective, appears classist and narrow-minded in consequence, in the sense of focusing on meager fictional connections instead of "the innumerable histories of this world" and our common humanness. The direct question Dickens poses about

Mr. Merdle's complaint also addresses the explanations readers might be speculating about; in both cases, Dickens answers the question immediately with what sounds like an irritable impatience with how narrowly readers were directing their imaginations toward simple plot solutions rather than common human plights.

One strategy Dickens uses for helping readers tolerate uncertainty about how both real and fictional lives have connected and will connect, then, is to use direct addresses that underscore the profoundly human nature of this uncertainty. He also shows characters vainly, sometimes pitifully, struggling to neatly order the past, present, and future in their minds. Hilary Schor has described multiple problems of storytelling featured in *Little Dorrit*.[67] Putting things in narrative, temporal order turns out to be one of the most fundamental, but also vulnerable and difficult, mental capacities for Dickens's characters— as, we have seen, it was for Dickens himself. In other words, this is a resonant, poignant struggle that underlies and surfaces in Dickens's work. Brooks describes how in *Great Expectations* Pip only moves ahead in his life by understanding the past, "since revelation, tied to the past, belongs to the future."[68] Miss Havisham is a more iconic but later version of *Little Dorrit*'s Mrs. Clennam, who tragically attempts to stop time by imprisoning herself in her bedroom. "I know nothing of summer and winter, shut up here," Mrs. Clennam says almost proudly, as the narrator notes how unnatural and inhuman this is: "Her being beyond the reach of the seasons seemed but a fit sequence to her being beyond the reach of all changing emotions" (46). While Mrs. Clennam is beyond the reach of all sympathy, other characters are more pitiful in their attempts to leave the past behind, like Mr. Dorrit, who, in the last dinner party of his life, "cancelled the dream through which [he] had since groped, and knew of nothing beyond the Marshalsea" (622). Amy Dorrit's attachment to her old life is similarly expressed as a kind of temporal confusion. When she is trying to learn new things in her new life of wealth, she tells Clennam, "All my planning, thinking, and trying go in old directions . . . and then I remember with a start that there are no such cares left, and that in itself is so new and improbable that it sets me wandering again" (452).

Lacking the ability to put a coherent narrative together is as often portrayed in a comic light as in this lyrical, sympathetic mode. Describing how Mr. Dorrit's affairs have long resisted narrative order, Dickens writes that when an attempt is made to construct a narrative of the debts that have landed him in the Marshalsea prison, "A dozen agents in succession . . . could make neither beginning, middle, nor end of them, or him" (74). Past, present, and future are repeatedly conflated or confused in the characters' thoughts and speech. When Mrs. Tickit sits at the window thinking of the Meagles family, she says, "all times seem to be present, and a person must get out of that state and consider before they can say which is which" (508). Dwelling on one thought in the novel tends to dislodge a character's usual sense of temporal order, much like Flora's recursion to the past causes linguistic disjunctions. Listening to Flora mix up past and present makes Clennam "lightheaded" (155); his confused emotions after his first evening back with the Casbys make Arthur "so much more lightheaded than ever, that . . . he might . . . have drifted anywhere" (162). An orderly narrative finally emerges only at the time that the novel ends. The church clerk present at Amy Dorrit's wedding to Clennam makes a novel out of her life: "Her birth is in what I call the first volume; she lay asleep on this very floor, with her pretty head on what I call the second volume; and she's now a-writing her little name as a bride, in what I call the third volume" (785).

For although Dickens's disparate plots do come together, in *Little Dorrit* this is essentially an afterthought; the novel draws out, as long as possible, the feeling of being subject to the unknowable conditions of human life. Characters who can see a hidden network of social connections in Dickens's novels often do so with dubious motivation or find the experience disordering. Within *Bleak House*, for instance, Garrett cites Tulkinghorn, Mrs. Snagsby, and Mr. Guppy as suspect detectives, and Jo as bewildered by the seeming likeness between Esther Summerson, Lady Dedlock, and her maid Hortense.[69] Even in *Bleak House*, where (as J. Hillis Miller argues) the professional detective Bucket comes in to solve the mystery and bring closure, Miller also points out how the Chancery suit resolves by self-combusting.[70] In *Little Dorrit*, Pancks appears to be a similar type of character as Bucket, but his "fortune telling," the mystery of the Dorrit family finances, which he resolves halfway through the novel, does not bring closure, and his process of solving the puzzle, like the puzzle itself, remains opaque to both characters and reader. Dickens describes how Pancks, "had felt his way inch by inch, and 'Moled it out, sir' (that was Mr Pancks' expression), grain by grain. How, in the beginning of the labor described by this new verb, and to render which the more expressive Mr Pancks shut his eyes in pronouncing it and shook his hair over them, he had alternated from sudden lights and hopes to sudden darkness and no hopes, and back again, and back again" (396). Pancks's process of "mol[ing] it out" circles back, has ups and downs, and appears mysterious, dizzying, and unintelligible, even and especially when Pancks pantomimes it. Early in the novel Amy Dorrit is "greatly confused" and "beyond measure perplexed" by him (283). In *Bleak*

House, Dickens describes the physical Bleak House's eccentric makeup as having a similar nature to the novel's formal structure. Similarly, in *Little Dorrit,* Pancks's process of "mol[ing] it out" manifests the nature of reading the novel: being taken for a wild ride without any idea of its destination, "as in life" (as Dickens described the effect he hoped to achieve in the novel).

Reading "as in life" is nearly the opposite of "reading as if for life": David Copperfield's mode of reading is joyful, abundantly imaginative, and escapist, while *Little Dorrit's* characters are anxious, bewildered, and cannot escape from their own, imaginatively starved minds, like the Victorian readers who frustrated Dickens.

"Always, Little Dorrit"

Little Dorrit's characters have painfully limited imaginations. On the night when Arthur Clennam is accidentally shut in the Marshalsea prison, he tries to sleep but cannot, for "[s]peculations . . . bearing the strangest relations towards the prison, but always concerning the prison, ran like nightmares through his mind while he lay awake." Dickens lists a parade of morbid questions that go through Clennam's mind like "involuntary starts of fancy" before one thought "held possession of him": that his mother imprisoned herself in her bedroom as atonement for having somehow caused Mr. Dorrit's imprisonment for debt (96). Neither form of imagining, uncontrolled speculation nor obsessive rumination, is a very pleasant or productive way of piecing together disparate plots, which is how these narrative strands appear at the time to both Clennam and the reader. In using prose style to convey the restricted nature of his characters' imaginative processes, Dickens can be seen linking the act of reading his novels to an imaginative plight that has broad cultural resonance for him.

Though Clennam and other characters sit in reverie trying to understand how they are linked together, their reveries become hyperfocused ruminations on one other character—or, at most, one family: as Mrs. Tickit (who sits by the window not reading a book whenever the Meagles family goes away) tells Clennam of what happens "when I do think of one thing and do think of another," "'I need hardly tell you, Mr Clennam, that I think of the family. Because, dear me! A person's thoughts,' Mrs Tickit said this with an argumentative and philosophic air, 'however they may stray, will go more or less on what is uppermost in their minds. They *will* do it, sir, and a person can't prevent them'" (508). Mrs. Ticket's "philosoph[y]" of mind sounds like a comic version of the associationist model of thinking prevalent in Victorian intellectual culture. As we know, Dickens was personally haunted by this contemporary way of thinking about minds that, "however they may stray," cannot get out of their own bounds. In a telling moment late in the novel when Clennam has himself been imprisoned for debt, he cannot get his mind off his own troubles enough to read and "release even the imaginary people of the book from the Marshalsea" (703).

Dickens uses the novel's prose style to immerse the reader in imagining, ironically, the oppressive experience of being underimaginative. The effect that living a "contracted existence" has on the capacity for imagination is essentially *Little Dorrit*'s keynote, a variation on the theme of his previous novel, *Hard Times*, which depicts a society whose keynote is "Never Wonder." Where *Hard Times* is satiric, however, in *Little Dorrit* Dickens uses the extreme physical and mental immobility of Mrs. Clennam to show the traumatic effects of a culture that brings its children up without fancy, as Arthur Clennam is brought up. Mrs. Clennam's immobility is made pitiful, but not sympathetic, essentially a state one is glad not to share. Dickens's mechanical repetition of words and phrases evokes the monotony of Mrs. Clennam's physical existence: "The same unvarying round of life. Morning, noon, and night, morning, noon, and night, each recurring with its accompanying monotony, always the same reluctant return of the same sequences of machinery, like a dragging piece of clockwork" (331). There is no redeeming mental activity in this alien, inhuman description. He goes on to "suppose" the effect that such a "long routine of gloomy days" would have on the sufferer's mind, emphasizing, at first, how separate this experience is from the narrator's or reader's experiences:

> The wheeled chair had its associated remembrances and reveries, one may suppose, as every place that is made the station of a human being has. Pictures of demolished streets and altered houses, as they formerly were when the occupant of the chair was familiar with them, images of people as they too used to be, with little or no allowance made for the lapse of time since they were seen; of these, there must have been many in the long routine of gloomy days. To stop the clock of busy existence at the hour when we were personally sequestered from it, to suppose mankind stricken motionless when we were brought to a stand-still, to be unable to measure the changes beyond our view by any larger standard than the shrunken one of our own uniform and contracted existence, is the infirmity of many invalids, and the mental unhealthiness of almost all recluses. (331)

The passage begins by guessing at Mrs. Clennam's thoughts ("there must have been many"), but soon shifts to a first-person plural perspective that positions the reader in imagining the "shrunken" outlook of "*our own* uniform and contracted existence." Though Dickens walks the reader step-by-step into imaginative projection, the passage has the air of a clinical diagnosis, explaining how mistaken imagining is characteristic of "invalids" and "recluses." That Dickens associates the position with invalidism and "unhealthiness" suggests what Amanda Anderson has shown about characters ruminating in Victorian novels: that these scenes convey the powerless and helpless social position of the character, "the ongoing *injury* of social disenfranchisement."[71] Reading about this type of character's absorption in "remembrances and reveries" does not have a stimulating effect on the reader's imagination but a dulling, numbing, and disempowering one.

Arthur Clennam's reveries are especially oppressive to read. Dickens's depictions of reverie in this novel differ from those that Elisha Cohn has identified as not-fully-conscious moments of respite from the rigorous work of self-culture that the Victorian novel demands of both character and reader. (It makes sense that Dickens is only mentioned briefly in Cohn's study of four other Victorian novelists.[72]) Dickens's prose style in narrating Clennam's reveries adds to the weighty mental experience being described. When Clennam is first seen in London, he sits in the window of a coffeehouse with "nothing to change the brooding mind, or raise it up," as Dickens says of all London on a Sunday. He remembers "a legion of Sundays, all days of unserviceable bitterness and mortification" (41–42). Dickens lists the Sundays using repetitive rhetorical structure, just as he lists the "subjects" in Clennam's mind as he walks to Twickenham for the first time. There are a lot of subjects and the descriptions are long:

> First, there was the subject seldom absent from his mind, the question, what he was to do henceforth in life; to what occupation he should devote himself, and in what direction he had best seek it. He was far from rich, and every day of indecision and inaction made his inheritance a source of greater anxiety to him. As often as he began to consider how to increase this inheritance, or to lay it by, so often his misgiving that there was some one with an unsatisfied claim upon his justice, returned; and that alone was a subject to outlast the longest walk. Again, there was the subject of his relations with his mother, which were now upon an equable and peaceful but never confidential footing, and whom he saw several times a week. Little Dorrit was a leading and a constant subject: for the circumstances of his life, united to those of her own story, presented the little creature to him as

the only person between whom and himself there were ties of innocent reliance on one hand, and affectionate protection on the other; ties of compassion, respect, unselfish interest, gratitude, and pity. Thinking of her, and of the possibility of her father's release from prison by the unbarring hand of death—the only change of circumstance he could foresee that might enable him to be such a friend to her as he wished to be, by altering her whole manner of life, smoothing her rough road, and giving her a home—he regarded her, in that perspective, as his adopted daughter, his poor child of the Marshalsea hushed to rest. If there were a last subject in his thoughts, and it lay towards Twickenham, its form was so indefinite that it was little more than the pervading atmosphere in which these other subjects floated before him. (189)

Dickens repeatedly elaborates Clennam's thoughts when in reverie at length. In fact, here Dickens suggests he is holding back from saying more ("That alone was a subject to outlast the longest walk"). Since he is gathering topics that have already been the subjects of other reveries, he refers to thoughts that have "returned" or Clennam has "again," as if using a kind of shorthand, acknowledging that, yes, the reader must return to the same thoughts when Clennam does. He also conveys the brooding nature of Clennam's mind, with its "leading and constant subject," through repetition, by repeating an initial phrase or term ("subject"), which acts like an anchor weighing down Clennam's thoughts. His thoughts also seem to be stuck in the present; when he tries to look ahead, his imagination is weakened. His mind either wanders back to some unknown injustice in the past, to the "the only change of circumstance he could foresee" for Little Dorrit, her father's death, or to an "indefinite" image of Pet Meagles. One common view of Dickens's daydreamers has been that reveries provide a vicarious substitute for action in their lives, but Clennam can hardly form a wish, let alone imagine it being fulfilled.

Dickens uses his prose style even more dramatically to conjure the experience of having obsessive, restricted thoughts when Little Dorrit overtakes any other subject in Clennam's mind. So obsessive does Clennam become that there is not space for his thoughts to vary between the repetitive openings of each clause, unlike when he is first walking to Twickenham: "He thought of his poor child, Little Dorrit, for a long time there; he thought of her, going home; he thought of her in the night; he thought of her when the day came round again" (258–59). Clennam's unelaborated thoughts sound unenlightened, dully repetitive, which conveys to the reader the sense of an unconscious limit within Clennam's mind that prevents his recognizing the real nature of his love for "his poor child." When Clennam is first imprisoned in the Marshalsea after his financial ruin, he sits and thinks "for hours" (690), his memory always turning to Amy Dorrit. "So always, as he sat alone in the faded chair, thinking. Always, Little Dorrit." Conveying the repetition of Clennam's single thought and the fact that he cannot see beyond it, Dickens's description of the contents of Clennam's thoughts is winnowed down to three words— "Always, Little Dorrit." As if this were not narrow enough, this monotonous reverie is itself repeated later in the chapter. Dickens's description on this occasion is longer—but only because he repeats the same words more times: "Little Dorrit, Little Dorrit. Again, for hours. Always Little Dorrit!" (702).

Amy Dorrit's own reveries are also narratively constricted on several levels. For one, Amy's reveries are as much about Clennam as his are about her, but Dickens is no Charlotte Brontë; while thoroughly implying Amy's love, he keeps the young female heroine's romantic feelings properly locked away, literally. Her reveries frequently occur at a barred window, an image that also symbolizes how her circumscribed experience of life, based in a prison, has limited her imagination. As Dickens describes Amy seated at the barred window of her room in the Marshalsea prison, his account of her reveries appears confined:

> Many combinations did those spikes upon the wall assume, many light shapes did the strong iron weave itself into, many golden touches fell upon the rust, while Little Dorrit sat there musing. New zig-zags sprung into the cruel pattern sometimes, when she saw it through a burst of tears; but beautified or hardened still, always over it and under it and through it, she was fain to look in her solitude, seeing everything with that ineffaceable brand. (284)

The attention of the passage is not on Amy's particular thoughts; Dickens never says directly what they are. Instead, the way Dickens narrates Amy's reverie conveys the experience of limitation within her mind. Here, he does this by extending his descriptions of everything else other than Amy's thoughts. He describes multiple ways in which the shadows replicate the bars on the window, literally redoubling the prison's sense of confinement. The rhythmic repetitiveness of the prose dramatizes the fact that this melancholy reverie is not only a prolonged but a frequent state for Amy: her musing drones on through "many combinations . . . many light shapes"; she sits looking out next to the barred window "always over it and under it and through it." And extending his description of the moving shadows accentuates the contrast with Amy's unchanging thoughts. The picture we get is not of the contents of Amy's imaginings but of the cramped space in which her imagination functions.

The reader's imagination has to function in this same cramped space in *Little Dorrit*, an experience Dickens may have designed in order to make the reader long for imaginative freedom. Later in the novel, after the Dorrit family has gained freedom from the debtors' prison, Dickens appears to offer a freer narration of the contents of Amy Dorrit's reveries, but in fact her mind goes over past experiences from earlier in the novel. When the family is in Italy, Dickens writes of her sitting by herself in the afternoons:

> She would think of that old gate, and of herself sitting at it in the dead of the night, pillowing Maggie's head; and of other places and other scenes associated with those different times. And then she would lean upon her balcony, and look over at the water, as though they all lay underneath it. When she got to that, she would musingly watch its running, as if, in the general vision, it might run dry, and show her the prison again, and herself, and the old room, and the old inmates, and the old visitors: all lasting realities that had never changed. (451)

The prose is lusher here, certainly more so than the mechanical style in which Dickens describes Clennam's reverie about "Little Dorrit." But Dickens again restricts Amy's thoughts. While he appears to offer the reader a glimpse of her private thoughts, he is actually describing events that the reader already knows because they happened in the first book. We, as readers, can, of course, picture what Amy is imagining: a few hundred pages back, when Dickens first describes these events, *we* were the ones imagining a "prison," an "old room," "old inmates," and "old visitors" who were not physically in front of us. Amy cannot get her mind out of prison, but neither can the reader, who becomes, like Clennam, wanting but unable to "release even the imaginary people of the book from the Marshalsea" (703). Dickens crafts a reading experience that stirs a longing to read like David Copperfield, and joyfully release fictional characters from their imprisonment in an author's imagination.

3

Reading Ahead in *Adam Bede*

JANE CARLYLE loved *Adam Bede* (1859), writing to John Blackwood, the novel's publisher, of how she "could fancy in reading it, to be seeing and hearing once again a crystal-clear, musical, Scotch stream, such as I long to lie down beside."[1] George Eliot was delighted with this warm response, even though Carlyle describes having a detailed mental picture that is nowhere present in the book. Eliot wrote to Blackwood, "Will you tell her that the sort of effect she declares herself to have felt from 'Adam Bede' is just what I desire to produce—gentle thoughts and happy remembrances."[2] That a book might prompt its reader to a wholly distinct, peaceful reverie is modeled within the novel itself.[3] In one moment late in the novel, Seth Bede sits with a volume in hand, "a newly-bought book, Wesley's abridgment of Madam Guyon's life, which was full of wonder and interest for him"; Seth, however, is also thinking of something else, his "blue dreamy eyes, as often as not looking vaguely out of the window instead of at his book." "Th' lad," Adam says of his brother, "liked to sit full o' thoughts he could give no account of; they'd never come t' anything, but they made him happy" (531). Putting the book aside not to dwell on its characters or events, but to think of private "thoughts and . . . remembrances," appears to have been "the sort of effect" Eliot sought.

Eliot was also conscious that most readers' imaginations could not simply be counted on to conjure "gentle thoughts and happy remembrances." Over the course of her career, Eliot found that many of her readers were busily engaged in an imagining of their own direction—and one far different from Jane Carlyle's "remembrances." By the late 1850s, when Eliot was beginning her career as a novelist, the novel had codified into its commercially successful, three-volume form, and readers were well versed in imagining the outcome of its typical marriage plot. Reading several of Eliot's novels in serial form, readers often guessed what the next installment would contain and guessed wrong.

Over the many months during which *Romola* (1863) or *Middlemarch* (1871–72)
first appeared, a complex relation developed between the realist author and
her forecasting audience, which became an increasing anxiety for the novelist.
As Blackwood recorded of a remark she made about her last novel, *Daniel
Deronda* (1876), "It was hard upon her that people should be angry with her
for not doing what *they* expected with her characters."[4] Eliot's recognition that
she could not control the wayward imaginings of readers was compatible with
the growing recognition in the period that the imagination was not easily con-
trollable. In the mid-nineteenth century, Victorian psychologists—among
whom Eliot's partner, George Henry Lewes, was a central figure—were beginning to theorize the unconscious workings of the imagination, which appeared
particularly immune to rational control or coaxing.[5]

   Critics have emphasized Eliot's controlling presence in her fiction, but Eliot
recognizes that her realist ambition to create a novel-world that mirrors things
"as they are" (222) can only be complete with the cooperation of the reader's
sometimes divergent imagination. In her letters, Eliot distinguishes between
the two widely different forms that, in her experience, readers' private imaginings took: uninvited wish fulfillment, which looks forward and seeks ideal
outcomes counter to the real, erring experience Eliot aims to represent, and
private recollection, in which the reader looks backward to authentic memories that can strengthen sympathetic continuities between the fictional and
"real" worlds. George Levine has described how nineteenth-century realism
defined itself against wish fulfillment in distinguishing itself from romance.[6]
Within her fiction, Eliot chastises readers for wish-fulfilling daydreams that
interfere with reading, and outright appeals to readers, at other times, to recollect experiences that have nothing to do with reading, in order to fill in unnarratable, real-life aspects of the story.[7] Seeing how this type of appeal emerges
along with the aims of midcentury realism fills in a longer history than we have
recognized to the value readers today afford to "relatability."[8]

A Culture of Conjecture

Novel readers had been writing to novelists in an effort to bend the plot toward
fulfilling their own wishes at least since Samuel Richardson received such letters about *Clarissa* (1748). After Richardson's readers asked for Clarissa to
marry Lovelace, the author was concerned that his moral didacticism was not
heard loudly enough; he altered subsequent editions to make clearer the moral
purity of Clarissa's character, which to him made such a marriage impossible.[9]

The serial format in which many Victorian novels were published heightened the readerly habit of predicting, if not influencing, the fate of characters. The original readers of *Middlemarch* spent more than a year learning the futures of Dorothea and Lydgate[10] and, in the spaces between bimonthly installments, were naturally inclined to speculate about plot development, to forecast ahead. Serial publication spread over many months, according to Linda Hughes and Michael Lund's comprehensive study, fostered "a community of readers [who] . . . shared the pleasure and excitement of anticipation."[11] Readers actively participated in attempting to construct the future of the narrative; according to Hughes and Lund, "during the expansive middle of the serial works," readers regularly engaged together in "provisional assumptions and interpretations about the literary world."[12]

This positive vision of serialization's pleasures rings true for Eliot's readers, for without the confusion that readers of Dickens frequently commented on, readers of Eliot's long, late multiplot novels could revel in the pleasures of speculation. One reviewer of the second installment of *Daniel Deronda* refers to the "ample time" ahead for "free social discussion of the characters, for speculation as to their unrevealed past and their unreached future."[13] As we have seen, serialization heightened the desire readers had to make sense of the unfolding plot, which, Peter Brooks suggests, is a natural outgrowth of the dynamic nature of narrative fiction: "that which makes us—like the heroes of the text often, and certainly like their authors—want and need plotting, seeking through the narrative text as it unfurls before us a precipitation of shape and meaning."[14] So heightened was serial speculation, however, that this same reviewer of *Daniel Deronda* even suggests a way Eliot herself might profit from the anticipation: "Opinions during the last month have been much divided as to what she intends to make of her heroine; bets have been freely laid, and the gifted authoress . . . might add indefinitely to the profits, if not to the artistic unity, of her work, by consenting to accept suggestions from interested parties."[15]

Eliot's interactions with readers recorded in her letters display her intimate understanding of, and frustrated response to, this culture of conjecture. While Victorian readers and reviewers were reveling in the pleasures of speculation about her work, Eliot found this "acuteness of conjecture," as Henry James called the general response to book 2 of *Daniel Deronda*, a "nightmare."[16] As she writes to Blackwood about letters she had been receiving from prophetic readers of *Daniel Deronda*: "People in their eagerness about my characters are quite angry, it appears, when their own expectations are not fulfilled—angry, for example, that Gwendolen accepts Grandcourt etc. etc. One reader is sure that

Mirah is going to die very soon, and I suppose will be disgusted at her remaining alive. Such are the reproaches to which I make myself liable."[17] Carol Martin, in her thorough study of Eliot's uneven relationship with serialization, suggests that the author's often-noted "morbid sensitivity" to criticism made such prolonged opportunity for critique quite trying—so much so that after *Scenes of Clerical Life* (1858), which first appeared as separate stories in Blackwood's *Magazine*, Eliot published her next three works only in volume form.[18]

In Eliot's case, her readers' active imaginations at times went beyond merely predicting events in the pauses between serial installments: they appropriated her fictions. "Over-authoritative fans," Leah Price has suggested, plagued Eliot throughout her career, requisitioning her work for sequels, stage adaptations, or outrageously claiming to have written the novels themselves.[19] At least one unauthorized sequel was written to remedy a novel's objectionable ending. *Gwendolen: A Sequel to George Eliot's "Daniel Deronda"* (alternately titled *Reclaimed* in other editions; 1878) appeared in America two years after the original novel's publication and opened with a reprinted "Review of *Daniel Deronda*" from the *North American Review* (1877), which refers to "the almost universal disappointment at the *unanticipated* conclusion of the story—a conclusion which many readers have resented as though it were a personal grievance or affront."[20] This review, if correct about the universal disappointment, offers insight into readers' minds: they wished to have their surmises confirmed, not to be surprised, suggesting that the act of forecasting could be a determining part of the reading process. *Gwendolen* itself offers further insight into what some of Eliot's readers may have wanted: Mirah does, as Eliot's correspondent predicted, "die very soon" (in childbirth, in the first chapter); shortly after, Daniel renounces Judaism and converts to Christianity and ultimately (if I may spoil the ending) ends up with Gwendolen.

Eliot's unusually extensive correspondence with one fan, an eccentric young Scotsman named Alexander Main, exemplifies her struggle with her fans' imaginations. Main wrote Eliot a letter in August 1871 asking her how to pronounce "Romola"; Eliot continued to respond for several years to his effusive letters in which she found, as she wrote to Main, "intense comfort . . . in the response which your mind has given to every 'deliverance' of mine."[21] Eliot and Lewes eventually allowed Main to collect excerpts from her novels and publish them as *The Wise, Witty, and Tender Sayings of George Eliot* (1873), a decision she seems to have regretted, as Price has recounted in detail. Critics and biographers tend to portray her overall relationship with Main, a flatterer, as an embarrassment.[22] Rebecca Mead's literary critical memoir, *My Life in*

Middlemarch (2014), is unique in portraying him sympathetically based on his still unpublished letters to Eliot. Mead suggests Eliot was touched by Main's appreciation of the higher moral purpose of her art.[23]

Blackwood aptly called Main "the Gusher," and what likely appealed to Eliot is that Main gushes not about the plot but about how rich in "spiritual nourishment" and "full of the tender yet strong Spirit of Humanity" her novels are.[24] Such an outpouring of emotion, in elevated, abstract language, contrasts with typical Victorian reviewers who discussed, for example, the banality of *Middlemarch* ending with Fred and Mary. As Lewes wrote to Blackwood, Main's letters "have been a source of extreme gratification and sustainment to Mrs Lewes ... because of the real insight and appreciation of her meaning on points where most critics and admirers seem to have been dead."[25] Eliot's letters to Main emphasize her satisfaction that his mind mirrors her own, while he writes about himself as if he were an idealized figure present in Eliot's mind as she is writing: "I feel (as both you and your noble husband have *made* me feel) that I am in some sense—in some very real sense—present to your thought."[26]

Eliot's correspondence with Main, however, reveals how even he could not resist the temptation of forecasting. Eliot repeatedly uses the word "receptivity" to talk about a reader's willingness, readiness, or capacity for grasping the author's whole vision; she contrasts this capacity with the teleological story "construction" that impedes it. She had to remind Main of the difference while he was reading and making recommendations to her about *Middlemarch*. After reading only as far as book 2, he suggested, half-jestingly, "You really must get that Casaubon quietly, decently, and gravely of course, *out of the way*, into another world (of which he may be found more worthy) and leaving Dodo into *the closest possible relation* with that mysterious youngster."[27] Eliot replied, "Nothing mars the receptivity more than eager construction—as I know to my own cost."[28] Eliot appears to be referring to her past experiences with readers who were "eager" to know the plot, for she then tries to persuade him that he will lose pleasure by forecasting: "Try to keep from forecast of Dorothea's lot, and that sort of construction beforehand which makes everything that actually happens a disappointment."[29] Though he responds by claiming, "I have given up guessing as to her future lot," in the same letter he goes on to make specific guesses: "Will she *write*, I wonder? Will she save Will Ladislaw as Maggie Tulliver saved Philip Wakem?"[30] Having changed his mind about Dorothea and the "mysterious youngster," far into *Middlemarch*'s serial publication, Main continued to describe to Eliot, in detail, why Will Ladislaw and Dorothea Brooke should part for life. He adds, in an act of both humility and bravura, "You must not be angry with me for having ventured to finish the novel in my own way."[31] Acknowledging his prescribed status as the novel's recipient, Main commands Eliot not to chastise him for overstepping it; he rationalizes to her that the very "interest this part compelled me to take in Dodo & Will & their relation to each other, present and future, would not give me rest till I had followed them, in imagination, to the close."[32] His letters reveal how much pleasure he derives from conjecture, but it is a pleasure that Gillian Beer describes as common to gambling and novel reading, which are both "acts of desire whose longing is to *possess* and settle the future."[33] Main's evident desire to possess Eliot's story sharpened the conflict between an ideal reader and a real one for Eliot. An ideal reader mirrors the author's own authentic affect; an actual reader uses his mind to predict the plot and preempt her authorial role.

Forecasting Characters, Curtailing Author

Eliot responded to this culture of "construction" throughout her career by attempting to intervene in the reading process. Her efforts to discourage wishful forecasting can be seen in two ways within her fiction: narrative interjections and character depictions. In one of her most explicit direct addresses to the reader, she denounces prediction altogether. After Will Ladislaw's first brief appearance in *Middlemarch*, the narrator cautions the reader, "Let him start for the Continent, then, without our pronouncing on his future. Of all forms of mistake, prophecy is the most gratuitous" (110). Despite the humor of this maxim, the futility of attempting not just to predict but to shape one's own future is one of Eliot's great themes. As the narrator also comments directly to the reader, early in the same novel, on the common tendency to guess whom among our acquaintance might figure prominently in our lives, "[d]estiny stands by sarcastic with our *dramatis personae* folded in her hand" (122). This section focuses on Eliot's cautionary depictions of characters engaged in forecasting in multiple novels, which can be similarly explicit. In *The Mill on the Floss* (1860), in one of the most direct references in her fiction to how this imaginative habit interferes with reading, Maggie Tulliver comments on the book Philip Wakem carries with him while on a walk in the Red Deeps. The moment forebodes that novel's own unhappy ending: "'The Pirate' . . . O, I began that once; I read to where Minna is walking with Cleveland, and could never get to read the rest. I went on with it in my own head, and I made several endings; but they were all unhappy. I could never make a happy ending out of that beginning. Poor Minna! I wonder what is the real end."[34]

"Poor Minna." With much of Eliot's fiction devoted to narrating her characters' consciousness, Eliot uses extensive depictions of characters engaged in forward-looking imagining to caution readers against, like Maggie, trying to make up their own, unrealistic happy endings. Whether it is Rosamond's "rapid forecast and rumination concerning house furniture" (301) or Hetty Sorrel's dreams that "some day she should be a grand lady . . . and dress for dinner in a brocaded silk" (196), Eliot's characters throughout her novels continually indulge in reveries about their own futures, and are often no less mistaken than her readers were in their predictions.[35] For like Rosamond and Hetty, many serial readers seem to have persistently anticipated happy, romanticized endings, which exacerbated their disappointment with the realist endings Eliot actually wrote. As Lewes wrote to Blackwood, with the reading public "greatly agog as to how *Middlemarch* will end . . . Mrs. Lewes feels perfectly sure that everybody will be disappointed."[36] The reviewer from *The Times* wrote, "The sober happiness and length of humdrum days accorded to Fred and Mary scarcely lighten the general gray of a sky which novelists usually make it a point of honour to flood with sunshine at the final hour."[37] It is Eliot herself who proved gifted at foresight, in grasping the reader's expectations and how her novels, with their "gray" endings, might fail to meet them.

In depicting the inner lives of her characters, then, Eliot highlights the forward-looking nature of their daydreams. As Elisha Cohn has shown, a moment of reverie depicted in a novel is one in which the forward movement of the plot stands still, while the subject of a reverie itself might be forward or backward looking.[38] Though Eliot's novels are deeply invested in the past—whether the historical past or the past as a basis for nostalgia or even blackmail—memory and history most often manifest as larger narrative tropes; her characters have surprisingly few specified memories.[39] Although *The Mill on the Floss* seems to begin with the narrator's reverie about the past, Eliot quickly destabilizes the reverie form. What appears to be the narrator's conscious daydream is suddenly cut short by an ellipsis and confession that the narrator had "dozed off" and was "dreaming . . . of Dorlcote Mill, as it looked one February afternoon many years ago" (8–9). The story about the past then resumes in the second person, "I was going to tell you," which frames the rest of the novel as oral storytelling, not reverie. In contrast, when the reader glimpses a character's private consciousness, Eliot reveals daydreams and wishes that are unknown to other characters.

In those crucial moments throughout Eliot's fiction, in which the reader's sympathy with a character is first generated through glimpsing a character's innermost life, we see Lydgate's medical ambitions, his "plan of his future" (178), how he "dream[s] of himself as a discoverer" (175), and his "reveries" about the "primitive tissue" (305); Casaubon's dreams of a Latin dedication *not* addressed to Carp; and Gwendolen Harleth's "fits of spiritual dread" (63), her moments of anxiety about the unknown future, in which "subjection to a possible self, a self not to be absolutely predicted about, caused her some . . . terror" (136). Eliot's investment in future-imagining is crystallized, even hyperbolized, in a set of characters throughout her fiction who do almost nothing but foresee: clairvoyants, such as Latimer in "The Lifted Veil" (1859), Mordecai in *Daniel Deronda*, and Dino and Savonarola in *Romola* (1863). Latimer, who is cursed by knowing absolutely what lies ahead, longs for the feeling once again of possibility, and celebrates the essential creativity of speculation. "So absolute is our soul's need of something hidden and uncertain, . . . that if the whole future were laid bare to us beyond today, the interest of all mankind would be bent on the hours that lie between. . . . Art and philosophy, literature and science, would fasten like bees on that one proposition which had the honey of probability in it, and be the more eager because their enjoyment would end, with sunset."[40]

On one hand, then, Eliot acknowledges how deeply embedded in human nature is the fallible tendency to construct a rosy future out of present materials. As the narrator of *Daniel Deronda* comments of Mrs. Davilow's imaginings when she first hears of Grandcourt as a possible suitor for Gwendolen, "A little speculation on 'what may be' comes naturally, without encouragement—comes inevitably in the form of images, when unknown persons are mentioned" (93). Indeed, wishful thinking, the activity of "aerial castle-building" (*Daniel Deronda*, 94) or "delightful aerial building" (*Middlemarch*, 334), is importantly not restricted to the Rosamonds and Hettys of Eliot's world. One of Eliot's more devoted aerial builders is the actual builder, Adam Bede, who daydreams in minute detail about both marriage to Hetty and ingenious designs for kitchen cupboards. Eliot even invokes the valorized language of building as a metaphor for Adam's aerial construction: "Adam no sooner caught his imagination leaping forward in this way—making arrangements for an uncertain future—than he checked himself. 'A pretty building I'm making, without either bricks or timber. I'm up in the garret already, and haven't so much as dug the foundation'" (255). But if there is one lesson Eliot's novels seek to teach, it is that fiction and wishes ought to have little traffic with one another. "Silly Novels by Lady Novelists" (1856), an essay Eliot wrote just as she began to contemplate a novelistic career, baldly critiques literary

productions that seem to her hardly more than the published daydreams of
their authors. "Such stories as this of 'The Enigma,'" she writes of one exem-
plary novel, "remind us of the pictures clever children sometimes draw 'out of
their own head.'"[41] In *Adam Bede* she indicts not only writers but imagined
"lady readers" who desire the novel to be "just what we like," or little more than
wish fulfillment (221–22).

As part of her realist project to sway readers against wishful forecasting,
Eliot frequently shows her characters' daydreams being curtailed. A dynamic
of daydreaming character and curtailing author recurs throughout Eliot's fiction. "Her reverie was broken" begins two of the four sentences in which the
word "reverie" appears in *Middlemarch* (71; 585), suggesting that the interruption stems from an outside source; "his brief reverie was interrupted" (566)
begins the third, while the fourth ends prematurely in sleep ("He had shut his
eyes in the last instance of reverie"; 638). In another instance early in the novel,
when Dorothea first suspects Casaubon's marital intentions, she sets out for a
solitary walk, for "[t]here had risen before her the girl's vision of a possible
future for herself to which she looked forward with trembling hope, and she
wanted to wander on in that visionary future without interruption" (49). Her
walk is, however, abruptly ended two pages later, as "Dorothea checked herself
suddenly with self-rebuke for the presumptuous way in which she was reckoning
on uncertain events." Despite the reference to "self-rebuke," the narrator makes
clear that a second, narratorial interruption was already, literally, on the horizon,
in the form of Sir James Chettam, as the sentence continues: "but she was
spared any inward effort to change the direction of her thoughts by the appearance of a cantering horseman round a turning of the road" (51–52).

With the emphatic doubling of interruption in this passage, and the repeated act of delimiting her characters' projections throughout her fiction,
Eliot makes clear that imagining ahead is to be held in check. Together with
her comments on forecasting in her letters, these depictions serve to forewarn
her readers against developing wishes for the future of her characters. In other
words, Eliot uses her characters' acts of forecasting as an analogue for the readers' forecasting, to dissuade her readers from the habit of taking the novel's
act of imagining into their own hands.[42] Serial readers were taking it upon
themselves to project the future and, in doing so, anticipating happy endings
that undermined their receptivity to the realist endings Eliot actually wrote.
As the characters within the novel, too, repeatedly attempt—and fail—to nar-
rate the future, a competition for the unfolding of the plot is continually being
staged as well as foreclosed.

The unintended effect of Eliot's inscribing this competitive dynamic between the author's aims and the reader's wishes into her narratives is to give a vulnerable quality to Eliot's distinctive, controlling presence in her fiction. Audrey Jaffe, in her study of omniscience in Dickens, argues that the figure of the omniscient narrator in nineteenth-century fiction is merely a "fantasy" of "unquestioned authority"; in fact, she claims, omniscience depends on a continual effort to mark the difference between the describer and the objects being described, the continual "assertion of narratorial knowledge and its absence in characters."[43] Eliot's characteristic narrative voice can be seen in an analogous light. Her continual assertion of control over other trains of thought—whether characters' or readers'—points to an awareness of needing to gain control over the novel genre's capacity for inspiring both realistic and wishful possibilities.

Kindling the Reader's Mind

By repeatedly attempting to curb the reader's train of thought, Eliot is implicitly recognizing that novel readers *have* highly fertile imaginations of their own. Critics largely discuss Victorian realist novels as depicting self-contained worlds brought into being by their authors' instructions, which are carried out by compliant, predictable readers.[44] Although the independent activity of the reader's mind was cumulatively to prove an aggravation to Eliot, her first novel, *Adam Bede*, reveals Eliot's hopeful attempts to enlist the reader's creative imagination as a resource for her fiction. Seeing Eliot's negotiation between kindling and controlling the reader's mental images in *Adam Bede*, before these attempts are complicated by her later frustration with her readers' real minds, reveals the extent to which an acute appreciation of the reader's private imagination lies at the heart of Eliot's conception of fiction.

Adam Bede was originally conceived as a possible fourth tale in *Scenes of Clerical Life*, whose stories were appearing serially in Blackwood's *Magazine*. But what Eliot refers to discreetly as "several motives" caused her to end the series with the story "Janet's Repentance."[45] In fact, her publisher's initial delight in the stories had been tempered by growing objections to the turns they were taking: the less than ideal ending of the middle story and the alcoholism portrayed in the last one. The difficulties with Blackwood's reservations continued even after she began writing *Adam Bede* as a full-length work; initial plans to publish it serially in his family-centered magazine faltered as well when he showed reluctance to commit before knowing how the story would end. She writes in her journal of his response to the first volume:

He still *wished* to have it for the Mag., but desired to know the course of the story; at *present*, he saw nothing to prevent its reception in Maga, but he would like to see more. I am uncertain whether his doubts rested solely on Hetty's relation to Arthur, or whether they were also directed towards the treatment of Methodism by the Church. I refused to tell my story beforehand, on the ground that I would not have it judged apart from my *treatment*, which alone determines the moral quality of art; and ultimately I proposed that the notion of publication in Maga should be given up.[46]

Given her later manifest anger at readers who forecast, it is striking that Eliot objects to Blackwood's desire to know the story "beforehand," and that she insists that plot should not be separated from the author's unique handling of it. Though the decision not to publish *Adam Bede* serially was agreed to be mutual, as Carol Martin has shown, this early experience with a critical editor— one whose criticism was, above all, anticipatory—contributed to Eliot's career-long sensitivity to the serialization of her work. As mentioned earlier, Eliot did not publish another work serially until *Romola*, three novels later. Blackwood, as an editor, was in a unique position to interfere with her narrative choices, and *Adam Bede*'s chapter on art, its defense of making supposedly unpopular artistic choices against the objecting voices of imagined "lady readers," has been seen as directly addressed to her publisher.[47] "Do improve the facts a little" (221), Eliot imagines a lady reader, "my fair critic," saying in an echo of Blackwood's sentiment. At the same time, Rosemarie Bodenheimer has demonstrated that such a critical, antagonistic reader, as a rhetorical figure, had already appeared throughout Eliot's early letters as a kind of boxing partner against whom the author worked out many of her ideas about art.[48] Along both avenues, perhaps, Eliot's tendency to think in terms of the reader's response was well developed by the time of her writing *Adam Bede*.

Adam Bede is concerned at several levels with predicting, prescribing, and exploring how the mind of the reader might work. Eliot's addresses to the "lady reader" in chapter 17 are only the most contrived among several images the novel offers of the reading mind. Nowhere in Eliot's highly didactic fiction is she arguably more directive than in this chapter, in which, as W. J. Harvey put it, "the reader is repelled by having his reactions determined for him."[49] But I want to suggest that these attempts at scripting her fictional reader's acts of imagining ultimately signal an acknowledgment that her real readers *have* minds of their own, for in contrast to other Victorian novelists, Eliot is remarkable for the extent to which she acknowledges that readers bring the private, affective content of their minds to bear on a text. In *Barchester Towers*, Anthony Trollope repeatedly refers to the reader's mind as if it were primarily stocked with the reading of other novels. In *Adam Bede* Eliot makes use of the deepest stores of her readers' inner lives in an effort to stir an imaginative response in its reader, which will ultimately have an outward effect in the world.

Throughout *Adam Bede*, Eliot exposes the novelist's unspoken dependence upon the real reader's capacity to envision. The novel opens with the comparison of the novelist to a conjuror of images: "With a single drop of ink for a mirror, the Egyptian sorcerer undertakes to reveal to any chance comer far-reaching visions of the past. This is what I undertake to do for you, reader" (49). Speaking directly to the reader acknowledges, and attempts to overcome, the underlying act of fabrication but also participates in a further invention: the "reader" referred to at such moments turns out to be himself conjured. If at times the reader is implied to be the real person holding *Adam Bede* in his hands, at other times this figure appears as a kind of minor character in the novel, imagined to evince a great many prejudices, deficiencies, and objections in the process of envisioning. "'This rector of Broxton is little better than a pagan!' I hear one of my lady readers exclaim," begins chapter 17 (221). Bodenheimer suggests that such exaggerated, ironic attributing of thoughts unsympathetic to the author's aims is meant to serve a rhetorical purpose rather than to impute the real reader's response: as in Eliot's early letters, she creates for herself an uninformed audience to whom she may explicate her views all the more earnestly.[50]

But alongside these addresses to a reader Eliot has constructed, at times *Adam Bede* also addresses the real reader, and does so in order to invite him to conjure his own images. When Eliot first introduces the Poysers' farm, she calls attention to the act of imaginative "license" that underlies fiction: "Yes, the house must be inhabited, and we will see by whom; for imagination is a licensed trespasser: it has no fear of dogs, but may climb over walls and peep in at windows with impunity" (115–16). The succeeding description of the house's interior is prefaced with a command that the reader participate in the act of invention: "Put your face to one of the glass panes in the right-hand window: what do you see? . . . And what through the left-hand window?" (116). While a description of the house follows, she starts off with open-ended, enticing questions. Eliot is unearthing what Elaine Scarry shows are the usually embedded instructions an author of a literary text gives the reader in order to increase the vivacity with which he envisions the fictional world.[51] But she is also appealing to a reader whose imagination is a "trespasser" who acts "with impunity," and may have begun to picture a beloved farmhouse from memory, and become absorbed in those pictures. Thus, the politeness of Eliot's appeal to the reader highlights the solicitation—rather than simply instructions—that takes place in reading between the author and the reader's autonomous faculty of envisioning. "I beseech you to imagine Mr Irwine," Eliot writes at another moment, laying bare the negotiation between author and reader, which determines how fully her vision of the novel is realized (242).

The more Eliot asks the reader to imagine on his own, the more she serves one of her stated aims: to develop the reader's capacity to see continuities between the fictional and real worlds. A particularly open-ended invitation to imagine appears in an early passage in which Hetty's beauty is first described. Like the blank page in *Tristram Shandy* on which the reader is asked to project the beauty of Widow Wadman, Eliot claims that only the reader's own store of mental pictures can supply Hetty's likeness:

> It is of little use for me to tell you that Hetty's cheek was like a rose-petal, that dimples played about her pouting lips, that her large dark eyes hid a soft roguishness under their long lashes, and that her curly hair, though all pushed back under her round cap while she was at work, stole back in dark delicate rings on her forehead, and about her white shell-like ears; it is of little use for me to say how lovely was the contour of her pink and white neckerchief, tucked into her low plum-coloured stuff bodice, or how the linen butter-making apron, with its bib, seemed a thing to be imitated in silk by duchesses, since it fell in such charming lines, or how her brown stockings and thick-soled buckled shoes lost all that clumsiness which they must certainly have had when empty of her foot and ankle;—of little use, unless you have seen a woman who affected you as Hetty affected her beholders, for otherwise, though you might conjure up the image of a lovely woman, she would not in the least resemble that distracting, kitten-like maiden. (128)

I have quoted this passage at length to demonstrate how much it differs from a blank page. Eliot does not entrust the reader with providing an image of beauty but rather attempts to prescribe what is envisioned. The iteration of authorial insufficiency here—"it is of little use for me to tell you"—is in a sense quite rhetorically conventional, when Hetty's image is given in such purple, sensuous detail. Despite the sumptuous luxury of the passage, which verges on irony, however, Eliot ends the catalog with a sincere appeal to the reader's memory: "unless you have seen a woman who affected you as Hetty affected her beholders." Though an image might be conjured for the reader, and a sensation even stirred up within him, neither carries the affect of real-life experience, which is seen to be beyond the novelist's representational ability, and yet is absolutely required to imbue the passage with deeper meaning in the reader's mind. Private, real-life memories outside of the novelist's reach convey the author's meaning *better* than her fictional description.

In inviting the reader to imagine his own past experience, Eliot not only recognizes but relies upon a form of readerly mental activity that directly contrasts her readers' forecasting. She sends the reader's thoughts backward rather than forward, out of the novel's pages rather than further along in them, and seeks affective authenticity rather than wishful invention. This private, independent type of imagining comes to the fore as the passage about Hetty continues, and Eliot again invites the reader to supplement the limited capacity of her words:

> I might mention all the divine charms of a bright spring day, but if you had never in your life utterly forgotten yourself in straining your eyes after the mounting lark, or in wandering through the still lanes when the fresh-opened blossoms fill them with a sacred, silent beauty like that of fretted aisles, where would be the use of my descriptive catalogue? I could never make you know what I meant by a bright spring day. (128)

Again, the claim of authorial insufficiency appears somewhat ironic when Eliot describes the sensations of spring in such evocative detail. Yet in her brief essay "Story-telling," she hints at why the reader's own memories might be more compelling than the author's words in conveying a story's affect: "The modes of telling a story . . . derive their effectiveness from the superior mastery of images and pictures in grasping the attention—or, one might say with more fundamental accuracy, from the fact that our earliest, strongest impressions, our most intimate convictions, are simply images added to more or less of sensation."[52] Eliot acknowledges not only the power of mental images in storytelling but the special power of images from one's past life, one's "earliest" and "most intimate" memories and convictions. They carry a depth of feeling beyond that contained in any "descriptive catalogue"—the depth of our "most intimate" feelings about a real person, as opposed to inevitably more shallow feelings about a fictional character. Alicia Mireles Christoff, in writing about the oscillating movement that characterizes Eliot's narrators, also suggests that the powerful appeal of her narration stems in part from what I call a need to appeal to the reader's private thoughts. Rather than "perform an unfailing omniscience," Eliot's narrators "move in and out of knowing," creating both a welcome sense that "someone out there might know us" *and* preserving a sense that each one of us is not simply transcribable but more than the sum of words on a page.[53]

Eliot hoped, through evoking such recollection, that her meaning would be "perfectly seized" and "repeated" in the reader's mind, that "the emotion which stirred one in writing is repeated in the mind of the reader" (as she wrote to a fan). Yet she also knew from a variety of causes, including her intimate knowledge of psychology, that "the mind of the reader" had a mind of its own.[54] As she later writes of attempting to evoke recollection, "In writing any careful presentation of human feelings, you must count on that infinite stupidity of readers who are always substituting their crammed notions of what ought to have been felt for any attempt to recall truly what they themselves have felt under like circumstances."[55] Eliot also knew that individual experiences so differ that even a single word can produce innumerable memories. In the opening of her essay "The Natural History of German Life," she indicates an awareness that the very "picture-writing of the mind," or the associations an individual has to a given word, is itself highly variable. The mental pictures called up even by the single word "railways," Eliot notes, differ widely in the railway engineer, traveler, or shareholder from those of the man "who is not highly locomotive" and visualizes only "the image of a Bradshaw, or of the station with which he is most familiar, or of an indefinite length of tram-road."[56]

"The picture-writing of the mind": such discussions point to the overlap between Eliot's understanding of how the mind conjures images and the work of her partner, George Henry Lewes. Lewes's range of writing in the fields of literary journalism, physiology, and natural history began to focus increasingly on the study of the mind from roughly 1857 until his death in 1878, the exact years of Eliot's novelistic career.[57] The work of psychology in which Lewes was engaged serves as an important context to Eliot's representations of mental activity, particularly in *Adam Bede*, for in the same small room in Richmond in which Eliot wrote much of this novel, Lewes was working simultaneously on *The Physiology of Common Life* (1860). In fact, with the two authors writing "at tables close to each other," Gordon Haight notes that "the scratch of pen and rustle of paper" were audible and, to Eliot at least, distracting.[58] This literal proximity of Victorian psychology to Eliot's own writing is a powerful emblem of its influence on her representations of mind. The importance of Lewes's work for Eliot has been well documented, as have the ways her perceptions of the mind also overlap with the writing of some of Lewes's colleagues, a number of whom, like Herbert Spencer and E. S. Dallas, were friends. I want, for a moment, to consider how several of these writers were discussing the very mental processes Eliot invokes, and how their ideas may have informed—and complicated—Eliot's own portrayal of imaginative activity.

In *The Gay Science* (1866), Dallas suggests that imagination has not been given adequate attention by previous writers on psychology, from Locke to his contemporary, Herbert Spencer. Dallas's own hypothesis is that imagination is not a separate faculty but rather a "special function" or state of activity in which the mind, largely at a subconscious level, is continually engaged. "Imagination is but a name for the unknown, unconscious action of the mind— . . . for the Hidden Soul," he writes.[59] The notion that a stream of thought might exist outside of consciousness had broad currency by the mid-nineteenth century; Dallas cites Leibniz, Mill, and Spencer as acknowledging the possibility (202), while William Carpenter claimed to have been the first to propose a theory of "unconscious cerebration" in his *Human Physiology* (1855).[60] The unconscious functioning of the imagination was said to be especially active during sleep. Carpenter, in his expanded work, *Principles of Mental Physiology* (1874), describes the free play of imagination that occurs during sleep and dreaming as "the exercise of our constructive Imagination, working automatically without guidance or restraint," and sees dreams themselves defined by a "want of volitional control over the current of thought."[61]

Dallas sees this state of "free play" as characterizing waking life as well, arguing that the mind continually carries on a "double life" in which the conscious part is diminished next to the "vaster life beyond it" of unconscious workings:

> One can accept Prospero's lines almost literally. For what is it? Our little life is rounded with a sleep; our conscious existence is a little spot of light, rounded or begirt with a haze of slumber—not a dead but a living slumber, dimly-lighted and like a visible darkness, but full of dreams and irrepressible activity, an unknown and indefinable, but real and enjoyable mode of life. (251)

In his description, the activity of imagination sounds much like a daydream: a "living slumber," a state rich in "dreams and irrepressible activity" that is barely visible but nonetheless "enjoyable." Dallas, in fact, regards both daydreams and sleeping dreams as the states in which the nature of imagining is most visible: "The type of imaginative activity is dreaming," he writes, referring to both "dream by night and reverie by day" (258). Since the imagination's life is carried on "automatically and secretly" (307), a supposed "absence of mind" for Dallas actually signifies that one is attending to the "under-currents of thought" (227), to that "absent mind which haunts us like a ghost or a dream" (199). The real absence is of will or control over this mind's workings: "We may coax and cozen imagination; we cannot command it" (258). One of Dallas's chief illustrations of this fact is the expression of sympathy, the sharing of affect, which is so crucial to Eliot's work: "There is no form of imaginative activity more wonderful than sympathy, that strange involuntary force which impels me to identify myself with you, and you to identify yourself with me" (274). Dallas's definition of sympathy chimes with Adam Smith's, which Rae Greiner argues predominated in nineteenth-century realist fiction.[62] Smith defines sympathy as "our imaginatively changing places with the sufferer, thereby coming to conceive what he feels or even to feel what he feels." However, Dallas calls sympathy an "unconscious imitation" (240). He suggests that the activity of sympathizing is a part of this uncontrollable life carried on by the imagination.

While Dallas's account of the imagination's "irrepressible activity" is overtly celebratory, other Victorian writers confirm his depiction of imagining, and particularly daydreaming, as characteristically profuse, dynamic, and uncontrollable states. "That imagination requires restraining nobody will doubt," James Sully writes in his *Outlines of Psychology* (1885). "Wild, disconcerting and injurious fancies must, it is plain, be dispelled."[63] In a chapter in *The Senses and the Intellect* (1855) that deals with imagination, Alexander Bain discusses in similar terms a particular subset of imaginative action that he calls "emotional constructiveness": "The daydreams of ambition in a sanguine temperament . . . will embrace a whole history of the future, the baseless fabric of a vision of wonders and triumphs, which is not only constructed without labour, but whose constructions no labour can arrest." Bain himself can hardly find terms unrestrained enough to describe this activity that overpowers the very faculties of reasoning: "stupendous constructiveness, unbounded originality, flow out at once as fast as thought can evolve itself"; "a power needing restraint"; "ready to flow out, at any moment when the feeling is roused." Above all, imaginative construction seems to be defined by its lack of regulation. Referring to the daydreamer who gets carried away by his ambitions, Bain suggests that had he attempted to bring his dreams and images of the future, his "string of airy successes," to accord "with the stern experience of human life," this more restrained activity would require another name: "The term 'imagination' would no longer be used to describe it."[64]

Given Eliot's proximity to the work in which Dallas and Bain were engaged, it is reasonably certain that she was familiar with such views of the imagination as a potentially overpowering faculty, and of its association with unconscious, unprompted mental workings. Theories of the unconscious began to proliferate in the 1860s;[65] Eliot herself writes in *Daniel Deronda* about Gwendolen Harleth's moments of unaccountable anxiety: "There is a great deal of unmapped country within us which would have to be taken into account in an explanation of our gusts and storms" (276–77). But while critics have noted Eliot's recognition of a significant, unconscious element to the mind in this, her last novel, the seed of this understanding is less familiar in *Adam Bede*.[66] Dallas himself, in his own "double life" as fiction reviewer for *The Times*, noted Eliot's interest in what he calls "the region of latent thoughts" in his review of *Adam Bede*:

> It will be evident that in order to establish the identity of man with man an author must travel a good deal into the region of latent thoughts, and unconscious or but semi-conscious feelings. There is infinite variety in what we express; there is a wonderful monotony in that great world of life which never comes into the light, but works within us like the beating of the heart and the breathing of the lungs—a constant, though unobserved influence. It is in this twilight of the human soul that our novelist most delights to make his observations.[67]

The activity of sympathizing, of feeling with her characters, that Eliot seeks to evoke in readers is, as we have already seen for Dallas, a function of that unconscious life carried on by the imagination ("that great world of life which never comes into the light"). In Dallas's account of Eliot's novel, the further one goes beyond conscious experience, the more that sympathy is realized.

Throughout *Adam Bede*, Eliot invokes just such a layer of mental functioning that is beyond the characters' conscious control. In one sense, Eliot's fiction as a whole is constructed so that the omniscient narrator, and the reader who has access to his narration, always understands a level beyond what the characters perceive in their own motives. But this state of half-knowledge also appears as an internal condition within the psyche, as in the scene in which Arthur breakfasts with Irwine and shies away from his intention to confess his flirtation with Hetty:

> Was there a motive at work under this strange reluctance of Arthur's which had a sort of backstairs influence, not admitted to himself? Our mental business is carried on in much the same way as the business of the State: a great deal of hard work is done by agents who are not acknowledged. . . . Possibly, there was some such unrecognized agent secretly busy in Arthur's mind at this moment—possibly it was the fear lest he might hereafter find

the fact of having made a confession to the Rector a serious annoyance, in case he should *not* be able quite to carry out his good resolutions? The human soul is a complex thing. (218)

Though the language of the "unrecognized," "complex" work of the mind is employed somewhat satirically in this passage, this bemused, ironic perspective is exactly the tone in which Eliot most often frames insights about human nature. At other moments in this novel, Eliot has characters speak of unconscious sources of feeling with a kind of religious solemnity. Love, in particular, is described repeatedly as "a mystery we can give no account of" (168). "Mother," Seth tells Lisbeth, "thee know'st we canna love just where other folks 'ud have us. There's nobody but God can control the heart of man" (89).

The mind's workings appear equally resistant to conscious control in the many moments throughout the novel in which a character is deeply absorbed in private reverie. Daydreaming repeatedly appears so engrossing as to make one oblivious to the surrounding world, regardless of whether it consists of constructing aerial castles or being absorbed in spiritual meditation. In the opening scene in the carpentry workshop, Seth forgets to add the panels to the door he is making: his unnarrated but clearly wandering thoughts ("which was ye thinkin' on . . . the pretty parson's face or her sarmunt, when ye forgot the panel?" Wiry Ben asks; 52) are literally situated as "constructions no labour can arrest," to use Bain's words. Seth is so prone to "wool-gathering," as Adam calls it, that "he'd leave his head behind him, if it was loose" (340). Hetty, under the "narcotic" influence of the affair with Arthur, goes about "in a sort of dream, unconscious of weight or effort" (144). Stalwart Adam, at Arthur's birthday dance, loses himself in "delicious thoughts of coming home from work, and drawing Hetty to his side . . . till he forgot where he was, and the music and the tread of feet might have been the falling of rain and the roaring of the wind, for what he knew" (331). Adam's enthusiasm repeatedly expresses itself in daydreams: when he first realizes his love for Dinah, he again so intently envisions "Dinah's face turned up towards his" that, "for a few moments he was not quite conscious where he was" (544–45).

Eliot's interest in the functioning of the mind in such deep states of imagining particularly coalesces in this novel in the character of Dinah, whose spiritual meditations might be an early version of the hallucinatory visions of Mordecai, the Jewish visionary in *Daniel Deronda*. "She was so accustomed to think of impressions as purely spiritual monitions, that she looked for no material visible accompaniment of the voice," Eliot writes of the moment when Dinah hears Adam call out her name, but does not think to look for him, as they meet on the hill near the end of the novel (576). Dinah's absorption in spiritual imaginings makes her appear particularly unconscious to the surrounding world. "It's my besetment to forget where I am and everything about me, and lose myself in thoughts that I could give no account of," she tells Mr. Irwine (135). Like Seth's "thoughts he could give no account of" while he has a book in front of him (531), Dinah's reveries—as with other states of deep feeling in the novel—are characterized not only by their unconscious nature but by their unnarratable one. As Adam says in defense of Mr. Irwine's aid during the crisis of his life, Hetty's trial for child-murder: "I know there's a deal in a man's inward life as you can't measure by the square, and say, 'do this and that'll follow,' and 'do that and this'll follow'" (227). It is in such moments of deep, unaccountable feeling, as with the description of Hetty, that Eliot appeals to her readers for their experiences, which have nothing to do with reading, asking them to supply mental images for an affect that cannot, the novel insists, be narrated.

A pattern, then, emerges in the novel. When Eliot refers to the scripted figure of her "lady reader," she depicts someone engaged (and sometimes enraged) with the novel itself, a reader misinterpreting, critiquing, proposing revisions to the written work. When Eliot addresses an unscripted, real reader, it is to call the reader's attention away from the book. Here is how it works: At several important moments in the narrative, Eliot invokes the second person to suggest that the reader might have private memories that resonate with the fictional images she is conjuring. Calling upon the reader to experience the fictional scene through the filter of these memories, she then imbues her own conjured image with the deeper affect of treasured, real-life experience. The pattern is exemplified in Eliot's lyrical discussion of Dinah and Adam dusting together in his study near the end of the novel:

> That is a simple scene, reader. But it is almost certain that you, too, have been in love—perhaps, even, more than once, though you may not choose to say so to all your lady friends. If so, you will no more think the slight words, the timid looks, the tremulous touches, by which two human souls approach each other gradually, like two little quivering rain-streams, before they mingle into one—you will no more think these things trivial, than you will think the first-detected signs of coming spring trivial, though they be but a faint, indescribable something in the air and in the song of the birds, and the tiniest perceptible budding on the hedgerow branches. Those slight words and looks and touches are part of the soul's language; and the finest

language, I believe, is chiefly made up of unimposing words, such as "light," "sound," "stars," "music." . . . I am of the opinion that love is a great and beautiful thing too; and if you agree with me, the smallest signs of it . . . will rather be like those little words, "light" and "music," stirring the long-winding fibres of your memory, and enriching your present with your most precious past. (537)

This long passage engages with the figure of the reader on several levels. The first direct address, "reader," speaks to the actual reader of the novel and, in commenting upon the foregoing "scene," calls attention to the act of imagining in which, to this point, he has been engaged. However, the address functions like a traffic marker, signaling to the reader a detour in the direction of his imagining back toward his own world. The succeeding, ironic reference to the reader's "lady friends" briefly replaces this real reader with a version of Eliot's imagined reader, that minor character in the novel. But as the passage continues, the real reader emerges once again, and now defined by more than just his state of reading at that moment. He appears to have a unique subjectivity and memory to which the author admittedly does not have access. As we saw in the previous section, Eliot rarely depicts her characters' acts of remembering; we can now modify that claim to add that she is instead interested in soliciting the *reader's* remembrance as a necessary means of conveying the affect of a particular moment in the story. In fact, to Eliot the functioning of the mind makes it inevitable that the reader's private images would be evoked at such stirring moments in the narrative: as she says of Adam's thoughts at another point, "a certain consciousness of our entire past and our imagined future blends itself with all our moments of keen sensibility" (245). (Or as Lewes later writes in *Problems of Life and Mind* [1875], expressing an organicist view common to nineteenth-century psychology: "If we see the bud, after we have learned that it is a bud, there is always a forward glance at the flower, and a backward glance at the seed, dimly associated with the perception."[68]) Eliot, however, is further attempting to cultivate and appropriate the emotional energy of the reader's private associations for her own aims.

The reader is not, in a sense, putting the book down at all in such moments, when thinking of the world beyond the book is exactly what the novel is concerned with at a deeper level. *Adam Bede* is deeply committed to a realist aesthetic of sympathy for one's "fellow-mortals," to bolstering the reader's relation to the "real breathing men and women" whom the reader is asked to recall in such moments (222), for if the reader is invited to bring his prior experience of the real world to bear on the novel in order to carry out the act of imagining the characters, reading the novel conversely makes the reader more capable of imagining real people in the world. As Eliot describes her aim for her writings in a letter, "Those who read them should be better able to *imagine* and to *feel* the pains and the joys of those who differ from themselves in everything but the broad fact of being struggling erring human creatures."[69] By evoking the reader's private images in some of the most lyrical moments of the novel, such as the scene with Adam and Dinah, Eliot frames the reader's memories within a pleasing, comforting context, which serves her aim that novel reading increases rather than diminishes the reader's affection for those outside the novel.

Eliot's novel, in turn, offers a frame that might impel readers to *want* to recollect. In *The Physiology of Mind* (1867), Henry Maudsley portrays reading as generating an unconscious bustle that ultimately has more to do with the reader's own memories than the words on the page: "When we are reading or listening to a conversation, or when the mind is in a state of reverie, associations of ideas go on spontaneously, without any effort of will, and even without consciousness of the train of thought, and we may be surprised to find that an idea sometimes occurs to us in this way through the revival of old associations which seemed to have been lost."[70] Reading and reverie bring "old," "lost" associations back to the reader's consciousness. Explicitly invited to recollect, readers of *Adam Bede* may have been prompted to do so by the implicit way in which their deepest, unverbalized mental images and feelings were evoked in a particularly lyrical, pleasing context—and thus not only kindled for the author's purposes but articulated for themselves. One early reviewer, Anne Mozley, suggested that *Adam Bede*'s wide popularity was in part due to how the novel "chimes in a telling, because natural and simple way, with associations and thoughts which have been lying half developed and struggling for expression in many minds."[71] Eliot described her own reading of Rousseau in such terms: "It is simply that the rushing mighty wind of his inspiration has so quickened my faculties that I have been able to shape more definitely for myself ideas which had previously dwelt as dim 'ahnungen' in my soul—the fire of his genius has so fused together old thoughts and prejudices that I have been ready to make new combinations."[72] Mozley also suggests that *Adam Bede*'s ability to move the reader derives from descriptions made rich by its author's own highly associative mind, in which private reflections "people every familiar scene with a pleasant, leisurely crowd of thoughts and fancies, till each salient point is hung and garlanded with these memorials, and haunted, as it were, by a summer hum of reverie."[73] Eliot even seems to have had this effect on other people in personal conversation. Rebecca Mead recites how "William Hale White, her co-lodger at 142 Strand, remarked that when she was talking with any sincerely engaged person, 'she strove to elicit his best, and generally disclosed to him something in himself of which he was not aware.'"[74]

Stirring the reader's faculties to "make new combinations," as Eliot described reading Rousseau, however, can bring reading itself to a stop. Reading Eliot's fiction had this effect on her publisher, Blackwood, who described to her how he put Book 5 of *Middlemarch* down out of very appreciation for it:

> I dallied for days over this Book, pausing and reading and rereading, and now when I sit down to write to you, instead of doing so out of hand I find myself turning over the sheets of the Book, looking at the different points and wondering what is most perfect, until if I do not take care the morning will be gone and no letters written at all, as has happened to me more than once before. When things please me particularly I sit back in my chair and begin dreaming.[75]

Though Blackwood describes "dall[ying]" over and meditating on the novel's perfections, this is no critical publisher's professional reading: he has been derailed into "dreaming," transported into a state of personal indulgence and pleasure in his own meditations. Blackwood shows how private imagining can become unruly instead of keeping to its prescribed role of being an enriching supplement. The danger is that such "dreaming" can become more absorbing than the novel itself.

Indeed, within *Adam Bede*, Eliot also stresses the precarious nature of the process whereby one's ideals are translated into effects, as she says of the not fully matured Arthur: "Our deeds determine us, as much as we determine our deeds; and until we know what has been or will be the peculiar combination of outward with inward facts, which constitutes a man's critical actions, it will be better not to think ourselves wise about his character" (359). Acutely concerned throughout this novel with a need to elicit the readers' own memories, she equally acknowledges that such imaginative engagement can run riot over the author's aims, for as we have seen from her experience with both readers and contemporary theories of the imagination, Eliot seems to have been mindful that her fiction depended on a capacity that had little to do with rational control. In soliciting the reader to imagine at key moments, Eliot was aware of summoning a faculty that was notably immune to coaxing, and that might engage as well (as her later readers did) in other unsolicited acts of wish fulfillment.

Adam Bede is filled with images of characters sitting with a book in front of them but absorbed instead in their own thoughts. Seth, as we have seen, appears more interested in his inarticulate thoughts than in his new book (531); Bartle Massey, concerned about Adam before Hetty's trial, is only "pretending to read, while he is really looking over his spectacles at Adam" (466); while Adam, with "shaking hands," tries to read the letter that informs Irwine of Hetty's arrest and cannot (455). Required for the enterprise of sympathy, recollection may prove as disruptive to the reading process as wishful forecasting, for just after the passage in which Eliot solicits the reader's daydreams of his own past love in order to conjure Dinah and Adam's, the characters themselves appear in this very dilemma: sitting with a book in hand but too absorbed in dreaming of each other to heed it. In the passage with which I began, Seth at least reads intermittently: his "dreamy eyes *as often as not* looking vaguely out the window." With Adam and Dinah, the absorption is total: Adam's mother awakens his feelings about Dinah while he attempts to read on a Sunday morning, so that he sits "looking down at the book on the table, without seeing any of the letters" (545), while Dinah, from the same cause, sits with a book by her side, not even opened (550).

Imagination and Sympathy: Acting and Reacting

The Janus faces of Eliot's relation with her readers' minds are emblematized in the chapter "The Two Bed-Chambers" in *Adam Bede*. Dinah appears on one side of the bedroom wall, her imagination and sympathy working harmoniously together to envision her cousin Hetty in future difficulty; on the other side, Hetty dreams of "fine clothes" (199). The two forms of imagining modeled, respectively, in the characters of Hetty and Dinah are not exactly parallel: Hetty-like, wishful imagining could take place among a community of readers, while Dinahesque imagining is by nature deeply private; Hetty's type of fantasy involves forecast, Dinah's recollection; and most significantly, Hetty-like readers overwrite the author's vision, while Dinahesque readers supplement it. What they share is what Dallas might term their "irrepressible activity," the fact that any type of independent imagining has the potential to eclipse the text that generates it. Moreover, Dinah's idealized sympathy relies upon the very same faculty of envisioning that Hetty employs in indulging her "vision" (197). Even in an ideal mind, the various faculties appear entwined, as Eliot writes of Dinah: "Her imagination had created a thorny thicket of sin and sorrow, in which she saw the poor thing struggling torn and bleeding. . . . It was in this way that

Dinah's imagination and sympathy acted and reacted habitually, each heightening the other" (203). This last part of the discussion of *Adam Bede* briefly examines the complex narrative interplay that develops as Eliot attempts to marshal the daydreams stirred up by her fiction and highlights the difficulty of separating desirable from undesired forms of imagining.

"Aerial building" has particular resonance in *Adam Bede*, as an inverse of that activity so valorized in the novel: carpentry. Lewes worried the novel would not sell because, as he wrote in his journal, readers "like to fancy themselves doing and feeling what the heroes and heroines do and feel"—an interesting insight into *his* view of readers' mental activity—and "no one would care to be a merely upright carpenter."[76] Building is idealized in the novel as the work of meliorism; oppositely, Jenny Uglow refers to the "magical thinking" in which Hetty and Arthur indulge, in which "dreams unchecked can *dissolve* the sure outlines of the familiar world."[77] But Adam, as we have seen, habitually daydreams, his mind most often "leaping forward" (255) while he is walking. The "walk" forms the organizing trope of Rousseau's *Les Rêveries du promeneur solitaire* (1782), while the "walking reverie," in Celeste Langan's term, proliferates throughout Wordsworth's poetry.[78] Particularly as an apparent allusion to writers whom Eliot admired, Adam's pedestrian daydreams appear to be less egoistic wish fulfillments than expressions of reverent love and enthusiasm.[79] As the narrator says of Adam's thoughts after Jonathan Burge has offered to make him a partner:

> So he gave his hand to Burge on that bargain, and went home with his mind full of happy visions, in which (my refined reader will perhaps be shocked when I say it), the image of Hetty hovered and smiled over plans for seasoning timber at a trifling expense, calculations as to the cheapening of bricks per thousand by water-carriage, and a favourite scheme for the strengthening of roofs and walls with a peculiar form of iron girder. (401)

The puzzle Eliot highlights in detailing Adam's dreams is that his generous but deluded visions of Hetty are inextricably bound up with his admirable, inventive visions of carpentry. Here Adam exemplifies the problem of distinguishing that form of imagining Eliot wishes to encourage in her reader—sympathy—from the distracting form of imagining she wishes to discourage: egoistic wish fulfillment.

If as a subject of Adam's visions Hetty symbolizes that brand of imagining Eliot wishes to discourage in her reader, the deterrent portrait is emphatic when Hetty herself daydreams. Hetty's imagination, far from fertile, is described by the frequent use of the words "little" and "narrow"; the narrator is frequently caustic toward her "little silly imagination" (145) and her "little trivial soul" (386). Hetty's narcissistic use of her limited capacities is the chief blame: "They are but dim, ill-defined pictures that her narrow bit of an imagination can make of the future; but of every picture she is the central figure, in fine clothes; . . . and everybody else is admiring and envying her" (198). Hetty is oblivious to Adam Bede's feelings over his father's death, absorbed instead in a "beatified world" of her own making: "Young souls, in such pleasant delirium as hers, are as unsympathetic as butterflies sipping nectar; they are isolated from all appeals by a barrier of dreams" (146). This description of Hetty as "unsympathetic" to another's grief might also be read another way, as a recognition that Hetty herself is "unsympathetic" as an object of readerly identification. That Eliot is crueler toward Hetty than almost any other character is a commonplace in Eliot criticism.[80] Hetty is triply extradited in the novel: from the village of Hayslope, from England, and, at the last gasp in the epilogue, from the living world itself.

Yet though the early part of the novel is devoted to demonstrating the shortcomings of Hetty's mental life, her dreams eventually become the very means through which Eliot stirs whatever degree of sympathy the novel has for her. The fact that her imagination has only one key, wish fulfillment, appears in a more sympathetic light beginning with her journey to find Arthur, when her persistent dreams, once of finery, become a pool in which she might drown herself. "At last she was among the fields she had been dreaming of, on a long narrow pathway leading towards a wood. If there should be a pool in that wood!" (430). Though the narrator's language still suggests that Hetty brought this crisis on herself, it is now insisted that her "little brain" (365) suffers disproportionately:

> Poor wandering Hetty, with the rounded childish face, and the hard unloving despairing soul looking out of it—with the narrow heart and narrow thoughts, no room in them for any sorrows but her own, and tasting that sorrow with the more intense bitterness! My heart bleeds for her as I see her toiling along on her weary feet, or seated in a cart, with her eyes fixed vacantly on the road before her, never thinking or caring whither it tends, till hunger comes and makes her desire that a village may be near. (435)

While Eliot acknowledges that Hetty is still unresponsive to the pain of others, her "narrow thoughts" are now the cause of intense suffering. In another moment describing Hetty's journey, Eliot invokes that "lady reader" whose responses, imagined to be antagonistic, provide the narrator an opportunity for ardent defense. As she writes of Hetty, "She knew no romance, and had only a feeble share in the feelings which are the source of romance, so that well-read ladies may find it difficult to understand her state of mind. She was too ignorant of everything beyond the simple notions and habits in which she had been brought up, to have any more definite idea of her probable future than that Arthur would take care of her somehow" (418). Invoking a fictionalized, prejudiced reader in this context makes that reader appear like Hetty: both lack the ability to sympathize and cannot freely imagine anything beyond their respective spheres of experience. Eliot's projection of the imagined reader not "understand[ing]" Hetty might even be read as a somewhat euphemistic intervention, an acknowledgment that the real reader might simply dislike Hetty. The real reader, then, may also be deficient in imagining, in the sense of engaging at such moments in little of that "wonderful" form of imaginative activity Dallas calls sympathy.

Eliot repeatedly punctuates her accounts of Hetty's daydreams with references to what a reader, real or imagined, might be thinking about Hetty. The novel thus offers suggestively interwoven portraits of these two activities of mind, the reader's novel reading and Hetty's daydreaming, for though Hetty is decidedly not a reader, she shares two of the readerly tendencies to which Eliot proved keenly sensitive from her first publishing experiences: a penchant for wish fulfillment and excessive anticipation. In Hetty's case, her persistent imagining ahead lays bare such "moral deficiencies" (200) as her indifference to those who have nurtured her: she "could have cast all her past life behind her and never cared to be reminded of it again" (199). The violence of Eliot's treatment of Hetty also resonates with the tone of the author's later reactions to those real readers whose imaginings—also about the future, though the future within the novel—are similarly persistent and misguided. Hetty in a sense appears as a figure for that element in her readership that prickled Eliot from the beginning of her career: that desire, as she says of Hetty, to see "all things through a soft, liquid veil, as if she were living not in this solid world of brick and stone, but in a beatified world" (144). One might imagine that it is Hetty complaining about the people of Hayslope, and not the "lady reader" of chapter 17 protesting pettishly about the novel, "What vulgar details! What good is there in taking all these pains to give an exact likeness of old women and clowns? What a low phase of life!—what clumsy, ugly people!" (223). Hetty, the reader might recall, "did not understand how anybody could be very fond of middle-aged people" (199–200).

Though much of *Adam Bede* is devoted to depicting this kind of reality-denying wish fulfillment, whether in Hetty, Arthur, Adam, or the imagined reader, it is also suggested that even reading a romance novel could have schooled them in necessary foresight. Early on, Arthur tries to dissuade himself from flirting further with Hetty by bringing his knowledge of old stories to bear on the situation: "No gentleman, out of a ballad, could marry a farmer's niece" (184). Later he is seen carrying Dr. John Moore's *Zeluco* (a story about a seducer) into the woods with him—but he throws it into the corner of the hermitage, unread. If further reading could have stirred up Arthur to imagine the consequences of his own actions, and thus averted deep trouble and suffering, Eliot considers how reading might have helped Hetty learn to narrativize. Imagining the future, that act that later has such resonance in Eliot's fiction, comes to have real stakes in *Adam Bede*, as Hetty's inability to do so is implicated in the tragedy of the novel: during her deepest crisis, when she is about to have her baby, she can only form "again and again the same childish, doubtful images of what was to come" (418). As Eliot writes of Hetty's thoughts of the future during the affair with Arthur:

> There was no knowing what would come since this strange entrancing delight had come. If a chest full of lace and satin and jewels had been sent her from some unknown source, how could she but have thought that her whole lot was going to change, and that to-morrow some still more bewildering joy would befall her? Hetty had never read a novel: if she had ever seen one, I think the words would have been too hard for her: how then could she find a shape for her expectations? (181)

Despite the irony regarding Hetty's inability to shape her feelings into a romance plot, the passage expresses a momentary sympathy toward Hetty in the suggestion that had she tried to read a novel, "the words would have been too hard for her." Forecasting appears almost desirable, as Hetty, unlike Eliot's later readers, is unaccustomed to novel reading, and is quite tragically unable to imagine a future for herself, to read ahead in her own story.

The relation between thoughts and deeds, wishes and their realization, preoccupies Eliot's fiction from the beginning. In *Adam Bede* Eliot explores several versions of this question of whether or not intentions translate into actions, including what work the novelist's own acts of imagining, in writing fiction, do. "Our deeds determine us," she says of Arthur's ultimately ineffectual ideals; on the other hand, the novel's defense of realistic art is concerned with the effect the novel itself has on the minds of readers, and with how the readers' thoughts might in turn affect the world beyond her book. She writes, "I would not, even if I had the choice, be the clever novelist who could create a world so much better than this, in which we get up in the morning to do our daily work, that you would be likely to turn a harder, colder eye on the dusty streets and the common green fields" (222). In imagining that reading a novel can have such an impact on its readers—even if, as here, it is conceived as a negative one— Eliot is in a sense writing her own version of wish fulfillment.

Wish fulfillment is explored in a new way in Eliot's last novel, *Daniel Deronda*, in which the deepest hopes and thoughts of several characters in fact appear to be achieved outside of themselves. During the few chapters that take place in Genoa late in the novel, Daniel learns that he is Jewish, which sets in motion the fulfillment of Mordecai's great wish that Deronda carry out his hopes for the Jewish people; at the same time, Gwendolen finds one of her own deepest wishes much more frighteningly realized. In the passage to which I alluded at the beginning of the chapter, she tells Deronda what happened in the boat the afternoon her estranged husband, Grandcourt, drowns:

> "I had cruel wishes—I fancied impossible ways of—I did not want to die myself; I was afraid of our being drowned together. . . . I knew no way of killing him there, but I did, I did kill him in my thoughts. . . . The evil long-ings, the evil prayers came again and blotted everything else dim, till, in the midst of them—I don't know how it was—he was turning the sail—there was a gust—he was struck—I know nothing—I only know that I saw my wish outside me." (695–96)

There are several narratives of agency in this chilling passage. On the one hand, Gwendolen expresses profound guilt in imagining her thoughts to be deeds: "I did, I did kill him in my thoughts"; "I saw my wish outside me." Moreover, the wish fulfilled so horrifically, if accidentally, in this passage, Andrew Miller has pointed out, is one that the reader who has endured six hundred pages of Grand-court's cruelty has probably also long entertained.[81] The reader, then, may share Gwendolen's feeling of guilt at this wish's consummation. Be careful what you wish for, Eliot appears to be cautioning her actively forecasting readers.

But on another level, Eliot also clarifies that Gwendolen's wishes are indeed only harmless thoughts, by repeatedly identifying them as "wishes," "fancie[s]," and "longings," all terms that emphasize a state of desiring rather than action. Even her "evil prayers" are not actually enacted but spoken of longingly and with a deep sense of futility: "If it had been any use I should have prayed"

(695). Indeed, Gwendolen appears strikingly helpless against the horrific translation of these thoughts into reality: "I know nothing," "I don't know how it was," "I knew no way of killing him." The reader, too, is perhaps being reminded throughout the passage that he has been, like Gwendolen, ultimately helpless to effect his wish ("I knew no way of killing him"). The reader is caught in a fantasy of agency, reminded (by the omnipotent author) of the poor power his wishes have over the text. Yet he is simultaneously freed from responsibility for these evil imaginings—imaginings that, after all, indicate a generous sympathy with Gwendolen's long misery.[82] After years of grappling with readers' imaginations, Eliot acknowledges that reading is a form of wishing, and one in which hoped-for sympathy with suffering, and dreams for its termination, might remain inevitably intertwined.

4

Middlemarch's Negations

WHO THAT cares to know George Eliot's fiction has not stumbled over her occasionally convoluted prose, has not had to ask himself or herself, "Wait, what did I just read?" Reading Eliot, I feel like I understand a whole paragraph, but I actually understand less when I look at its individual sentences. Take, for example, the first words of *Middlemarch* (1871–72), which my first sentence echoes: "Who that cares much to know the history of man, and how the mysterious mixture behaves under the varying experiments of Time, has not dwelt, at least briefly, on the life of Saint Theresa, has not smiled with some gentleness at the thought of the little girl walking forth one morning hand-in-hand with her still smaller brother, to go and seek martyrdom in the country of the Moors?" (25). Reading this sentence, I feel as if I am being tapped as one who "cares" to learn about vexed, mysterious human nature as it has acted in the world, and that the narrator is offering to show it to me. However, far from affirming my status as one among like-minded readers who wish to understand human nature more fully, Eliot's sentence puts the case negatively, frames it as a rhetorical question, and focuses on an unidentified subject who has *not* performed the described meditations. As Anthony Trollope wrote of reading *Daniel Deronda* (1876), "There are sentences which I have found myself compelled to read three times before I have been able to take home to myself all that the writer has intended."[1]

There are many kinds of strangeness in Eliot's sentences, but her use of negation is a cause of confusion that stands out against the backdrop of her preoccupation with readers who formed their own narratives of what they thought *should* be in her books. Within Eliot's prose, what a character does not know, or what a character does not look like, often becomes entangled in her sentences with what does exist within the contours of the fictional world. This rhetorical construction, of describing something by saying what is not the case, appears twice in the opening sentence of the prelude (who "has not dwelt," "has not smiled"), and Eliot goes on to use it throughout *Middlemarch*. She calls up detailed mental images only to identify them as not being part of the novel's realized world. For instance, when introducing Nicholas Bulstrode's character, the narrator first describes what not to picture and then offers a second "actual" image: "Do not imagine his sickly aspect to have been of the yellow, black-haired sort: he had a pale blond skin, thin gray-besprinkled brown hair, light-gray eyes, and a large forehead" (151). The initial description of what Bulstrode does not look like is fleeting, a half-sentence that appears especially brief in contrast to Jane Austen's extended descriptions of hypothetical marriage plots. But speed here is crucial: within a single sentence, Eliot has her reader form two contradictory images of what comprises the fictional world in quick succession. The correct image (pale, brown-haired) follows the incorrect one (yellow, black-haired) so soon that there is not time for erasure. The effect is to create images that layer on top of one another: the brighter yellow skin and black hair conjured in the first part of the sentence persist under the pale, thin, light second image. Instead of the reader's imagining a two-dimensional face drawn from a flatly narrated catalog of features, Eliot cultivates a mobile, three-dimensional structure of imagining in the reader's mind using a technique of layering similar to one Elaine Scarry has described.[2] In another moment, when the narrator asks the reader whether she pictures Rosamond Vincy revealing any sign of her scheming, the described image of Rosamond's scheming remains vivid despite the much briefer phrase that denies its visibility: "Do you imagine that her rapid forecast and rumination concerning house-furniture . . . were ever discernible in her conversation, even with her mamma? On the contrary" (301).

As these examples suggest, Eliot's negations include a variety of ways in which a statement is nullified, denied, or the reader is told in detail what is not rather than what is. The use of negative statements to convey an opposite meaning has a long history in both philosophy and classical rhetoric, in the form of litotes.[3] Traditionally used for ironic understatement, such statements are not simple (the Greek meaning of litotes) but rather complex, rhetorically elevated, and call to mind the epic tradition.[4] George Orwell thought negative constructions were pretentious and decadent, and objected to their overuse in his essay "Politics and the English Language" (1946), in which he tries to rally readers "to laugh the *not un-*formation out of existence."[5] Eliot's frequent use of this high rhetorical construction in *Middlemarch* may suit her larger ambition to write a "home epic," and has, as we will see, the effect of elevating the "incalculably diffusive," that which is invisible within or resists being circumscribed by conventional definition. When Eliot uses an overwhelming number of negative constructions in a single passage, she affirms the novel's investment in the intangible and rare nature of inward life, which can only be understood by rejecting ready-made, easily named images.

These "no" and "not" statements about characters have a counterfactual status in the text, but they differ from the plot-oriented focus of recent discussions of unrealized narrative possibilities. Rather, they prompt the reader to *visualize* something that is said to be counter to how it appears within the fictional world. Counterfactual acts of imagining what Catherine Gallagher describes as "possible but unrealized alternative *consequences* that might have resulted," whether in historical events or fictional lives, have drawn recent critical attention through the searching work of Gallagher and Andrew Miller.[6] That which does not happen has been seen particularly to haunt Eliot's fiction, as well as the experience of reading it. Victorian reviewers regularly expressed disappointment with the plot outcomes of Eliot's novels and belatedly suggested alternative endings.[7] Among critics, Barbara Hardy originally identified in Eliot's fiction "a strong and deliberate suggestion of the possible lives her characters might have lived"—a sense of multiple possibilities that she sees as most poignant at moments of moral crisis.[8]

This focus on alternate possible lives and consequences, on the characters' actions and choices, does not take into account that for Eliot plot provided an erroneous structure for the reader's imaginings. Knowing Eliot's attitude toward readers who forecast their wishes for their favorite character's "lot," it should not be surprising that trying to imagine a more desirable sequence of events in a character's life can result in vague, overly narrow, or humorous images in *Middlemarch*. In Dickens's fiction, thinking about "what might have happened" is often a profitable mental act, described in detailed terms, as Miller has shown throughout *Great Expectations* (1861). Likewise, in *David Copperfield* (1850), David describes in painful detail after Dora's death how "I had thought, much and often, of my Dora's shadowing out to me what might have happened, in those years that were destined not to try us; I had considered how the things that never happen, are often as much realities to us, in their effects, as those that are accomplished" (824–25). In contrast, dwelling on alternate plot possibilities becomes humorous, rather than morally instructive, when Mary Garth calls Fred Vincy out on being idle and extravagant, and he offers a bland, subjunctive description of himself having had more means. "I should not have made a bad fellow if I had been rich," Fred says (166). Given

Eliot's larger concern with the ways the conventions of a three-volume novel governed and thinned out her readers' imaginative reception of her work, her frequent use of negation suggests that her concern with the problematic forms that imagination was taking in novel readers' minds penetrates to, and haunts her at, the level of individual clauses and sentences.

In *Middlemarch* Eliot asks us to imagine alternatives not on the larger scale of plot but at the level of the sentence, in the descriptions, scenarios, and knowledge she describes as not being realized in the novel's world. Recently, some critics have been looking closely at how a writer's style influences a reader's creative engagement with a novel.[9] The effect of Eliot's negative constructions is to invite her readers to fill out "the scenery of the event" (510) by holding multiple, contradictory mental pictures in their minds at one time.[10] As we will see, her relentless use of negative constructions paradoxically helps to create that "impression of expansiveness" that has been so often commented on by readers of *Middlemarch*, of "life going on beyond this particular selection of life" (as Barbara Hardy memorably describes it).[11] The novel's habitual negations also create an impression of life going on, inwardly, that cannot and even should not be contained within ordinary positive definition. Since we are used to thinking of Eliot as having a very controlling narratorial presence, it is surprising to find her innovating a range of strategies, at various formal scales, to keep her readers' minds open to multiple possibilities.

Do Not Imagine

Eliot is known for telling readers what to imagine—not for telling them what they should *not* imagine. Yet multiple direct addresses within *Middlemarch* simultaneously direct the reader in what to envision and how not to imagine a character or scenario. In commanding the reader to create mental images that she explicitly says are not part of the fictional world, Eliot is using an opposite narrative technique to that which operates in *Adam Bede* (1859). As we saw in chapter 3, in her first full-length novel Eliot uses direct addresses that prompt readers to picture their own private, unscripted remembrances and to bring that real-life affect to bear on depicted scenes within the novel. By the time of the later novel, she had more experience with, and arguably less confidence in, real readers of her fiction. In *Middlemarch* she often uses a rhetorical structure that repeatedly scripts what readers should imagine and then excludes those images from the novel's represented world. Both forms of readerly imagining— unscripted and scripted by the author, invited in and excluded from the novel's depicted world—suggest that the reader's imagination of what is beyond the described fictional world is needed to create a fuller image of what she aims to represent. Though it seems counterintuitive, Eliot uses commands *not* to imagine in order to bring what she felt was a much-needed sense of flexibility, depth, and realism to the novel reader's mental pictures.

How does the rhetorical tic of negation result in such nuanced layers of imagining? Recent criticism focused on Eliot's syntax and image making have taught us to examine her sentences at a minute level.[12] The first thing to notice about Eliot's negative commands is that many of them engage the reader in a precise, expansive imagining of mental pictures, not events. In prompting the reader to imagine different versions of what she calls "the scenery of the event" (510)—the filled-in background of a narrative—she prolongs a moment that is independent of plot. Eliot's description of Bulstrode's appearance in *Middlemarch* is just such a neutral moment: a moment free of the kind of readerly, plot-based wishes that narrow thinking. When Eliot suggests that the reader might have an instinct to imagine the opposite, and describes what should not be pictured, she ends up drawing out the moment of envisioning. Each of the novel's many negations guides the novel's reader through this complex mental construction of forming multiple, contradictory images at once. As Laurence Horn discusses in his comprehensive work on the philosophy and psychology of negation, negative statements take longer to process than the corresponding positive ones, in part because negatives tend to be first converted to positives in the hearer's mind.[13] Thus, Eliot's negative descriptions create tension between the sequential imagining required by narrative and the additional, lateral imagining required to picture negated alternative images. The result is that the novel's sentences hold back its plot; they slow down the forward narrative thrust of reading. The value of moments of stasis, within or as a quality of longer narratives, has been increasingly recognized within recent critical work on the nineteenth-century novel.[14] In *Middlemarch*, these moments of imaginative proliferation can be individually minute, but they have a cumulative effect: over the lengthy experience of reading her prose, the imagining of alternatives becomes a nearly unconscious habit in readers' minds, and ultimately works to create a less teleological and more imaginatively capacious reading experience.

The second thing to notice about many of Eliot's negative commands is that they are structured not only to extend imagining but to correct it. When we are told explicitly what Bulstrode does not look like, and what he does, these are not offered as two viable alternatives, either of which could characterize the novel's fictional world. Rather, Eliot makes a meaningful drama of correcting an unattuned and often hastily imagining reader. In Bulstrode's case, Eliot appears to be addressing a natural tendency to form quick, conventional images as the narrator warns us not to form an image we have, perhaps, already pictured to ourselves. "Do not imagine his sickly aspect to have been of the yellow, black-haired *sort*" uses shorthand terms to refer to a "sort" of sickliness as if it were a known type, as if a reader would be predisposed to associate the word "sickly" with a formulaic picture of a jaundiced face. In contrast to the ease of calling up a clichéd image, Eliot puts the reader through mental gymnastics. She simultaneously commands the reader to picture and reject this melodramatic image with the oxymoronic phrase "do not imagine"; she describes an image in bright, vivid colors, which makes the canceled image harder to suppress in the reader's mind, and then she directs the reader to envision, feature by feature, a less obviously peevish face. The cognitive challenge of this moment mirrors its moral complexity, as the reader is also prompted to rethink stock moral assumptions, such as that genuine ill—physical *and* moral ill, in Bulstrode's case—shows itself in a particular type. We are familiar with Eliot's investment in widening narrow ways of thinking as a moral and ethical precept; diversifying readers' minds away from narrow forms of imagining describes Eliot's realist aesthetic as well.[15]

Correcting a reader's erroneous imaginative assumptions is a construction that Eliot uses throughout her career. As I discussed earlier, Rosemarie Bodenheimer argues that Eliot sets up an imaginatively deficient reader, throughout her early letters and fiction, as a kind of boxing partner against whom she could articulate many of her early ideas about art.[16] From "Silly Novels by Lady Novelists" through *Middlemarch*, Eliot continues to educate her reader about realistic art by rejecting incorrect, unrealistic uses of the imagination. Through both positive direct addresses *and* negative commands, then, Eliot sets up her art as an alternative form of storytelling that resists predictable forms. This picturesque moment, in which the villagers gather together in *Adam Bede*, forms a template for Eliot's negative method of direct address. She lingers over a scenic moment—a moment independent of plot—as she corrects the reader's clichéd imagining of it:[17]

> The men were chiefly gathered in the neighbourhood of the blacksmith's shop. But *do not imagine them* gathered in a knot. Villagers never swarm: a whisper is unknown among them, and they seem almost as incapable of an undertone as a cow or a stag. Your true rustic turns his back on his

interlocutor, throwing a question over his shoulder as if he meant to run away from the answer, and walking a step or two farther off when the interest of the dialogue culminates. So the group in the vicinity of the blacksmith's door was *by no means a close one*, and *formed no screen* in front of Chad Cranage, the blacksmith himself, who stood with his black brawny arms folded, leaning against the door-post. (63; my emphases)

As Eliot is well known for doing in another chapter, "In Which the Story Pauses a Little," she interrupts the diegesis to address the reader—here, as if presuming that the reader has begun to imagine in an unrealistic, overhasty way. Though the tone is not as chastising as other moments of direct address in *Adam Bede*, the fictionalized, urbane reader being confronted knows little about the habits of "villagers" and "true rustic[s]," and has to be stopped from importing a familiar image of men closely gathered, as on a city street. However, in the course of preventing or correcting a supposedly uninformed reader figure, Eliot adds detail to what the actual reader is *not* supposed to picture. She describes the hypothetical villagers in picturesque terms, never "swarm[ing,]" "whisper[ing,]" or forming a "knot" or "screen." In one of the novel's stranger negations, she even invites the reader to imagine a couple of farm animals talking, as she suggests the men are "almost as incapable of an undertone as a cow or a stag." Following this narrative sequence becomes an intricate mental exercise in distinguishing realistic images from unrealistic images (the talking cow), and images realized in the novel's world from unrealized ones. The complicated imaginative process that unfolds over the course of the passage gives the "true rustic" an added claim to lifelike verisimilitude when the multidimensional, compound image that emerges is compared with the initial, vague image of men "gathered in the neighbourhood of the blacksmith's shop."

What happens to the first canceled image that we learn is erroneous only after, as in the case of Bulstrode, she has evoked a vivid picture of a jaundiced man? As Freud describes in his essay on "Negation," in psychoanalysis, a patient's denial of having thought something is irrelevant—once the content has come to the surface, even if framed by a denial, it cannot be re-repressed. So, in such a moment Eliot calls into the reader's mind two images in quick succession, almost coexisting—one negated and the other "actual." Negated images and unrealized possibilities become subtly but continually integrated with the actual world of the novel. Eliot describes a similar dynamic happening within Lydgate's thoughts after Mrs. Bulstrode cautions him that he has been paying too much attention to Rosamond. "It must be confessed also that momentary speculations as to all the possible grounds for Mrs Bulstrode's hints had managed to get woven like slight, clinging hairs into the more sub- stantial web of his thoughts" (334–35). The action of the mind Eliot describes is of sketchy suggestions not disappearing but lingering and intermingling into more developed, conscious thought. In the case of Lydgate's unconsciously developing feelings for Rosamond, these "slight, clinging hairs"—Mrs. Bul- strode's hint and Lydgate's speculations about their basis—become interwo- ven with his "web" of thoughts. The web is Eliot's most recognizable metaphor to characterize the social network in which a person is enmeshed, and a similar sense of connection appears to be at work within the individual mind; no set of thoughts can be disconnected from the others and disowned. In fact, thoughts are all too likely to become entangled, as she writes about Casaubon, "We all of us, grave or light, get our thoughts entangled in metaphors, and act fatally on the strength of them" (111). Not being able to distinguish the real from the metaphoric, the speculative from the substantial, is a common but consequential condition of mind for Eliot.

Thus, the pervasiveness of Eliot's negations is not just stylistic, but rather this repetition has a cognitive effect on the novel's reader. By describing something absent, Eliot brings the described image vividly into the reader's mind. What is "not" becomes inextricably mixed in among the stream of images the novel asks the reader to envision. This is especially the case when a single negative statement contains a dizzying number of negations, which makes it all the more difficult to separate what is not true from what is, as in the following sentences about various characters:

> Perhaps it was *not* possible for Lydgate, under the double stress of outward material difficulty and of his own proud resistance to humiliating conse- quences, to imagine fully what this sudden trial was to a young creature who had known *nothing* but indulgence. (640–41; my emphasis)

> He had *no* sonnets to write, and it could *not* strike him agreeably that he was *not* an object of preference to the woman who he had preferred. (85; my emphasis)

> But *no one* stated exactly what else that was in her power she ought rather to have done—*not* even Sir James Chettam, *who went no further than the negative prescription* that she ought *not* to have married Will Ladislaw. (894; my emphasis)

J. Hillis Miller, who refers to "the strangely multiplied negatives" in another passage of *Middlemarch*, is known for describing Eliot's effort in the novel as "negative" in a larger sense: that she is dismantling "the metaphysical system of history" and the characters' metaphysical notions of what human lives are like.[18] But I am suggesting that Eliot's negative syntax has another effect that is constructive rather than deconstructive. As she spells out in detail how to imagine something that is denied to the novel's world, reading the description evokes the image nonetheless, and can even evoke a corresponding affect. In the first example above, in the service of describing Lydgate's mind, which cannot sympathetically envision Rosamond's pained mind, the sentence begins to cultivate feeling for this suddenly vulnerable-sounding "young creature." The reader provides the sympathy that Lydgate, at this moment, cannot. The second example, which describes Sir James's feeling after learning Dorothea is to marry Casaubon, also uses negations that construct and convey a character's affective state to the reader. In this case, the reader has to disencumber the grammatical complexity of three successive negatives ("no sonnets . . . it could not strike him . . . not an object of preference"), each of which "acts as a kind of dam to the stream of understanding," in Laurence Horn's words.[19] The result is a perplexing, discomfiting experience for the reader, much like what Sir James is feeling. The denied images that comprise these moments become an established part of the holistic, inclusive mix that is *Middlemarch* in the reader's mind. Gillian Beer has described how "the book's boundaries are permeable," and were especially so to Victorian readers, due to Eliot's wide-ranging allusions and because Eliot calls upon "a stock of common knowledge" known to them.[20] I am suggesting that the novel's habitual syntax assists in creating the illusion that what is technically not in *Middlemarch* is part of the imagined world that forms in the reader's mind.

As negated images become interwoven with the more "substantial" world of the novel, they give an illusion of depth to the reader's mental picture of that world. This sense of depth is enacted through the different levels of awareness Eliot frequently refers to when she describes what is not true about the novel's realized fictional world. Early in the novel, Eliot narrates Lydgate's life prior to arriving in the town, only to reveal directly afterward, at the very end of the chapter, that this narrated history lies outside of the characters' knowledge:

> *No one* in Middlemarch was likely to have such a notion of Lydgate's past as has here been faintly shadowed, and indeed the respectable townsfolk there were *not more given* than mortals generally to any eager attempt at exactness in the representation to themselves of *what did not* come under their own senses. (183; my emphasis)

This sentence—which does, as Trollope says, probably need to be read three times before it makes sense—is an ontological puzzle in which layers of statements that describe what is *not* the case take precedence linguistically over what does exist. The sentence refers to what characters do not know, the mental habits they do not possess, and what they do not directly perceive. The sentence establishes that there can be several different mental pictures of the same character, Lydgate, depending on the varying gradations of awareness in the minds of different actors. First, there is the reader being addressed by the narrator, who here learns that he or she knows more in this instance than the novel's characters. Second, there is the more knowledgeable narrator, who refers to a narration that "has here been faintly shadowed," as if there is more to the story than the narration contains. And finally, there are the anonymous "townsfolk," who are as little knowledgeable as their real counterparts, "mortals generally," and as unlikely to even try to imagine with any accuracy. With a single sentence focused on describing what is *not* true of Middlemarchers, Eliot produces an image of Lydgate that has the stereoscopic depth of both intimacy and distant acquaintance. As in a stereoscope, separate two-dimensional images fuse together to create an image with more lifelike substance.

Eliot uses the technique of denying some knowledge to one set of characters while revealing it to the reader more than once when establishing Lydgate's character in the town. The effect is to set up a comparison between a privileged circle of wider thinkers that includes the narrator, Lydgate, the reader, and a background of "nobod[ies]" whose imaginations she gently ridicules. She writes of the town gossip in his favor, "Nobody's imagination had gone so far as to conjecture that Mr. Lydgate could know as much as Dr. Sprague and Dr. Minchin" (171). Although this is a grammatically simple sentence, especially compared to the contorted syntax of some of her negative constructions, a surprising number of different imaginative abilities are referred to within it. Most obviously, Eliot refers to the imaginative limits of the townspeople, who can only conceive of Lydgate's capacities as also having a limit. In doing so, she pokes a little ironic fun at those who judge from a narrow range of experience that they think is vast. By describing what is *not* being conjectured, Eliot enacts for the reader the experience of surpassing the curtailed imagining ascribed to Middlemarch gossips. Throughout the novel Eliot refers to other characters' finite images of Lydgate, which are set against the reader's own increasingly nuanced, multidimensional image of him. In Rosamond Vincy's imagination, Lydgate is like a paper cut-out figure: "In Rosamond's romance, it was not necessary to imagine much about the inward life of the hero" (195). Even here, Eliot uses the negation of what it was "not necessary" for Rosamond to picture, in this case for ironic understatement; the reader shares in this belittling humor with the narrator. Received, conventional, clichéd images narrow the mind in art as they do in morals, and Eliot not only makes such stunted imagining morally unappealing, but she repeatedly creates the experience for the reader of transcending it.

As I have been showing on a minute scale, the level of the sentence, Eliot repeatedly underscores the difference between a narrower, flatter, less realistic mental image and a multidimensional, imaginatively engaging one. She first asks the reader to imagine something conventional or generic and then pushes the reader to recast the familiar type: to question and add lifelike depth to the original mental image. She crafts a habitual experience for the reader of developing this realistic, imaginative depth as a narrative process or experience that unfolds over the course of a description. "Character too is a process and an unfolding," Eliot writes, a phrase that takes on different meaning in this context, as a technique Eliot uses that gradually develops a character's multidimensional inner life (178), for in *Middlemarch* there are consequences when one character does *not* imagine another's inward life—and consequently marries him or her. In discussing Rosamond Vincy's daydreams after meeting Lydgate, Eliot chides the reader for possibly forming too hasty an image. In this case, Rosamond's own undetected, imaginative "prematureness" transcends the reader's knowledge:

> Do you imagine that her rapid forecast and rumination concerning house-furniture and society were ever discernible in her conversation, even with her mamma? On the contrary, she would have expressed the prettiest surprise and disapprobation if she had heard that another young lady had been detected in that immodest prematureness. (301)

As with the initial image of Bulstrode, Eliot's question first implies that her readers might have pictured Rosamond's behavior as conforming to a distasteful but easily identifiable type. Then, calling out such a mistaken imagination with a curt "on the contrary," she suggests the more insidious reality that calculating persons can pass for uncalculating ones. Even as Rosamond may be imagining a plot for herself as conventionally romantic as any cited in "Silly Novels by Lady Novelists," Eliot suggests that she has one up on readers— who would, in this case, have a hard time pegging and dismissing her as such a frothy-minded heroine. In fact, Eliot has us imagine Rosamond showing herself superior to any other "young lady" who does not take such care to hide her frothy ambitions. Conventional as her "rumination concerning house-furniture" is, then, her mind appears—to the reader at least—as a calculating force to be reckoned with. Lydgate, with "spots of commonness" in his vision of women (179), demonstrates the tragic consequences of not having such layered vision: he is unable to imagine that the mind of a conventionally pretty woman might not match her outwardly docile appearance.

Eliot's commands not to imagine, like the above passage about Rosamond, tend to share the ironic, bemused tone of the novel's narrator, but the tonal gentleness of the irony at either the character's or reader's expense is a notable change from Eliot's early fiction. The caustic portrayal of lady readers in "In Which the Story Pauses a Little" does indeed appear to have served a developmental function for Eliot, for in the later novel, the opposition often sounds toned down. In place of the boxing match dynamic that Bodenheimer aptly describes between the narrator and an antagonistic reader in Eliot's early writing, in *Middlemarch* the boxing match appears staged within the reader's mind, as an opposition set up between stereotypical and realistic images. In the later novel irony takes the form of overpoliteness, as when the narrator addresses a reader whom she figures as (like Lydgate) underestimating Rosamond's surprisingly vivid power of imagining: "If you think it incredible that to imagine Lydgate as a man of family could cause thrills of satisfaction which had anything to do with the sense that she was in love with him, I will ask you to use your power of comparison a little more effectively, and consider whether red cloth and epaulets have never had an influence of that sort," she writes (196). It is Rosamond who bears the brunt of Eliot's satire in such moments, not an imagined "lady" reader. After "ask[ing]" the reader with exaggerated politeness to do better in picturing the depth of Rosamond's superficiality, Eliot makes ironic references to romantic conventions that the actual reader might recognize and disdain. The narrator moves to the inclusive, forgiving "our" as the passage goes on: "Our passions do not live apart in locked chambers, but, dressed in their small wardrobe of notions, bring their provisions to a common table and mess together, feeding out of the common store according to their appetite" (196). Moments in which Eliot instructs the reader in what and what not to imagine are frequently aimed at a wider "any one," are offered as maxims, or weigh the instance against a general rule. As she also writes about Rosamond, "Any one who imagines ten days too short a time—not for falling into leanness, lightness, or other measurable effects of passion, but—for the whole spiritual circuit of alarmed conjecture and disappointment, is ignorant of what can go on in the elegant leisure of a young lady's mind" (334). As here, Eliot repeatedly figures a reader who has a preconceived idea and does not think realistically about thinking—about "what can go on" in another person's mind, especially Rosamond's.

What Eliot's negations rely on, as well as further test, is the flexibility, multiplicity, and fluidity of readers' minds. Eliot is exercising the reader's ability to distinguish what is and is not realized in a novel, a cognitive ability regularly employed in novel reading, which Lisa Zunshine describes as "tracking sources." Zunshine argues that fiction relies on our ability to keep track of "who thought what, when."[21] I am suggesting that Eliot is especially exercising this faculty of the reader's mind, seeking to make it all the more limber, because of her concern that the overwhelming desire for certain plot outcomes makes readers' minds rigid and linear—because of, as she calls it, "the vulgar coercion of conventional plot."[22] In her brief essay "Story-telling," she complains that the reading public is resistant to formal experimentation: "Why should a story not be told in the most irregular fashion that an author's idiosyncrasy may prompt? . . . The dear public would do well to reflect that they are often bored from the want of flexibility in their own minds."[23] *Middlemarch* as a whole is "told" in a different fashion from Eliot's earlier fiction, as her first explicitly multiplot novel, a structural multiplicity that penetrates to the level of its syntax.

We have been seeing how Eliot's individual sentences refuse to be read for the plot and instead open up an "irregular" space of continually imagining several realities at once. This can be hard work for a reader. During *Middlemarch*'s original serial publication, her publisher, John Blackwood, commented, "The public mind has been wonderfully exercised by the book and exercised for good."[24] He also wrote of an incident in which his wife tried and failed to read Book 5 while traveling. "It is utterly impossible to read *Middlemarch* with your head and heart half out of the window," he reported her saying, adding his own belief that "[i]t requires the most undivided attention."[25] "Half" out of the window is a metaphor that repeats a key word from the novel: some way in which the novel contains opposing forces, as if any one statement is only half of the picture.[26] In reading Eliot's novels we never get to relax into the ontological closure and familiarity of, say, a Sherlock Holmes story. At the same time, the possibilities are not endless—we are specifically told what not to imagine in relation to what is realized in the fictional world, just as there are two halves in a whole. (That the possibilities are dealt out in a controlled way from the author's hand keeps the reader from Mr. Brooke's fate of having a mind that ranges over too many possibilities. As Eliot writes satirically about his contradictory beliefs, "It is a narrow mind which cannot look at a subject from various points of view"; 91.) Isobel Armstrong has discussed Eliot's dialectical thinking, which echoes Hegel's, in which confrontations of opposites create something new.[27] Eliot's negative constructions often follow a dialectical structure in which a conventional image is negated and, through the process of correcting the initial image, a multidimensional vision created in its place.

The "Fitful Simmer of Many-Hued Significance"

For Eliot a "multitudinous," abundant, or range of possible meanings is inherent in our very comprehension of language. Eliot's deep knowledge of psychology included an awareness that the foundational act of reading, forming mental images to go with the words on the page, depends on the individual and variable memories, associations, and visual images a reader brings to the text. Frustrated with readers who single-mindedly focused on imagining the endings they wanted, Eliot writes in her essays and letters about her belief that provoking multiple images in the mind of a person reading a novel enables the reader to get as close as possible to a lifelike mental picture, when the reader is imagining a world made up from the imperfect medium of words.

That the act of reading naturally calls to mind multiple possibilities is for Eliot inherent in our comprehension of individual words. While her fascination with the mind's functioning is well known, we have only begun to examine her fascination with the direct effect individual words have on the receiver's mind. Melissa Raines has illuminated Eliot's layered, historical understanding of words. "The Natural History of German Life" (1856) begins with an account of the different mental images that might arise from the word "railways" in the minds of two people who have had very different experiences: the "fixity" of images formed by a man who is "non-locomotive" and the imagistic "variety" characteristic of a man who has worked in every conceivable aspect of railway business and travel. Eliot writes, "It is probable that the range of images which would by turns present themselves to his mind at the mention of the *word* 'railways,' would include all the essential facts in the existence and relations of the *thing*."[28] In other words, the more images a word elicits, the subtler and more essential its meaning becomes. As she says similarly of Ladislaw's aesthetic enjoyment of Rome's miscellaneous quality, its multitudinous variety, it "made the mind flexible with constant comparison, and saved you from seeing the world's ages as a set of box-like partitions without vital connection. . . . The fragments stimulated his imagination and made him

constructive" (245). It is not only the accumulation of images but the genera-
tive relations between them (Rome's fragments "made the mind flexible with
constant comparison") that give mental pictures a sense of vitality and of capturing "the essential facts in the existence and relations of the *thing*."

The aesthetic potential of individual words comes up repeatedly in Eliot's nonfiction writing. She acknowledges in several contexts that the vari-
ability of images in each individual's mind is the reason for both the indefi-
niteness and the potential resonance of a writer's words. In "The Natural
History of German Life," she describes the wavering subtlety of language
as a medium of communication, "an instrument which scarcely anything
short of genius can wield with definiteness and certainty." As she goes on
to defend the transcendent quality that individuality gives to language, her
slight tone of irony gives way to lyrical sincerity, as often happens with
Eliot:

> Suppose, then, that the effect which has been again and again made to con-
> struct a universal language on a rational basis has at length succeeded, and
> that you have a language which has no uncertainty, no whims of idiom, no
> cumbrous forms, no fitful simmer of many-hued significance . . . a patent
> deodorized and non-resonant language, which effects the purpose of com-
> munication as perfectly and rapidly as algebraic signs. . . . With the anoma-
> lies and inconveniences of historical language you will have parted with its
> music and its passions, and its vital qualities as an expression of individual
> character, with its subtle capabilities of wit, with everything that gives it
> power over the imagination.[29]

Notice that Eliot uses negation here in describing what a universal language
would *lack*. In explicating the qualities of language, she uses the familiar structure of rejection: a hypothetical image she finds fault with is followed by an
explication of what makes real language positively unique. Within this structure she defends the multifariousness of language, elegantly describing the
"fitful simmer of many-hued significance" created by uncertainties and multiple possible meanings. Even before she began writing fiction, then, Eliot was
articulating the belief that the aesthetic potential of language—its "music," its
"power over the imagination"—rests in single words evoking multiple, fluctuating images rather than a single, static one.

For Eliot verbal art uniquely draws out the reader's own deep store of images, as opposed to creating one "superfici[al]" image. Within *Middlemarch*,
Eliot features a conversation between Will Ladislaw and the painter Naumann

in which Will describes language's unique power over the imagination in such terms. He says of words, against pictures: "Language gives a fuller image, which is all the better for being vague. After all, the true seeing is within; and painting stares at you with an insistent imperfection" (222). In Will's commentary, language elicits a "fuller" picture than a single, static image like a painting, because it calls up multiple associations from "within," enlisting the reader's own images in a way that forms a "fuller image" of what is being described. Even words, though, can be paltry, thin things depending on the listener's experience; in an early letter Eliot expressed a belief that no writer's words can ever fully communicate to another person our innermost, "sacred" experience.[30] "Words are very clumsy things—I like less and less to handle my friends' sacred feelings with them," she wrote. "For even those who call themselves 'intimate' know very little about each other—hardly ever know just *how* a 'sorrow' is felt."[31] This melancholy sense that individual words cannot be counted on to transmit the writer's meaning is the inextricable other side of Eliot's relishing the potential that language has to evoke an unknown multitude of meanings in the receiver's mind.

Eliot characteristically uses the term "full" to describe the depth and richness of a mental picture, particularly one captured in and conveyed by a work of art. Explaining to a correspondent why she included so much historical detail in *Romola*, she writes, "It is the habit of my imagination to strive after as full a vision of the medium in which a character moves as of the character itself."[32] Fullness is a quality a writer has to "strive after" and is noteworthy when achieved. Indeed, Plato suggests that paucity is a defining feature of imagination; Scarry suggests that writers use specific strategies that mimic actual perception in order to overcome the inherent feebleness of imagined visions. Another thing working against imaginative richness is plot. In a brief essay on "historic imagination," Eliot describes with sarcasm how striving to reconstruct enough historical context to make past events meaningful requires

> freedom from the vulgar coercion of conventional plot, which is become hardly of higher influence on imaginative representation than a detailed "order" for a picture sent by a rich grocer to an eminent painter—allotting a certain portion of the canvas to a rural scene, another to a fashionable group, with a request for a murder in the middle distance, and a little comedy to relieve it.[33]

For Eliot, the aesthetic quality of fullness flourishes when there are no generic types or conventions to fulfill. In the glowing review of Elizabeth Barrett

Browning's prose poem *Aurora Leigh* (1857), which Eliot wrote for the *Westminster Review,* she praises it as a long narrative in which plot is of secondary importance to "fullness of thought and feeling": "The story of 'Aurora Leigh' has no other merit than that of offering . . . certain situations which are peculiarly fitted to call forth the writer's rich thought and experience," she writes.[34] It features "a full mind pouring itself out in . . . its natural and easiest medium."[35] Realism gets defined in Eliot's work as an aesthetic of full, rich, thick description that comes from a "full mind"[36]—a "multitudinous assemblage," as she describes comically in the essay "Looking Inward" from *Theophrastus Such* (1879): "My illusion is of a more liberal kind, and I imagine a far-off, hazy, multitudinous assemblage, as in a picture of Paradise, making an approving chorus to the sentences and paragraphs of which I myself particularly enjoy the writing."[37] Of course, once again Eliot comically portrays how the mind can become too "liberal" in Mr. Brooke, with his bric-a-brac conversation and "assemblage" of contradictory, coexisting beliefs. Eliot is always conscious of how exactly ideals might fail to be achieved.

In her letters Eliot continually distinguishes between readers who do and do not see "the fuller image" she envisioned in writing her novels. This may help to explain her claims to wanting a small audience. One difference for her lies in whether a reader is focused on the whole work, rather than parts, as she writes, expressing reservations about allowing her fan Alexander Main to edit a book of extracts from her novels: "Unless my readers are more moved towards the ends I seek by works as wholes than by an assemblage of extracts, my writings are a mistake."[38] By 1871, when she was writing *Middlemarch,* Eliot had plenty of experience with reviewers who indeed saw her work narrowly and in fragments, and not with that depth of perception that comes from a more stereoscopic vision. She perceived critics as reading selectively, expressing preferences of their own, and focusing on the wrong thing.[39] The highest compliment she gives to reviewers and readers is that they have looked to the whole work to understand her "aim and delight in writing": "Correspondents whose culture . . . enables them to judge of a work as a whole and not merely, as Goethe's Theaterdirektor says, pick out morsels to suit their own palate, are necessarily rare."[40]

Eliot's suggestion that a fuller, more absorbing image comes from having multiple and even contrasting associations called up simultaneously contradicts how absorption is often thought of: as a single-minded focus, blocking out other perceptions, a state of being singly immersed (absorption is "the state of being engrossed in *something*"; *OED*). Yet Eliot's alternate understanding chimes with scholarship by Nicholas Dames, John Plotz, and others that has recast how Victorians understood paying attention, especially paying attention to a novel, as an oscillating or partially immersed experience. Eliot sees the aesthetic enrichment to be gained—the "fuller image"—through the mind's expansive, back-and-forth movement between what is in the words and what is in the reader's mind. "There must be a systole and diastole in all inquiry," Lydgate says. "A man's mind must be continually expanding and shrinking between the whole human horizon and the horizon of an object-glass" (690). Eliot uses another optical image, of "mirroring," to refer to the image of the fictional world that forms in a reader's mind. "With a single drop of ink for a mirror, the Egyptian sorcerer undertakes to reveal to any chance comer far-reaching visions of the past," *Adam Bede* begins (49). The mirror of fiction may be made of ink, of words, but instead of a two-dimensional mirror, it is a pier glass comprised of many different perspectives. Though language can never fully communicate to another person our innermost experience, a variety of connected images is how Eliot envisions coming as close as possible to reproducing her own fictional vision in the reader's mind.

Negative Characters

The previous two sections discuss novel reading as Eliot would like it to happen. In reality, Eliot knew her readers were not only reading *Middlemarch* in parts (albeit longer parts, designed to contain more of the whole than a typical serial installment) but focusing as they read on their favorite parts. They were, as she thought was all too common in reviewers, "pick[ing] out morsels to suit their own palate[s]." As we saw in chapter 3, in her letters Eliot uses the word "receptivity" to talk about a reader's willingness or capacity for grasping the author's wide vision, in contrast to the teleological, wishful story "construction" that impedes it. "Nothing mars the receptivity more than eager construction—as I know to my own cost," she wrote to Main, whose speculation about Dorothea's future, Eliot thought, impaired his ability to take in her whole fictional vision.[41] *Middlemarch*'s characters have many such moments of narrowed imagining. Instead of being instructed by a narrator to imagine first one and then a second alternative, as readers are, her characters focus on a wished-for image and fail to imagine other undesired alternatives.[42] Lydgate comes to call Rosamond's capacity to block or reject undesired possibilities her "negative character—her want of sensibility, which showed itself in disregard both of his specific wishes and of his general aims" (702). The remainder of the chapter examines how Eliot uses structures of negation not only ideally to expand her readers' imagining, as we have seen, but also to ponder the problem of imaginative selectivity, at once ironizing and sympathizing with her characters' many denials and limitations. "She likes giving up" (41), Celia says about Dorothea's horseback riding, which, we are told, "she always looked forward to renouncing" (32). Eliot uses these moments of negative characterization to meditate on the humanness, as well as consequences for achieving aesthetic fullness, of the tendency Victorian readers and her characters share, whether consciously or not, to imagine only what they desire.

Eliot's characters tend to be guilty of a different imaginative error than the overhasty, fictionalized reader she addresses. Her characters' imaginations are limited by desire, not an overfamiliarity with narrative conventions. There is an obvious moral valence to the satiric negations that describe her characters stopping short from envisioning what is not personally desirable. As Caroline Levine has written about the selfishness of imagination for Eliot, her characters "are constantly imposing their own imaginative impulses onto the world."[43] As Mrs. Garth puts it in a "salutary general doctrine," which she pointedly tells Fred Vincy: "Yes, young people are usually blind to everything but their own wishes, and seldom imagine how much those wishes cost others" (619). As in this reference to what is "seldom imagine[d]," Eliot repeatedly uses negation to refer to her characters' inabilities to picture undesirable possibilities, as in Fred Vincy's "unsuccessful efforts to imagine what he was to do" to earn a living (601); Mrs. Vincy's "trying unsuccessfully to fancy herself caring about Mary's appearance in wedding clothes" (691); or how Lydgate "could not imagine himself pursuing [science and medicine] in such a home as Wrench had" (389). Phrasing her characters' visionary deficiencies as negations has the traditional effect of litotes, of ironic understatement about what is obvious to everyone except the person wishing otherwise: Rosamond "had been little used to imagining other people's states of mind except as a material cut into shape by her own wishes" (834); Dorothea "had thought that she could have been patient with John Milton, but she had never imagined him behaving in this way" (316). The gently belittling irony here is directed at the characters' assumptions that unimagined possibilities conveniently do not exist.

There is less humor when Eliot describes characters failing to imagine what is in the mind of another person—as almost every major character does at some point—especially when their actions "wound" another. When Will delivers his cutting remarks to Dorothea in Rome about Casaubon not knowing German scholarship, he "only thought of giving a good pinch that would annihilate that vaunted laboriousness, and was unable to imagine the mode in which Dorothea would be wounded" (240). "Why had he not imagined this beforehand?" Will asks himself when he sees that "Dorothea was perhaps pained" by his appearing at Lowick church one Sunday (513). Eliot often uses the word "beforehand" (forty-seven times in the novel), particularly to refer to characters who do not anticipate the negative effects of their actions on other people. About Fred's borrowing money from Caleb Garth, Eliot writes that his "pain in the affair beforehand had consisted almost entirely in the sense that he must seem dishonorable" and "he had not occupied himself with the inconvenience and possible injury that his breach might occasion them, for this exercise of the imagination on other people's needs is not common with hopeful young gentlemen" (281). This mildly sarcastic comment on Fred's moral selfishness contains a working definition of sympathy, the utmost moral good for Eliot, as the "exercise of the imagination on other people's needs." "Exercise" is different than incapacity, and the above instances refer to Fred and Will recognizing their blindnesses, and even somewhat taking themselves to task for them, afterward. What sets Rosamond chillingly apart is that her nature is "inflexible in proportion to its negations," such that Lydgate has to "make up his mind to [Rosamond's] negations" and "the need of accommodating himself to her nature . . . held him as with pincers" (718). Eliot's caustic tone toward Rosamond matches the intensity of Rosamond's effort (she "held him as with pincers") to not imagine what eventually *makes* itself seen in Eliot's novel-worlds, however inconveniently: the needs of other people.

The plot around Featherstone's fortune particularly dramatizes how multiple people with conflicting, selfish desires can each imagine the same set of events to suit themselves, and implicates the novel's reader in such willful acts of imagining. Referring to each of the siblings' covetous perceptions of Featherstone's postmortem plans, she writes, "Probabilities are as various as the faces to be seen at will in fretwork or paper-hangings: every form is there, from Jupiter to Judy, if you only look with creative inclination" (337). Eliot refers to the "probabilities" a viewer might make out specifically in a work of artistry: fretwork or paper hangings. While the scene of Featherstone's two wills being read aloud is about a legal rather than artistic document, it is hard not to think of a novel and its audience: a crowd of people listening raptly with different, desirous wishes for how a written document will determine a particular individual's fate. Perhaps Eliot fantasized about denying readers their wished-for outcomes; if so, she realizes that fantasy virtually in this scene in the form of a mean, posthumous trick played by a reprehensible human being. In fact, the fictionalized reader whom she likes to satirize, the type who in *Adam Bede* prefers "unobjectionable people," makes a rare appearance within *Middle-march* in the scene. When introducing Joshua Rigg, she addresses a fictional reader who dislikes reading about "low people." She gives this reader satiric instructions to recast the characters:

> [W]hatever has been or is to be narrated by me about low people, may be ennobled by being considered a parable; so that if any bad habits and ugly consequences are brought into view, the reader may have the relief of regarding them as not more than figuratively ungenteel, and may feel himself virtually in company with persons of some style. Thus while I tell the truth about loobies, my reader's imagination need not be entirely excluded from an occupation with lords; and the petty sums which any bankrupt of high standing would be sorry to retire upon, may be lifted to the level of high commercial transactions by the inexpensive addition of proportional ciphers. (375)

Turning "loobies" into "lords": Eliot gives explicit, satiric directions here in how to imagine otherwise. This moment in *Middlemarch* even sounds, tonally, like it belongs in *Adam Bede*, in its animus toward a reader who substitutes "persons of some style" for the mixed, tangled "truth" she portrays about the everyday realistic world. That the passage is facetious does not make it less pointed: satire uses humor "to expose and criticize prevailing immorality or foolishness" (*OED*). The actual knowing reader may recognize his or her difference from this foolish-figured reader, but the ending suggests a wider audience may be guilty of such practices, in a more minor degree, in Eliot's calling attention to how easily practiced and "inexpensive" (to the reader) the imaginative habit of "addition" is. As we have seen, the author pays the price: as Eliot wrote to Main, "Nothing mars the receptivity more than eager construction—as I know to my own *cost.*"[44] Eliot's habitual humor about imagining that is partial, selective, or misshapen based on the perceiver's desires can sound like it covers over—as humor often does—a persistent hurt or worry, such as the peril she expressed in a letter of trying to convey in language "just *how* a 'sorrow' is felt."

Eliot's tone is at once ironic and compassionate in writing about the failure of Featherstone's own single-minded wish to annoy his would-be legatees. She at once points out how the joke is on him and uses her characteristic tone of condescending patience with human error about what "we . . . all of us" in "fellowship" do. She comments:

> We are all of us imaginative in some form or other, for images are the brood of desire; and poor old Featherstone, who laughed much at the way in

which others cajoled themselves, did not escape the fellowship of illusion. In writing the programme for his burial he certainly did not make clear to himself that his pleasure in the little drama of which it formed a part was confined to anticipation. (358)

Imagination here displays the same chief qualities as elsewhere for Eliot: it naturally tends toward "illusion" or wish fulfillment; in its fullest form, it is comprised of "images"; and it often takes the form of "anticipation." Like Eliot's readers, Featherstone also "forecasts" what he wants to happen in the form of a plot or "little drama" instead of imagining multiple perspectives on the scene "beforehand." Forming a desired image is natural; where Featherstone fails is that desire prevents him from imagining an alternative, less pleasing picture as well. At the same time, the tone of condescending pity for us "poor" people who have our "little drama[s]" hints at Eliot's serious awareness of how little in control of error-prone imagination we actually are, as her contemporaries like E. S. Dallas were theorizing.

The willful imaginative failures of Eliot's characters are on a continuum with those blind spots she sees as barely conscious and even necessary to "ordinary human life." With Eliot's knowledge of how the unconscious mind was being theorized at the time, she seems to recognize that denial and repression are not always in the individual's control. Eliot coyly does not answer the question of how culpable characters are in limiting their own cognition. She refers to Dorothea's agency in insisting to herself that Sir James's chivalrous attention is that of a future brother-in-law rather than a suitor: "It is difficult to say whether there was or was not a little willfulness in her continuing blind to the possibility that another sort of choice was in question" (56). The passage immediately moves on to Dorothea's other conscious thoughts, leaving the phrase "whether there was or was not a little willfulness" open to interpretation about how much of Dorothea's repressing an unpleasant truth is conscious. Her tone is more distinctly ironic when she exposes how commonly we, as humans, acquiesce in being blind to other possibilities. In the novel she repeatedly uses the subjunctive tense ("if" clauses) to refer to a state that transcends ordinary imaginative or perceptual limits and compares this thought experiment to our perceptually limited reality. Referring to how Will Ladislaw "stopped his ears" against the "dirty business" involved in electioneering, Eliot writes, "Occasionally Parliament, like the rest of our lives, even to our eating and apparel, could hardly go on if our imaginations were too active about processes" (544). The most often-quoted sentences from the novel make this point lyrically, elaborating with a vivid hypothetical image:

> If we had a keen vision and feeling of all ordinary human life, it would be like hearing the grass grow and the squirrel's heart beat, and we should die of that roar which lies on the other side of silence. As it is, the quickest of us walk about well wadded with stupidity. (226) [45]

These sentences create an aural image that she goes on to say is *not* heard: "hearing the grass grow and the squirrel's heart beat." But as with other negations, for a moment—nine words—the reader has a tiny experience of imagining that other possibility beyond ordinary perception. As we know, negations prompt expansive thinking: they create an awareness, an image, and perhaps a longing for, something else, while simultaneously curtailing it. Negations like this take mental effort to imagine: What does growing grass sound like? The hypothetical description in the first sentence that stretches the reader's imagination is lyrical and moving; the second sentence is brutish and short, suggestive of Eliot's disappointment with those whose imaginations are difficult to stretch. It is the tone that she uses at times about real readers in her letters. In the rest of *Middlemarch*, she vents her criticism in gentler irony about "well-wadded" Mr. Brooke, who repeatedly tells others—using negative speech— what happened when he ventured beyond his comfort zone early in life: "I saw it would not do; I pulled up" (39, and many more). These two comic sentences, however, could emblematize Eliot's relationship with her readers throughout her career. Eliot optimistically tries to stretch her readers' imaginations beyond conventional bounds—and acquiesces, somewhat forgivingly and somewhat angrily, when they "pull up."

With Eliot suggesting that perception can all too easily be guided by wishes and comfort, it is not surprising that critics have found one imaginative block in the novel to be unnatural: Will and Dorothea's total lack of any thoughts that could be construed as adulterous or scheming. Though this lack of imagination is necessary on moral grounds, Barbara Hardy finds it unconvincing. She refers to the "marked and sometimes irritatingly innocent absence of . . . speculative fantasy which might well mark such a relationship."[46] Eliot herself acknowledges the "strange" absence in a passage describing Will as he hangs around Middlemarch after he has announced his departure. She begins defensively, with an admission that "it may seem strange" to the reader that he does not fantasize about what might naturally occupy anyone else—the realization of his wishes in a conventional romantic plot:

It may seem strange, but it is the fact, that the ordinary vulgar vision of which Mr Casaubon suspected him—namely, that Dorothea might become a widow, and that the interest he had established in her mind might turn into acceptance of him as a husband—had no tempting, arresting power over him; he did not live in the scenery of such an event, and follow it out, as we all do with that imagined "otherwise" which is our practical heaven. (509–10)

For once, Eliot does not ironize selective imagining but rather praises Will for his lack of interest in such an "ordinary vulgar vision." ("Vulgar" is how Eliot repeatedly describes clichéd plots, as in "the vulgar coercion of conventional plot" she indicts in "Leaves from a Note-Book.")[47] The larger passage of which this forms a part uses negations repeatedly to establish Will's exceptionalism, basing his value on what he rejects: "Will was not one of those whose wit 'keeps the roadway'" (509); "Will, we know, could not bear the thought of any flaw in his crystal" (510); "it was not only that he was unwilling to entertain thoughts which could be accused of baseness" (510). This specific claim about his rejection of fantasy may be phrased defensively because marrying the mon-eyed widow is the very plot in which he will eventually figure and Eliot knows that, by chapter 47, this plot has likely occurred to any attentive reader. It has certainly occurred to Casaubon, who is making his will at this point in the novel, as it did to Main, who wrote to Eliot after reading only as far as book 2: "My dear Mrs. Lewes, you really must get that Casaubon quietly, decently, and gravely of course, *out of the way*, into another world . . . and leaving Dodo into *the closest possible relation* with that mysterious youngster."[48] Though Eliot has to establish Will's mental innocence in order for their feelings not to be seen as adulterous, it appears equally important to separate his feelings for Dorothea from those of readers like Main and elevate them above this typical, "vulgar" readerly form. Critics may find this elevation unconvincing, though, because the rhetorical energy of the passage is in fact devoted to elaborating how ut-terly compelling the rest of us find wishful imagining to be. Eliot describes how we "*live* in [its] scenery," driven by the "tempting, arresting power" of some-thing "we all do," all the time. For Eliot this engrossing power is needed to fill out the "scenery" of her imagined vision in the reader's mind. The crux for Eliot is that this valuable capacity to imagine has to be wrested away—and was not easy to wrest away—from its natural inclination toward wish fulfillment. Ever optimistic, late in her career, Eliot puts the reader's imagination through rhetorical puzzles that subtly, grammatically wrest us away from single-mindedly wishing our way through the fictional world.

No Great Name

Middlemarch's use of negation as part of Eliot's project to elevate the reader's imagination above the conventional, ready-made, and vulgar, culminates in the finale, which sums up Dorothea's life by describing what does not happen in it. With its many negative statements describing closed-off opportunities, it is little wonder feminist critics have objected to the hemmed-in afterlife Eliot gives Dorothea, as she does other heroines. But the overwhelming number of negations, which relentlessly call to mind what Dorothea's life is not like, also affirm the novel's positive investment in a life that can only be understood by rejecting ready-made and easily named images. In closing, then, I return to the amplifying effect that repeated negations have and Eliot's belief that there are "sacred feelings" that language cannot fully convey. Through the finale's many negations, Eliot paradoxically creates a positive sense of possibilities unfolding beyond the defined, largely conventional world the novel portrays—the incalculable diffusiveness that readers have long cited as a unique effect of reading her novels.

It is worth quoting the finale's negative sentences at length, in the order they appear (all my emphases), for their collective effect:

> Dorothea herself had *no dreams* of being praised above other women, feeling that *there was always something better which she might have done,* if only she had been better and known better. (893)

> She *never repented* that she had given up position and fortune to marry Will Ladislaw, and he *would have held it the greatest shame as well as sorrow* to him if she had repented. (893–94)

> *No life would have been possible* to Dorothea which *was not filled* with emotion, and she had now a life filled also with a beneficent activity which *she had not* the doubtful pains of discovering and marking out for herself. (894)

> Dorothea *could have liked nothing better,* since wrongs existed, than that her husband should be in the thick of a struggle against them. (894)

> *No one stated* exactly what else that was in her power she ought rather to have done—*not even* Sir James Chettam, who went *no further* than the *negative prescription* that *she ought not* to have married Will Ladislaw. (894)

> Sir James *never ceased* to regard Dorothea's second marriage as a mistake. (896)

Those who *had not* seen anything of Dorothea usually observed that *she could not have been* "a nice woman," else she *would not have married* either the one or the other. (896)

Certainly those determining acts of her life were *not* ideally beautiful. (896)

For there is *no creature* whose inward being is so strong that it is *not greatly determined* by what lies outside it. (896)

Her finely-touched spirit had still its fine issues, though they were *not* widely visible. (896)

Her full nature, like that river of which Cyrus broke the strength, spent itself in channels which had *no great name* on the earth. (896)

That things are not so ill with you and me as *they might have been* is half owing to those who lived a hidden life and rest in *unvisited* tombs. (896)

This barrage of negatives (there are a few more) creates a subtly double sense of Dorothea's life. On the one hand, her life appears delimited and hemmed in, as feminist critics in particular have long noted. The repeated structure of "no ____" makes the phrases increasingly emphatic as one reads: "no dreams," "no life," "no further," "no great name." On the other hand, the lyricism of this repeated rhetoric, describing Dorothea's life by labeling what it lacks, over and over, builds a sense that there is some nobility to a life that exists outside of conventional, recognizable terms. Her life is outwardly unremarkable and yet defies positive description. These sentences create a subtle, atmospheric sense of a life that is "incalculably diffusive" ("incalculably" itself is a negation; 896), that takes place in an imaginative space that is not materially recognized by the narrow-minded people who surround Dorothea. Earlier, comically, Celia's imagination is not up to the unconventional task of imagining another life for Dorothea after she has been widowed. In response to Sir James expressing it "a pity she was not a queen," Celia responds: "'But what should we have been then? We must have been something else,' said Celia, objecting to so laborious a flight of imagination" (580). The sense that something undefinable has been created, that Eliot seems to be saying something more than the sum of the words, has been commented on as one of the remarkable effects of reading *Middlemarch*. It's the effect I began with: *feeling* like I understand a whole paragraph, even though Eliot makes me, like Trollope, read its sentences three times before I actually understand its meaning.

5

Daniel Deronda and Us

BEING REPULSED by another human being is not a response usually associated with George Eliot's fiction.[1] More familiar is Eliot's eminently quotable, affirmative language about art's ability to expand a reader's fellow-feeling for other, real people. *Daniel Deronda* (1876) has long been seen as the novel in which Eliot questions, "severely qualifies," or finds a limit to such sympathy's efficacy.[2] However, critical discussion has largely stopped with her depiction of the overreadiness and overapplication of what Eliot calls Deronda's "too reflective and diffuse sympathy" (364). What affective experience does the novel cultivate through reading if *not* the development of sympathy? The novel is full of situations that feature the opposite response toward another person: situations in which characters intensely reject one another. Most of the novel's characters experience "repulsion," "repugnance," or "revulsion" at one point: Gwendolen is repulsed by Lush, Grandcourt, Lydia Glasher, and Rex Gascoigne; Mirah is repulsed by Gwendolen and Lapidoth; Grandcourt is disgusted by most people; poor Rex repulses himself; and Deronda (oversympathetic Deronda!) feels repulsed by Gwendolen, the Cohens, Joseph Kalonymos, his mother, and Lapidoth. The novel's characters feel so much disgust for one another that at one point the narrator jokes about Gwendolen having to assert herself to claim her portion of it: "Gwendolen would not have liked to be an object of disgust to this husband whom she hated: she liked all disgust to be on her side" (602).[3]

This pattern of feeling repulsion toward another character within *Daniel Deronda* mirrors how Eliot expected many readers to feel toward the novel's Jewish characters and plot.[4] Throughout her career Eliot struggled with the additional imagining her novels stimulated in readers. She faced a different obstacle in anticipating that *Daniel Deronda*'s audience would be resistant to imagining one of her novel's fundamental aspects at all. She wrote to Harriet

Beecher Stowe of her expectation "from first to last in writing it, that it would create much stronger resistance and even repulsion than it has actually met with" toward the novel's Jewish elements. She sought, she wrote to Beecher Stowe, to "rouse the imagination of men and women to a vision of human claims in those races of their fellow-men who most differ from them in custom and beliefs."[5] Eliot's familiar goal of seeing all beings as having "human claims" is lyrically phrased. But Eliot knew that to use one's imagination at all "is to extend self, or to grasp the world outside self, or to face what is uncongenial and undesirable," as Barbara Hardy puts it, and that such extensions "of the spirit are hard for all striving human beings."[6] Eliot's use of an effortful, disruptive verb, to "*rouse* the imagination," suggests the friction she anticipated, so that the loftily phrased rest of her aim, "to a vision of human claims," sounds more aspirational than achievable. More concrete are the frank terms she goes on to use, in the same letter, to blame "the intellectual narrowness—in plain English, the stupidity" of the average English person who is uninterested in "any form of life that is not clad in the same coat-tails and flounces as our own."[7] Much of value has been said about the internally conflicted nature of Eliot's cosmopolitan ideals in writing the novel. Less has been said about her bluntly worded expectation that some readers would simply not entertain those ideals.[8] A stubborn unwillingness to recognize the equal claims of those who seem different from oneself is a powerful and persistent phenomenon, as we unfortunately still know.

Within the novel, Eliot repeatedly depicts situations that could inspire identification and sympathy but result, instead, in the revulsion she thought readers would feel toward the novel. Such dramatizations inscribe into her fiction the authorial anxiety Eliot expressed to Beecher Stowe about whether she could rouse "narrow" minds to willing sympathy. And so, also within the novel, Eliot brings her most iconic rhetorical gesture, her use of the first-person plural pronouns "we" and "us," to bear on reshaping Victorian readers' willingness to imagine Jewish characters. Eliot is known for using "we" in moments of direct address in order to underscore the universality of the experiences she is depicting. Yet our understanding of how she uses first-person plural pronouns has remained surprisingly one-dimensional despite their ubiquity and intrusiveness in her fiction. "We" has been seen as a condescending intruder into the diegesis of her novels, representing the Eliot who is inclusive but bossy, who compels "us mortals" to sympathize.

In *Daniel Deronda*, Eliot's career-long use of "we" to cultivate sympathy on the basis of communal experience appears fluid and multidimensional, as the pronoun helps to carry out Eliot's larger project of unsettling and making more inclusive the cultural boundaries of sympathy in potentially anti-Semitic Victorian readers. Alicia Mireles Christoff comments on how mid-nineteenth-century novels construct "the powerful and exclusionary 'we'" as comprised of "white, British, middle-class" readers, in reflecting on her own use of "we" to refer to a more inclusive imaginary readership.[9] Yet in Eliot's last novel, Eliot herself was seeking to expand who constitutes "we," who belongs to the human imaginary, in the minds of predominantly Christian, English readers. Accustomed as Eliot was to coaxing her readers' imaginations toward unwelcome acts, in her last novel she strives to develop readers' self-consciousness of their own exclusionary, hateful feelings. Ultimately, *Daniel Deronda*, in seeking to lead readers into a "self-abhorrence that stings us into better striving" (699), illuminates how some novelists beginning in the 1860s and 1870s were finding productive reasons to immerse readers in characters and states of feeling that do not naturally elicit sympathy but are uncomfortable and even repulsive to imagine.

"No Class of Sympathizers" with *Daniel Deronda*

Sympathy has so dominated criticism of Eliot's novels—and Victorian novels broadly—that we have yet to explore a larger economy of affects operating in her last novel.[10] Eliot and the theorizing of disgust in Victorian culture have seemed to have little to do with each other.[11] Yet *Daniel Deronda* examines in depth a repulsion so accepted and widespread that, she suggests, it is accepted unthinkingly. Eliot's formulations of affective states overall owe a great deal to Spinoza's *Ethics*, which she spent two years translating, "fascinated . . . [by] the intricacy of Spinoza's emotional and social logic," as Isobel Armstrong writes.[12] Eliot echoes Spinoza's understanding that affective states develop from images formed in the mind as she describes a mental image of Gwendolen stirring as much negative feeling in Mirah as Gwendolen's physical presence could: "Gwendolen, who was increasingly repugnant to her—increasingly, even after she had ceased to see her; for liking and disliking can grow in meditation as fast as in the more immediate kind of presence" (653). Eliot expresses her hope that the fictional images in her novels will similarly stir lifelike feelings in readers in an often-quoted letter to Charles Bray: "The only effect I ardently long to produce by my writings, is that those who read them should be better able *to imagine and to feel* the pains and joys of those who differ from themselves in everything but the broad fact of being struggling erring human creatures."[13]

Linking feeling and imagining as she does, Eliot would have anticipated that *Daniel Deronda*'s images of fictional Jews would "rouse the imagination" of some readers to intensely negative feelings—as intense as real encounters.[14]

In her one novel that portrays contemporary high society, Eliot depicts a social world that broadly condoned anti-Semitism. In Victorian high society, as Armstrong describes, "anti-Jewish contempt is a reflex."[15] Her direct addresses in the novel at times imply, at the very least, the reader's familiarity with hateful, stereotypical images and a widespread acceptance of them. At the time Deronda meets Mirah, he exemplifies the way that even the most sympathetic-minded Victorians might exclude Jews from their "interest" and instead feel "repugnan[ce]": "Spite of his strong tendency to side with the objects of prejudice, and in general with those who got the worst of it, his interest had never been practically drawn toward existing Jews, and the facts he knew about them, whether they walked conspicuous in fine apparel or lurked in by-streets, were chiefly of a sort most repugnant to him" (206). Eliot alludes to the pervasiveness of anti-Semitic "ugly stories" after Daniel rescues Mirah: "Deronda could not escape (who can?) knowing ugly stories of Jewish characteristics and occupations" (206). The phrase "(who can?)" assumes, or creates, a readership living amid ubiquitous anti-Semitism, a common recognition of "ugly stories" as a moment of bonding between narrator and reader. Outside of the novel Eliot also projected that negative attitudes would unite her reading public, in anticipating that the novel's Jewish plot "seems to me likely to satisfy *nobody*."[16] References to a united attitude in the collective body of readers pervade Victorian reviews of the novel, which repeatedly describe how "there can be no class of sympathizers" with the hero, whose Zionist aspirations "can scarcely interest the warm sympathy of the general reader."[17]

Eliot's exploration of the limits of sympathy within the novel is, in fact, mirrored in the language Victorian reviewers apply to the novel in excluding Jewish subjects from "the general reader[s']" sympathies or tastes. Many reviewers saw the book as too partial, not recognizing that this is the model of sympathy and interest that the novel, or at least its hero, deliberately chooses. "The sympathies to which it appeals are not, as in the case of *Adam Bede*, the sympathies of all the world," one reviewer claims, establishing that "all the world" is opposed to the world of Jews.[18] Another reviewer, who makes a point of saying he is not anti-Semitic, also objects that the book's narrow focus on a particular creed excludes too many readers, asking "whether the phase of Judaism now exhibited, the mystical enthusiasm for race and nation, has sufficient connection with broad human feeling to be stuff for prose fiction." He continues, dwelling (as other reviewers do as well) on how Mordecai's character "excludes fellow feeling":

> Now the "Samothracian mysteries of bottled moonshine" (to borrow a phrase from *Alton Locke*) into which Mordecai initiates Deronda are not thus connected with anything broadly human. They are not only "will-worship," but they have a provincial character which excludes fellow feeling. . . . They are not the stuff of which the main interest or even a prominent interest, or anything but a very carefully reduced side interest, or prose novels should be wrought.[19]

Cultivating "broad human feeling," what is "broadly human," and "fellow feeling" are usually terms that describe Eliot's idealized aim for her art. But in reviews of *Daniel Deronda*, these terms are used to accuse Eliot of betraying her own ideals. How could she, the repeated, confident assertions of the passage intimate, conceive of treating Judaism as more than "a very carefully reduced side interest"? The literary culture of the time was shaped by the vast commercial success of novels, a success that depended on fiction being "broad" in its appeal in order to draw in many readers. But both Daniel Deronda the character and *Daniel Deronda* the novel ultimately reject an all-encompassing, universal sympathy as "*too* diffusive" (my emphasis).[20] Just as Eliot sought to find ways around publishing in the commercially successful format of serialization, she claimed that she sought a more select audience for her later work. As *Romola* (1863) began serial publication, Eliot described that novel as purposely "addressed to fewer readers than my previous works." She writes, with some frustration, "If one is to have freedom to write out one's own varying unfolding self, and not be a machine always grinding out the same material or spinning the same sort of web, one cannot always write for the same public."[21] Strikingly, Eliot degrades the kind of monotonous, predictable writing she rejects as the "same sort of *web*," the image she is best known for using positively to convey the interconnectedness of "all the world." But here those interconnected beings are "the same public" who oppress Eliot with a demand for the easily imaginable and inoffensive—the conventional—as opposed to the authenticity and originality of "writ[ing] out one's own varying unfolding self."

I have been showing how reviewers tacitly and sometimes explicitly, even insistently, define the reading public as uninterested in or unmoved by Jewish subjects. The vehement language some Victorian reviewers use suggests the novel actually incited unwelcome emotions. In her journal Eliot commented on being "made aware of much repugnance or else indifference towards the Jewish part of Deronda, and of some hostile as well as adverse reviewing."[22] "Repugnance," "hostile," and "adverse" reactions sound like they overshadowed the "indifferent" response reviewers ascribed to the reading public, or at least loomed large in Eliot's perception. Deronda's marriage to Mirah elicited strong language from a reviewer who protested that when a young English gentleman "finishes off with his wedding in a Jewish synagogue, on the discovery that his father was a Jew, the most confiding reader leaves off with a sense of bewilderment and affront."[23] This reviewer suggests that a "confiding reader"—a reader who feels intimately attached to the novel—experiences a dramatic, deeply personal sense of betrayal from its ending.[24] The sense of "affront" toward a novel in which one is invested reappears with similar vigor in the early twentieth century, when F. R. Leavis gives the novel prominence as part of "the great tradition" of English fiction and proposes (and followed through on creating his own version) violently cleaving the "Jewish" from the "English" portions of the story.[25] He notoriously described the "Jewish" parts as "the deadweight of utterly indifferent matter that George Eliot thought fit to make it carry."[26] As Claudia Johnson shows, both F. R. Leavis and Q. D. Leavis, who was Jewish, had a complicated relationship with the novel in which their "many disidentifications with the not-English . . . are themselves responses to prior and equally powerful identifications."[27] While a resurgence of critical interest in character has been identifying different kinds of relationships readers have to fictional characters, the focus has tended to be on a positive "sense of something shared" (as Rita Felski puts it).[28] Critics like the Leavises dramatically reject a likeness they would rather not recognize—a type of response to fictional characters that, we will see, recurs within the novel.

Anti-Semitism is only one expression of repulsion circulating in the novel's social world. As recent work on antisociability has shown, feeling disgust toward another person was a social emotion in Victorian culture.[29] Repulsion in *Daniel Deronda* is not kept private but rather, even without being spoken, is legible between two people who are inescapably tied to each other. Gwendolen's disgust toward Grandcourt draws him to her, so that he proposes because of it: her knowing about Lydia "spurred him to triumph over that repugnance" (301). He later delights when he thinks that the diamonds "had at once created in Gwendolen a new repulsion for him," as if it were a new intimacy in their marriage (425). The repulsion a character feels toward another person is often recognized by multiple people without being explicitly expressed. Gwendolen's repulsion is particularly legible to other characters without their being told of it. Deronda guesses correctly that Gwendolen's poverty "had urged her acceptance where she must in some way have felt repulsion" (324), based on the events of her courtship with Grandcourt. Gwendolen's feeling toward Lush is not only known to Grandcourt but amuses him: "Gwendolen's repulsion for him being a fact that only amused his patron, and made him none the less willing to have Lush always at hand" (158). Sympathy is rare within Gwendolen and Deronda's social world, in which repulsion binds people more tightly together and "the beings closest to us, whether in love *or hate,* are often virtually our interpreters of the world" (672; my emphasis).

So far I have grouped together "hate," "repulsion," "repugnance," "revulsion," "aversion," and "disgust" as terms Eliot uses in the novel that convey the intensity of a character's "strong emotional reaction against something" (as the *OED* defines "revulsion"). In fact, these terms are used to define one another, and their definitions sound interchangeable: disgust is "strong repugnance, aversion, or repulsion" (*OED*); "hate" is "intense dislike or aversion towards a person or thing" (*OED*). Similarly, throughout the novel these various terms are used to describe many different sources of repulsion in many different characters, with one exception I discuss below. One effect of using many terms for a "strong emotional reaction against something" gives the impression that to have intensely negative feelings toward another person is a prevailing psychological experience in the world she is portraying, much as "the Inuit dialect spoken in Canada's Nunavik region has at least 53" words for snow.[30] Eliot does repeat one term consistently, "repugnance," in referring to how Gwendolen's "irreconcilable repugnance affected her even physically" (273). Not surprisingly, Gwendolen especially feels "repugnance" when confronted with sexuality, a response that Eliot distinguishes from other more socialized manifestations of repulsion in the novel. Gwendolen objects "with a sort of physical repulsion, to being directly made love to" (70); Eliot refers multiple times to her "revulsion" or "repugnance" toward Lydia and her illegitimate children ("her repugnance to certain facts" [669] and "her repugnance to the idea of Grandcourt's past" [314]); in poor Rex's case, "she had turned from his love with repugnance" (710). Gwendolen's antipathy toward expressions of sexuality is particularized, set apart as an involuntary physical response to physical stimuli. In contrast, much of the other repulsion that occurs throughout this hateful social world appears not to have a justifiable physical cause.

Eliot takes a semiscientific approach to analyzing social repulsion as she classifies different types and degrees to which this affect corrupts a person's worldview. On this scale, Grandcourt's general disdain for most other people is merely a kind of snobbery. Armstrong argues that Eliot critiques this society by making the character who has the prospect of being wealthier than the novel's other characters feel the most disdain toward other people. Gwendolen initially shares this sentiment toward everyone except her mother: "In this critical view of mankind there was an affinity between him and Gwendolen before their marriage, and we know that she had been attractingly wrought upon by the refined negations he presented to her" (671). Grandcourt's "refined negations" are, in Gwendolen's eyes, a pose that expresses his class status. But Grandcourt also knows what "personal repulsion" is: as Eliot writes, "nobody better; his mind was much furnished with a sense of what brutes his fellow-creatures were, both masculine and feminine" (670–71). Thinking of others as "brutes" expresses more disdain than having a "critical view of mankind." This affect, still concentrated on other people, fills the person feeling it with hate. Both Grandcourt's wide, universal disgust and Gwendolen's deep, soul-consuming hatred for her husband are labeled as "personal repulsion." From "refined negations" to "personal repulsion," the novel progresses to dramatizing "moral repulsion," which exceeds even Grandcourt's understanding. "He had no idea of a moral repulsion, and could not have believed, if he had been told it, that there may be a resentment and disgust which will gradually make beauty more detestable than ugliness, through exasperation at that outward virtue in which hateful things can flaunt themselves or find a supercilious advantage" (671). Grandcourt's worldview exemplifies how repulsion can become a broad phenomenon that colors one's view of all things. Eliot's novel targets a similarly diffuse repulsion in the Victorian social world, which largely accepted hateful views of Jewish people—the kind of "ready repugnance" Deronda imagines the kindly Meyricks will feel toward Mirah's "too Judaic brother" (578).

The repulsion that occurs between Jewish characters in the novel is not an expression of such socially accepted, generalized hatred. The novel's Jewish characters appear justly repulsed by "the beings closest" to them who commit egregious betrayals of one of the most fundamental human feelings: parental love. Deronda's mother makes him feel "the pain of repulsed tenderness" so strongly that he "turned pale with what always seemed more of a sensation than an emotion" (634); Mirah's "repulsion" toward her returned father mingles with other feelings (737), while he makes Deronda feel "a repulsion that was even a physical discomfort" (780). Generalized repulsion, in the form of Jewish self-hatred, is condemned. During their intellectuals' club meeting in the pub, Mordecai uses strong language to describe self-hating Jews who "despise" their "inheritance" and "brotherhood" just as Gentiles do (527). He says to Gideon:

> You are one of the multitudes over this globe who must walk among the nations and be known as Jews, and with words on their lips that mean, "I wish I had not been born a Jew, I disown any bond with the long travail of my race, I will outdo the Gentile in mocking at our separateness," they all the while feel breathing on them the breath of contempt because they are Jews, and they will breathe it back poisonously. (528)

Mordecai denounces Jewish people who identify with but want to dissociate themselves from a "race" that has an inferior social status. Through Mordecai, Eliot describes how each exercise of Jewish self-hatred adds to a social atmosphere of "contempt," just as anti-Semitism among Gentiles does, and leads to living amid more contempt. In portraying a society suffused with "the breath of contempt," Eliot is holding a mirror up in which her original readers could, if they chose, recognize their own anti-Semitism and how it shapes their experience of reading the novel.

Averse to Sympathy

Eliot's particular interest in sympathy as a state of not only feeling with another person, but feeling compassion for his or her sufferings, is usually traced back to Adam Smith, even though Smith defines sympathy as fellow-feeling with *almost* any passion. In arguing that sympathy develops through a process of imaginative identification, Smith does use "misery" as an example: "This is the source of our fellow-feeling for the misery of others, that it is by changing places in fancy with the sufferer, that we come either to conceive or to be affected by what he feels."[31] Theorists as well as researchers have long understood sympathy to thrive on certain kinds of negative emotion. Suzanne Keen argues that "empathetic responses to fictional characters and situations occur more readily for negative emotions," noting that psychological researchers believe "that empathy with pain moves us more surely towards sympathy and altruism than shared joy does."[32] This is certainly true for Deronda, for whom "difficulty and struggle . . . had a predominant attraction for his sympathy" (324). However, there are some strongly negative emotional states, like rage, that Smith suggests rouse strong emotions that make sympathy impossible, emotions that "nature teaches us to be more averse to entering into." The expression of such emotions like rage "arouse[s] no sort of sympathy; they serve rather to disgust and provoke us against them."[33] In situations that could evoke sympathy, the alternative is to respond with disgust.

Models of how sympathy forms through the act of reading are far more abundant in Victorian studies than models of how repulsion develops, as Sianne Ngai has pointed out.[34] Some of the most recent and insightful models for envisioning the relationship that develops between a reader and a nineteenth-century novel have included love, marriage, mentoring, and psychoanalysis.[35] These models on the whole explicate fiction's positive, often therapeutic, effects, even as they illuminate what Deidre Lynch calls the "edginess and complexities" of a reader's intimate relationship with literature.[36] We understand less about how Victorians perceived this intimate relationship when it results in intensely negative affects.

Resistance to sympathizing with another whose unfortunate or shameful circumstances are similar to, but more visible than, one's own is a dynamic repeatedly dramatized within *Daniel Deronda*. With virulent emotion, characters in the novel repel "the beings closest to us"—beings with whom they might otherwise sympathize, and who even, at times, mirror themselves (672).[37] What Eliot depicts is not outright rejection of another but a complex negotiation between identification and denial—much as we saw some of the novel's critics exhibit. The situations I am thinking of suggest the possibility of imaginative identification, which Laura Green defines as "the subject's perception or projection, willing or reluctant, of significant similarity between herself and another."[38] Instead of experiencing similarity as a feeling of connection, however, characters feel intensely uncomfortable emotions toward a part or version of themselves they would rather not identify with.[39]

The first such moment occurs when Eliot describes how thirteen-year-old Deronda puts down the book he is reading, the *History of the Italian Republics*, to ask his tutor why the priests and popes in the book had so many nephews. In this unwelcome moment of knowledge becoming conscious, he identifies himself as Sir Hugo Mallinger's illegitimate "nephew" for the first time. Though he is mistaken, as Audrey Jaffe discusses, Deronda's realization that the deep-seated prejudice of his own social world applies to him turns out to be wrong only in its cause—the shameful secret of his birth is that he is Jewish, not illegitimate.[40] Eliot emphasizes that Deronda has not previously made this connection, even though he has encountered such images before. While describing Deronda's "new mental survey of familiar facts" (166), Eliot describes the Mallinger family portraits, in which "the appropriate nose of the family" appears at times accurately, at other times inaccurately, but, she writes, "In the nephew Daniel Deronda the family faces of various types, seen on the walls of the gallery, found no reflex" (166). Visual art has not previously revealed Deronda's difference to himself; neither has history or literature: "Having read Shakespeare as well as a great deal of history, he could have talked with the wisdom of a bookish child about men who were born out of wedlock and were held unfortunate in consequence. . . . But he had never brought such knowledge into any association with his own lot, which had been too easy for him ever to think about it" (167). Eliot here describes recognition being kept apart from oneself and suggests a reason for such dissociation: identification means being "held unfortunate in consequence," with the incursion of shame into his previously "easy lot." José Esteban Muñoz argues that minority subjects confronted with a demeaning image of themselves in the dominant culture transform these images, or practice disidentification, for "cultural, material, and psychic survival."[41] Deronda practices avoidance. His conscious identification of himself with his mother, whom he assumes was in some way outcast, causes him to avoid further self-knowledge even when visually confronted with it: "His own face in the glass had during many years been associated for him with thoughts of some one whom he must be like—one about whose character and lot he continually wondered, and never dared to ask" (186). Eliot emphasizes that Deronda repeatedly keeps himself from knowledge of his birth, about which he "never dared to ask" and "checked himself" though he "longed to try" the lock of the cabinet containing the Mallinger family tree (171).

Deronda's reading about the pope's nephews is set up to be a classic moment of Eliotic sympathy: Deronda could come to understand, with a wider perspective, how his own "easy" lot might be shared with "unfortunate" others. Eliot even relates his newfound awareness of his own disadvantage to that of a child who has long lived in poverty. She writes in lyrical, moving terms how, "Some children, even younger than Deronda, have known the first arrival of care, like an ominous irremovable guest in their tender lives, on the discovery that their parents, whom they had imagined able to buy everything, were poor and in hard money troubles" (167). Like other Eliot characters who have known abstractly what suffering is before they have felt it, for Deronda a bookish knowledge that has been unaffecting suddenly takes embodied form; he reacts "as if something had stung him," and "started up in a sitting attitude" (165) with a "deep blush" (166). Eliot uses highly physical language to describe Deronda's "newly-roused set of feelings" (168)—he is "stung to the quick" and he "inwardly used strong words, for he was feeling the injury done him as a maimed boy feels the crushed limb which for others is merely reckoned in an average of accidents" (169–70). Eliot herself sounds like she is yearning for "strong words" here, for an image that might evoke actual physical aversion even in imagining it, like a "crushed limb." Deronda's response to this intense hurt is to conceal and turn away, not to feel fellowship with others who are also treated unjustly: "He would never bring himself near even a silent admission of the sore that had opened in him" (171).[42] Though Deronda later develops, through this self-knowledge, a compensatory "sympathy with certain ills" (175), it is worth noticing that in the moment he is not drawn on to the heightened awareness of others' pain, which for Eliot constitutes sympathy. Rather, Deronda's reverie ends when his tutor points out that he is, unaware, "sitting on the bent pages of [his] book" (167).

The Smithian sympathy that has dominated discussions of Victorian fiction is not a useful model for understanding the effect of feelings to which one is "averse." Deronda's response has much in common with the psychological coping mechanism Freud later identified as "repression."[43] Daniel is so preoccupied with this new, uncomfortable self-knowledge gained through reading that he unconsciously represses the source that revealed it to him in the sense that he physically crushes the book. In a short essay on repression, Freud writes that "the essence of repression lies simply in turning something away, and keeping it at a distance, from the conscious."[44] Seeing a connection to another person who shares one's unfortunate traits or—particularly in Victorian society, shameful status—is an experience of self-knowledge that can be unwelcome. Imaginatively identifying with a situation one does not want to be in can trigger mechanisms of resistance, so that self-knowledge is denied or remains not fully conscious.

When Eliot describes Deronda's "newly-roused set of feelings" (168) about his birth, Eliot echoes the aim she expressed for the novel to "rouse the imagination of men and women to a vision of human claims in those races of their fellow-men who most differ from them in custom and beliefs." Those "human claims," or recognizing that other human beings are also human beings (imagine that!), sounds like knowledge that prejudiced readers have, in a sense, repressed. Indeed, the effect on Deronda of meeting Mirah, who "was like others . . . in never having cared to reach any more special conclusions about actual Jews," is that "Mirah's longings roused his mind to a closer survey of details" (206). The novel's aim is to bring about a realization like Deronda's in which repressed, unwelcome knowledge can no longer remain conveniently unseen. Rita Felski describes such a dynamic between reader and character as an "irritation situation," in which a text functions as a mirror, but "the mirror it offers does not flatter."[45]

"A Sacred Aversion to Her Worst Self"

Within the novel, seeing an image, experiencing intense discomfort at the likeness, and turning away or wanting to turn away can actually begin a process of "self-abhorrence that stings us into better striving" (699). The benign fellow-feeling that Eliot eulogizes in other novels is not intense enough to counter racialized hatred; violent "self-abhorrence" is needed for redemption. Through Gwendolen, Eliot models the painful process of recognizing one's own hatred and developing "that self-disapproval which had been the awakening of a new life within her" (697). By the end of the novel Gwendolen at least glimpses that there are other human beings who have equal claims, the realization Eliot hoped to bring about in her readers.

Initially, Gwendolen reacts with violent disidentification toward images that prefigure her future self. When she sees the image behind the hinged panel in the drawing room at Offendene, the "upturned dead face from which an obscure figure seemed to be fleeing with outstretched arms," her own face is distorted in response: she turns to her mother "with a face which was flushed in reaction from her chill shudder" (27).[46] Gwendolen's sister predicts the image of the dead face, and the fleeing figure will haunt her ("You will never stay in this room by yourself, Gwendolen"; 27.) That is in a sense what happens near the end of the novel, when she is haunted by Grandcourt's drowning face. She feels a more concrete "revulsion" when she sees Lydia Glasher with Grandcourt's illegitimate children (152). Gwendolen, like the young Deronda, has not yet applied the generalized understanding she has gained from reading to herself: "Gwendolen's uncontrolled reading, though consisting chiefly in what are called pictures of life, had somehow not prepared her for this encounter with reality" (155). Despite replying that she will not stand in Lydia's way, her affective response to Lydia's plight is not sympathetic but explicitly antipathetic: "The revulsion within her was not tending to soften her. Everyone seemed hateful." Though Lydia aligns herself with Gwendolen—"when he first knew me, I too was young"—Eliot detaches Gwendolen from the person immediately before her even as she recognizes her potential fate in Lydia's. "Gwendolen, watching Mrs Glasher's face while she spoke, felt a sort of terror: it was as if some ghastly vision had come to her in a dream and said, 'I am a woman's life'" (152). Gwendolen both makes the connection and puts it further off from her: she "watch[es]" Lydia rather than feels for her, and sees her in generalized terms as living "*a woman's life*." Deronda represses unwelcome knowledge about himself; Gwendolen projects such knowledge outward until "Everyone seemed hateful."

Who would want to sympathize with, in the sense of imagining and feeling, such "averse" feelings as Gwendolen's? Gwendolen thinks what she most needs is Deronda's sympathy, sympathy directed toward her from another person, but he gives it with anxiety and dread, feeling that (after Grandcourt drowns), "He dreaded the weight of this woman's soul flung upon his own with imploring dependence" (689). Eliot eventually shows that the cathartic process Gwendolen needs to go through is seeing her own hateful feelings *as if* they exist in another person and subsequently feeling sympathy toward herself for the misery that feeling hate causes her. Throughout her writing, fiction and nonfiction, Eliot portrays having sympathy for others as cathartic for the person feeling sympathy. Aristotelian catharsis requires separation: seeing a painful experience cause misery in another person becomes therapeutic by occurring safely at a distance from the spectator or reader's self.[47] In narrating the events of Grandcourt's death to Deronda, a dissociated Gwendolen imagines watching her feelings "outside" herself, as if another being were feeling them. In the boat with Grandcourt before he falls overboard, Eliot writes:

> She was not afraid of any outward dangers—she was afraid of her own wishes, which were taking shapes possible and impossible, like a cloud of demon-faces. She was afraid of her own hatred, which under the cold iron touch that had compelled her today had gathered a fierce intensity. As she sat guiding the tiller under her husband's eyes, doing just what he told her, the strife within her seemed like her own effort to escape from herself. (681)

In Eliot's figurative language, Gwendolen's own emotion takes on a concrete shape outside herself, her "hatred" appearing to her "like a cloud of demon-faces," which she experiences as a separate, living entity. While she is "afraid" of these materialized wishes, by splitting off the "fierce intensity" of her hatred, she has enough of a respite from its intensity to be able to perceive "strife": there is another, better part of herself making an effort to escape.

Thus, a complex structure develops, similar to what Gwendolen experiences earlier in the novel when she sees Lydia Glasher and is confronted with an image that she simultaneously recognizes as like herself and rejects. Describing Grandcourt's drowning, Gwendolen speaks of herself as if she were witnessing another unwelcome person and does not deny the likeness. In a haltingly dissociated way, she tells Deronda, "I had the rope in my hand—I don't know what I thought—I was leaping away from myself—I would have saved him then. I was leaping from my crime, and there it was—close to me as I fell—there was the dead face—dead, dead" (696). Gwendolen recognizes her worst self in this complex confession: the abundant use of "I," "myself," and "my" claims a sense of agency for her actions. She also identifies herself as a figure fleeing a dead face, like the image on the panel at Offendene, which she once repulsed. At the same time, she describes several times fleeing from this recognition of herself: "leaping away from myself," "leaping from my crime." As her narrative goes on to reach the climactic moment of Grandcourt's falling overboard, the balance between the two selves within her shifts; her "evil longings" and "evil prayers" increasingly become the active agents, as entities in themselves; while she herself is innocent and helpless: "I don't know how it was—he was turning the sail—there was a gust—he was struck—I know nothing—I only know that I saw my wish outside me" (696). Grandcourt turns the sail and the wind gusts, while all that the first-person "I" claims is "I know nothing," "I saw my wish outside myself." By splitting off part of herself in her mind, Gwendolen is able to bear seeing "her worst self" and does not try to deny it. Instead, she feels what Eliot describes as "that sacred aversion to her worst self—that thorn-pressure which must come with the crowning of the sorrowful Better, suffering because of the Worse" (697). Gwendolen subtly models, for the reader who might be repulsed by Jewish characters, how recognizing one's hate materialized outside oneself can be a means of turning that repulsion toward others into a "*sacred* aversion" toward oneself. Within literature generally, Ngai has shown, "ugly feelings" such as envy or disgust can make a subject turn inward rather than sympathetically outward, and engage in metareflection about the powerlessness of a person feeling such emotions.[48]

In the context of Eliot's aim for the novel to free readers to feel something other than repulsion toward Jews, it is striking that repulsion is repeatedly gotten over in the novel. Gwendolen intends to give a "final repulsion" to Grandcourt's courtship multiple times (292, 297), and ultimately accepts his offer of marriage; overcoming this repulsion only breeds more bad feeling, however: "She was appalled by the idea that she was going to do what she had once started away from with repugnance" (311). By the novel's end, however, she is able to see likeness to those she had held "a long way off from me": "I used to think I could never be wicked. I thought of wicked people as if they were a long way off me. Since then I have been wicked. I have felt wicked" (692). Gwendolen has gotten over her revulsion enough to accept an unbecoming view of her "wicked" self and consequently have a more capacious, forgiving, less judgmental view of other people. More specifically, Eliot shows Deronda, multiple times, getting over his socially ingrained anti-Semitism. He embraces the Jewish people he at first is repulsed by, including the Cohen family ("his first sense of repulsion at the commonness of these people was beginning to be tempered with kindlier feeling"; 520) and the elderly stranger in the synagogue in Frankfort, Joseph Kalonymos, toward whom Deronda initially has a "strongly resistant feeling" (368). Deronda even overcomes repulsion toward an imagined idea, as Eliot hoped her readers would, when he "feel[s] his imagination moving without repugnance in the direction of Mordecai's desires" (545). Eliot particularly notes how the repulsion Jewish characters initially feel toward one another is resolved into "kindlier feeling." In a climactic moment, Deronda's mother, after repulsing his tenderness, "did not seem inclined to repulse him now" (638). There is actually less repulsion felt in the novel's last fifty pages, as if the resolution, or rather dissolution, of that emotion is part of the closure the novel needs to reach.

Who Are "We"?

A great deal of repulsion is overcome within *Daniel Deronda*, but Eliot knew she had less control over whether some readers would get over their repulsion toward the novel's Jewish characters. In fact, Eliot knew that Jewish "fellow-men" might be so habitually excluded from the sympathies of mainstream Victorian readers that they might not figure into how readers picture those persons she refers to in the novel as "we" and "all of us," and readers might not even be conscious of the exclusion. Particularly in Eliot's early novels, "we" has been said to create a tone that, while bossy, is also "nostalgic, possessive, and personal."[49] Barbara Hardy characterizes Eliot's "inclusive use of 'we'" as "communal" gestures.[50] Yet Eliot's use of "we" is not only a rhetorical feature but also projects a body of persons outside the novel's depicted, realized world who share certain emotions, behaviors, and experiences. In *Daniel Deronda*, rather than simply appearing as a benignant—or, more suspiciously, a coercive—feature of her narrative voice, Eliot's first-person plural interventions construct constantly changing social bodies. Within the novel, the implied composition of who "we" are subtly shifts: sometimes the addressed persons appear to share the social attitudes and experiences of the mainstream reading public, including its anti-Semitism, and sometimes appear to include all those who feel human feelings. Eliot uses this flexibility of making "we" sometimes appear to include Jewish people, and sometimes not, to unsettle readerly prejudices. She expands who is included in "we" in such a fluctuating, barely perceptible way that readers hardly notice the cumulative effect that her prose might have on weakening a biased reader's not-fully-conscious exclusions.

Eliot's use of "we" is one of few aspects of her work that still evokes an image of the overbearing, moralizing Victorian sage. However, even as an idealized feature of Eliot's narrative voice in her early novels, the first-person plural is often characterized by a tone of longing to bring common feeling into being; as a result, "we" can sound more tentatively aspirational than the authoritative tone usually ascribed to Eliot's narrative interjections. In *Adam Bede*, for instance, such pronouns often fall into one of two categories: first, her bemused, facetious commentaries on how "the wisest of us" ordinary beings are united by common faults (198). This is the confidently ironic Eliot, who dresses down all those who share human failings: "We are none of us aware of the impression we produce on Brazilian monkeys of feeble understanding," she quips (249). However, Eliot's other frequent way of using "we" in *Adam Bede* is less assured and more yearning. At times she uses "we" to articulate "very sublime feelings" in terms that strain to be lyrical and emotional enough to *create* the profound, difficult-to-access feeling in the reader's mind. As she writes about Seth being in love with Dinah:

> Our caresses, our tender words, our still rapture under the influence of autumn sunsets, or pillared vistas, or calm majestic statues, or Beethoven symphonies all bring with them the consciousness that they are mere waves and ripples in an unfathomable ocean of love and beauty; our emotion in its keenest moment passes from expression into silence, our love at its highest flood rushes beyond its object and loses itself in the sense of divine mystery. (81)

As in Dinah's preaching, which uses "we" extensively, "our" here focuses on a loss of egotism in the most sublime, "divine" moments of feeling. Such truly selfless moments of feeling are not easily achieved. Late in the novel as Eliot describes how Adam's sorrow over Hetty has softened him, she uses an overabundance of first-person plural pronouns, as if anxiously reasserting the hardwon sense of commonality:

> It would be a poor result of all *our* anguish and *our* wrestling if *we* won nothing but *our* old selves at the end of it—if *we* could return to the same blind loves, the same self-confident blame, the same light thoughts of human suffering, the same frivolous gossip over blighted human lives, the same feeble sense of that Unknown towards which *we* have sent forth irrepressible cries in *our* loneliness. Let *us* rather be thankful that *our* sorrow lives in *us* as an indestructible force, only changing its form, as forces do, and

passing from pain into sympathy—the one poor word which includes all *our* best insight and *our* best love. (531; my emphases)

That "we" would feel in tandem with one another appears to be contingent in multiple ways. For one, the growth of sympathy is dependent on overcoming the stubborn egotism that, in her other way of using "we," makes "us" appear by nature self-absorbed. Second, in this passage Eliot could be describing the effect she desires her novel to have, as a result of the reader's imagining and feeling the characters' pain along with them, yet she prefaces that hope with a projection of sympathy *not* being achieved.

Even this brief look at Eliot's early use of "we" shows how the pronoun asserts an ideal that Eliot's art hopes to cultivate but is conscious of striving to achieve. Stylistically, Eliot's use of "we" differs later in her career. Critics have noted that there are fewer and shorter narrative "intrusions" in *Daniel Deronda* than in Eliot's early novels, a shift that has been read as the maturing of Eliot's style.[51] "We" also gains complexity in *Daniel Deronda* by becoming a fluctuating projection, not always of unity. If "we" is a fictional group of human beings outside the novel's pages, imagined to share some particular experience or emotion that Eliot has just depicted, the fictionality of "we" becomes especially visible when Eliot appends "mortals" ("mortals," "we mortals," "us mortals" "our fellow mortals") or "all" ("all of us in our turn," 238; "Imagine—we all of us can—," 495) to "we" or "us." This projected community of "we mortals" or "all of us" is comprised of limited, fallible creatures (mortal, not immortal), not one of whom is better than any other (all of us). Moreover, thinking about the first-person plural not in terms of tone or style—in which case "we" sounds ideally inclusive—but as an imagined group of persons outside of the novel has a subtly alienating effect, for paradoxically, the more Eliot develops this communal sense, the more "we" appears to be a fictional invention that does not include "me," the actual person reading the novel. She uses the pronoun when turning an expression of personal feeling into a general claim about human experience, so that she attributes to this imagined body a feeling I, as reader, had felt in myself. Displacing the emotion that a scene has stirred up onto a category of made-up persons adds to the disruptive effect (as many Victorian reviewers saw them) of Eliot's narrative intrusions on the dramatic action. One Victorian reviewer of *Daniel Deronda* described how Eliot's "superfluous moralizing" can "delay the action of the piece to press home truths" and feel like a "painful jar."[52]

Other Victorian critics recognize this feature of Eliot's novels as a kind of "chorus," and Eliot's interjections do often show the outline of a citizenry much as a Greek chorus does. Leslie Stephen, defending Eliot's use of this literary technique in the obituary he wrote for her, describes how the author "acts occasionally as chorus."[53] In Greek tragedy the chorus represents the shared views of fellow citizens, and in scattered moments throughout the novel, Eliot offers a hint or outline of people who have specific social dimensions in her choral-like addresses. She refers to specifically English readers with the expressions "we English" (102), "this realm" (584), and "our foggy London" (196). At other times she singles out concrete types of readers, "those," "some," or "any" people, who have had specific experiences or are of specific ages: "Those who have known an impassioned childhood" (167); "We whom the years have subdued" (289). Sometimes her tone is facetious in such instances: "(Here should any young lady incline to imitate Gwendolen, let her consider)" (69); "most of us dainty people" (381). I want to underscore two perhaps obvious things about these varied examples: first, quite a number of Eliot's addresses, even those that use "we," are directed toward a circumscribed group of people, not all of "humankind"; and second, the specific audience being addressed, and the tone in which it is addressed, varies so that the narrator does not always have the same relation to "us."

It has been noted multiple times that the narrator's voice in the novel is closest to Deronda's perspective, that he appears to embody the detached, sympathetic narrative voice of Eliot's previous novels.[54] At times, "we" aligns with his perspective, but this is not the case in satiric moments, for (to put it frankly) Deronda has less of a sense of humor than Eliot. Sometimes "we" share traits or attitudes that Eliot identifies with the English reading public and sought, through ironic prodding, to change: what she described to Beecher Stowe as "the intellectual narrowness—in plain English, the stupidity" of the average English person who is uninterested in "any form of life that is not clad in the same coat-tails and flounces as our own."[55] When Eliot's narrator voices a similarly myopic perspective, the tone can be gently ironic and the first-person plural a means of making the critical judgment less abrasive and more gently instructive to the reader. Commenting on Mrs. Meyrick's hope that Mirah will give up her Judaism, the narrator does not accuse her of prejudice but rather suggests almost confidentially that the narrator belongs to a group of persons outside the novel who feel similarly: "We sit up at night to read about Sakya-Mouni, Saint Francis, or Oliver Cromwell; but whether we should be glad for anyone at all like them to call on us the next morning, still more, to reveal himself as a new relation, is quite another affair" (567). Rather than convey universality, here "we" implies an attitude of exclusion, accepted but not usually admitted among more general company, and harder to accept comfortably when voiced outright. Eliot similarly establishes Deronda's initial attitude toward Jewish people as familiar to an "us" who might not think "we" are anti-Semitic: "I suppose we should all have felt as Deronda did, without sinking into snobbishness or the notion that the primal duties of life demand a morning and an evening suit, that it was an admissible desire to free Mirah's first meeting with her brother from all jarring outward conditions" (544). In fact, many uses of "we" assume certain class-based knowledge, like the apparel of "a morning and an evening suit," or assume that "we" will understand specific cultural allusions: "Most of us remember Retzsch's drawing of destiny in the shape of Mephistopheles playing at chess with man for his soul" (455). Although the image Eliot refers to, the German artist Moritz Retzsch's *The Chess-Players*, was published in a penny magazine in the 1830s, suggesting its relatively wide circulation in England, the easygoing tone in which Eliot projects that "most of us remember" a forty-year-old German Romantic illustration inspired by Faust conjures an audience with more sophisticated tastes than the universal "we" that has been associated with her fiction.[56]

"We," then, at times marks out a limited group of imagined persons, defined by its specific cultural knowledge or attitudes, and at other times refers to a limitless, all-inclusive humankind; the distinction can be hard to tease apart. While this variation occurs to some extent throughout Eliot's fiction, in *Daniel Deronda* the pronoun carries the added meaning of Eliot's project to stretch the cultural boundaries of sympathy in her readers. Eliot's flexible use of the same pronoun to imply more and less inclusive groups of people is one narrative technique she uses to make these boundaries more elastic. A variety of meanings of "we" are entangled when the narrator comments ironically on Anna Gascoigne's dress: "I like to mark the time, and connect the course of individual lives with the historic stream, for all classes of thinkers. This was the period when the broadening of gauge in crinolines seemed to demand an agitation for the general enlargement of churches, ballrooms, and vehicles" (88). Eliot's description of making her characters' "individual lives" relevant to "the historic stream," and doing so for "all classes of thinkers," captures a genuine aim of her fiction as well as the specific narrative technique of commenting on the novel's action in generalizing terms. But in the second, more ironic sentence, a figure becomes just visible, an imagined addressee the tiniest bit more in focus, as someone who might recognize that moment in English sartorial history; the humor depends on it. The moment has the tone of addressing a culturally defined audience and the wording of speaking to "all" of us who are part of the "historic stream" of human life. As the meaning of who comprises "we" fluctuates from sentence to sentence, so does the reader's vision of who is sharing the same experiences and claims as "all of us." To see Eliot's broad aspiration to change readers' attitudes toward those different from themselves concretely at work in her use of a plural pronoun may seem familiar: in the early twenty-first century, third-person plural pronouns have become a means of acknowledging nontraditional gender identities.

In *Daniel Deronda* the assumption that Eliot's characteristic use of "all of us" refers to common human experiences, then, comes into friction with the subtle sense that she is addressing an audience that, she knew, thought about "fellow mortals" in anti-Semitic, exclusionary terms. In many cases, the "all of us" she *addresses* appears to share the characteristics of (and sometimes caricature) the English reading public; the fictional body of "we mortals" whose experiences she *describes* tends to point to all human beings who have numerous failings. For instance, Eliot often uses the particular construction "we all" or "us all" when she is identifying certain human emotions, patterns of thought, and behaviors, much as a social scientist might make a claim that implicitly applies to every human being. Here is a sampling:

> *We all of us* carry on our thinking in some habitual locus where there is a presence of other souls. (482)

> Deronda had that objection to answer which *we all* have known in speaking to those who are too certain of their own fixed interpretations. (661)

> That mingling of inconsequence which belongs to *us all*. (475)

> The often painful night watches, when *we are all* liable to be held with the clutch of a single thought. (479–80)

> *We all of us* carry on our thinking. (482)

> *We should all* have felt as Deronda did. (544)

> *We are all* apt to fall into this passionate egoism of imagination. (796)

Poor us, we who thought our consciousness was our own, distinct from other people's minds. There is a kind of coerciveness to "we all," a sense that the narrator, or novelist, who has such insight, who has found out such deeply hidden truths about human beings, is showing us the truth about ourselves, unfamiliar as it may seem. However, my point is that not every use of "we all" inspires this feeling of truthfulness; in many cases, "all" makes the persons referred to appear all the more invented. No schematic chart of who "we all" refers to is possible; the boundaries of this group of persons are constantly moving. For instance, "we all" can also have a hint of a culturally specific profile in the imagined addressee: "What should *we all* do without the calendar, when we want to put off a disagreeable duty?" (379); "the four superfluous girls, each, poor thing—like those other many thousand sisters of *us all*—" (229). These occasions when "us all" refers to socialized phenomena familiar to the mainstream English reading audience, which Eliot refers to in a confidential, one-of-us tone of voice, become nearly seamless with other occasions when Eliot evokes the image of a more inclusive social body. So subtle and barely detectable is the difference that she expands and contracts who is sharing these experiences, potentially without our even noticing that "we" are imagining the collective social body we belong to being made up differently.

What Eliot also makes less distinguishable in the novel, compared with her earlier works, is the very gesture of asking the reader to put the novel down and imagine his or her own experiences outside of the novel. Self-directed reflection, in the double sense of inviting the reader to have independent thoughts about his or her self, becomes seamlessly integrated into Eliot's prose (remember how she commands the reader to daydream in *Adam Bede*). Eliot's generalizing in the novel indeed takes forms that are woven into the fabric of the novel's depictions, particularly the form of a simile that directly connects the single depicted instance with an experience "we" recognize: "such as we give to a possession that we have been on the brink of losing" (755); "Deronda saw these consequences as we see any danger of marring our own work well begun" (377). Using "we" in figurative terms like this invites more back-and-forth in the reader's mind between the clearly fictional world and the part-fictionalized, part-real realm of "us" outside the novel. Her direct addresses in the novel often take the form of brief asides integrated into the narration in parentheses or midsentence (sometimes both), as in the reference to not being able to "escape (who can?) knowing ugly stories" of Jews (206). These asides are frequently rhetorical questions to which the unspoken answer is "no one," questions that tend to drive home the inescapability of being like other people: "Who can all at once describe a human being?" (111); "Who is absolutely neutral?" (382); "(Who has not seen men with faces of this corrective power . . . ?)" (331); "in a mood of rebellion (what human creature escapes it?) against things in general" (623). In addition to these direct addresses, many generalizing comments that employ "we," "our," or "us" take the form of single- or half-sentence references to something outside of the novel that is parallel, "akin," or "of this kind," with the action or description. These quick juxtapositions also ask the reader to affirm the fictional world's truth with real experience, particularly about psychological phenomena, such as how "our" thoughts work. There are too many examples to list; this rhetorical pattern pervades the novel, but it is particularly poignant when the subject of the sentence is as far from the "general reader" as possible: Mordecai's vision of "the awaited friend," "the imagery of his most passionate life." "It was Deronda now who was seen in the often painful night-watches, *when we are all liable to be held with the clutch of a single thought*—whose figure, never with its back turned, was seen in moments of soothed reverie or soothed dozing" (479–80; my emphasis). These moments that turn attention fleetingly to "we all" or "all of us" function as opportunities for self-reflection and self-knowledge. Eliot is partial to mirror images in other novels as well, and her moments of plural direct address turn the text into a mirror: they ask the reader to see a similarity between his or her own experience and that of the fictional characters. Integrating these reflections on human experience into the novel's prose makes novel reading into an opportunity for ongoing self-realization.

Eliot not only knew that we like to think about ourselves, but she made use of this desire to interest readers in a novel they might otherwise repulse. Eliot is best known for protesting that egoism can narrow one's perspective, as she writes of Casaubon in *Middlemarch*: "Will not a tiny speck very close to our vision blot out the glory of the world, and leave only a margin by which we see the blot? I know no speck so troublesome as self" (456). *Daniel Deronda* may have been unpopular because the novel appears to foreground sympathizing with an unfamiliar other, when, according to at least one reviewer, Victorian readers wanted to feel they were reading about themselves. As this rare reviewer wrote:

> And why should we not, for once in a way, travel away from ourselves? By risking the immediate disappointment of a large number of her most ardent admirers, George Eliot has paid us a higher compliment than if she had given us another Silas Marner. She has practically refused to believe the common libel, upon us who read fiction, that we only care to look at our own photographs and to be told what we already know.[57]

As this reviewer playfully alludes to, Eliot herself knew that "a large number" of readers might want to see themselves in a novel. Her fiction as a whole provides this opportunity continually by asking "us who read fiction," "all of us," to see and know ourselves more fully, to own up to our blemishes. This career-long interest is intensified thematically in *Daniel Deronda*, whose two principal characters are engaged in struggles to know and accept themselves. Indeed, Gwendolen, who at first feels so much complacent "self-delight" (229) that she actually kisses her smiling image in the mirror, gradually instead develops a very Eliot-like sense of fellow-feeling toward her imperfect self and looks in the mirror "not in admiration, but in a sad kind of companionship" (430). Literary critics have long regarded the readerly desire to recognize one's self in a novel's characters as a trait of common, uncritical, popular readers.[58] In *Daniel Deronda* George Eliot turns this impulse to see oneself in a novel into a complex dynamic of reckoning with who "we" are. Subtly, even unconsciously, Eliot's pronoun invites her readers to see more than just likenesses of themselves among their mental images of "us."

"Thus and Not Otherwise"

In closing I want to underscore the strangeness of Eliot's addressing the revulsion she anticipated readers would feel toward *Daniel Deronda*'s Jewish elements by cultivating negative affective experiences all the more. Narratively, the novel immerses the reader in long explications of intensely negative feeling states, such as Gwendolen's hatred toward herself and others; for the relatively long time it takes to read such descriptions, the reader is as helpless as the character to escape. "Things about me raise bad feelings—and I must go on—I can alter nothing—it is no use," Gwendolen tells Deronda (609). The novel literally "rais[es] bad feelings" for the reader, too, in the sense of conjuring them in painful and relentless detail, but the reader also "must go on" in the one-sided, teleological experience of reading a narrative and "can alter nothing." In *Daniel Deronda*, as Eliot thinks through other affective dimensions of the character-reader bond that can develop beyond the wished-for sympathetic identification usually associated with her fiction, she pays particular attention to the experience of being thwarted in imagining otherwise.

Eliot was not alone in the 1860s through the 1880s in depicting characters and states of feeling that readers might be averse to imagining. Anthony Trollope's *The Small House at Allington* (1864) and Henry James's *The Portrait of a Lady* (1881) also focus on the psychological and narrative consequences of choosing the wrong suitor early on—consequences from which Trollope and James, unlike Eliot, arguably refuse to rescue their misguided heroines.[59] For instance, while Trollope's other heroines collectively spend thousands of pages engaging in what Margaret Oliphant had already protested against as "the uncomfortable vacillation between two lovers which has been for some time past his favorite topic,"[60] in *The Small House at Allington*, Trollope deliberately upends his own novelistic practices and the conventions of the courtship novel more generally. He seems to fulfill the expectations of the genre's reader all too easily as the story of Lily Dale's being courted by and becoming engaged to Crosbie is told in a sentence, fifty pages in. Instead of the discomfort of prolonged indecision, narrative possibilities are emphatically foreclosed; Trollope even says that Lily knows the risks of so fully giving herself up to Crosbie, and yet "would not provide for herself any possibility of retreat."[61] All three novels enable an "irritation situation" (to use Felski's term) comprised of the heroine's discontent, the reader's malcontent with the heroine's marital choice, and the lack of realizable alternatives to persist for hundreds of pages.

As *Daniel Deronda*'s characters repeatedly struggle to think of alternatives for themselves, Eliot once more depicts her characters experiencing an affective dilemma that mirrors what she knew might be going on in readers' minds. By the time of Eliot's writing *Daniel Deronda*, her characters are no longer having concrete daydreams about their wishes coming true, as Eliot's characters do in *Adam Bede*. *Daniel Deronda*'s characters suffer throughout the novel because "things in general are thus and not otherwise." Eliot writes this when Deronda is in Genoa waiting to meet his mother, and he appears in a "mood of rebellion (what human creature escapes it?) against things in general because they are thus and not otherwise" (623). This is Eliot's signature gesture in the novel: a midsentence, parenthetical questioning aside that insinuates that all "human creature[s]" have had the experience she is representing, that no one "escapes it." What the narrator is commenting on, too, is the human dilemma of not being able to evade the limitations of reality. Deronda acts as Eliot's surrogate gospel of the "not otherwise," telling Gwendolen, "We must find out duties in what comes to us, not in what we imagine might have been," not in "foolish wishing of that sort" (701); after Gwendolen finishes her narrative of what happened in the boat when Grandcourt drowns, Eliot writes that anything Deronda said would be "sacrilege," but, "[i]f he had opened his lips to speak, he could only have echoed, 'It can never be altered—it remains unaltered, to alter other things'" (697). Unable to "alter" things, Gwendolen fails to find comfort in alternatives either: she "often pursued the comparison between what might have been, if she had not married Grandcourt, and what actually was," with no benefit (429). "Let her wander over the possibilities of her life as she would, an uncertain shadow dogged her," Eliot writes (430). At the end of the novel, writing to Deronda, Gwendolen can only haltingly refer to a vague future in which "it shall be better with me because I have known you," though "I do not yet see how that can be" (810).

Such repeated incapacity is instructive. Gwendolen, unable to alter what surrounds her, ends the novel with a faint recognition that something can be altered in herself, the lesson Eliot hoped her readers might take from the novel. At one point Eliot advises the reader that picturing the "might have been" between the novel's characters is so similarly "futile" as to not be worth the imaginative effort. Describing Rex Gascoigne and Gwendolen Harleth, the narrator comments, "One is tempted to that futile sort of wishing—if only things could have been a little otherwise then, so as to have been greatly otherwise after!" (68). Wishing the novel were even "a little otherwise" is not a viable use of imagination, Eliot explicitly tells us. What the novel does create space for is turning the temptation to imagine otherwise toward the more achievable aim of altering what is repulsive in ourselves.

The Reader's Part from Virginia Woolf to Relatability

LITERARY CRITICS today have been debating the relative truth values of different academic methods of reading but have said little about the sophisticated aesthetics of so-called common reading.[1] In this respect, little has changed in a century. Beginning with Henry James, Anglo-American literary criticism shifted wholesale from being centered on the reader to focusing on the writer, as Nicholas Dames posits.[2] A few scholars interested in discipline formation, in understanding why literary criticism takes the shape it does, are just beginning to break down surprisingly durable distinctions between what Wayne Booth long ago described as "the common reader's demand that he should be deeply and emotionally involved in what he reads" and the sophisticated reader's "willing[ness] to take his pleasure from 'aesthetic' and 'intellectual' qualities."[3] We have to look outside of academic criticism for continued theorizing about the common reader's practices in the twentieth and twenty-first centuries.

First, then, I turn to Virginia Woolf, arguably the best-known theorist of the imaginative, subjective nature of reading literature since the nineteenth century. At first glance, what Woolf describes in *Orlando* (1928) as doing "a reader's part in making up from bare hints dropped here and there" appears to depend on the omissions that characterize high-modernist narrative technique. "Bare hints" seem to have little in common with writing from the nineteenth century, a time when (according to Woolf's facetious description in the same novel) "sentences swelled, adjectives multiplied, lyrics became epics, and little trifles that had been essays a column long were now encyclopaedias in ten or twenty volumes."[4] In fact, throughout her writings Woolf explicates a personalized mode of reading that depends on the reader's individualized acts of imagination, much like the Victorian writers this book has examined.

Second, and finally, I turn to the literature classroom. Faculty today, like novelists in the nineteenth century, often grapple with how the personal associations students bring to bear on literature both enhance and supersede aesthetic appreciation. Students who value literature for its "relatability" are often dismissed as "uncritical" readers, much as newly literate Victorian readers were—although, as we now know, this unscripted, personalized mode of reading has a long tradition behind it as a worthwhile practice. In closing, then, I suggest how recognizing the tradition this book traces may urge us toward more nuanced terms to reckon with the readerly subjectivity that figures prominently in today's classrooms and, though as critics we have long sought to deny it, our criticism.[5]

Woolf, a quintessential modernist, figures the artistic nature of the reader's imaginative participation in much the same way major Victorian writers did. Woolf enables us to see how at least one modernist writer was not only reacting against Victorian fiction and its attendant reading practices, but she also fully articulates a role for the reader's imagination within the artistry of the novel, which Victorian novelists and critics had begun to value in a more conflicted way. As a result, we can finally fill in a missing part of the novel's history as a genre: how critics and novelists came to see that dreaminess novel reading inspires not as a quixotic danger but as a truth about the reader's cocreation of the imagined novel-world—and how they began to see this earlier than we think they did.

When Woolf theorizes the work performed by the reader's imagination in multiple essays, her prose enacts the mental processes, the flights of fancy, she describes. "Theorize" hardly captures how she revels in the imaginativeness of common reading, narrating in stream-of-consciousness detail how a reader of literature creatively supplements, goes on tangents, and replaces what an author describes with spontaneous mental images of his or her own. Woolf's literary critical essays are written in a lively, jaunty voice, sometimes exaggerated to the point of irony, and are filled with metaphor; her prose is suited to conveying the inspirited, creative high, the state of "flow," that reading literature induces for her. Although Woolf borrows Samuel Johnson's formulation of a "common reader" as the title for her two collections of literary essays, she differs from Johnson in the mental faculties she sees as exercised in reading literature. She quotes Johnson in the opening essay of the *First Series*: "I rejoice to concur with the common reader; for by the common sense of readers, uncorrupted by literary prejudices, after all the refinements of subtilty and the dogmatism of learning, must be finally decided all claim to poetical honours." Where the Enlightenment-era Johnson points to "the common *sense* of readers," Kate Flint suggests that for Woolf, "the activity of reading may function as a kind of mental springboard, the reader being led to create as well as to assimilate."[6] In introducing the *First Series*, Woolf uses elaborate figurative terms to describe the common reader as engaged in a creative project of his or her own:

> Above all, he is guided by an instinct to create for himself, out of whatever odds and ends he can come by, some kind of whole—a portrait of a man, a sketch of an age, a theory of the art of writing. He never ceases, as he reads, to run up some rickety and ramshackle fabric which shall give him the temporary satisfaction of looking sufficiently like the real object to allow of affection, laughter, and argument. Hasty, inaccurate, and superficial, snatching now this poem, now that scrap of old furniture, without caring where he finds it or of what nature it may be so long as it serves his purpose and rounds his structure.[7]

The language of piecing together, constructing, running up, and creating repeatedly characterizes Woolf's exuberant descriptions of the reading process. Repurposing becomes a means of absorbing and responding to the original text, but an author's work merely provides the pieces, for the rhetorical flourish of the passage is devoted to emphasizing how the reader's creative drive becomes more compelling than the contents of the author's work. The reader takes up "whatever odds and ends he can come by . . . without caring where he finds it or of what nature." Though Woolf refers to her reader as "he," his practice is domesticated and, in the process, democratized, a "fabric" made of "old furniture." Reading figures as an art of improvisation that can be practiced in the home, in which the reader, now the artist, spontaneously remakes the author's words in the course of processing them.

Like the Victorian critics of novel reading that I refer to in the introduction, Woolf claims that exercising independent imagination during reading deepens the reader's appreciation of literary artistry. Critics such as Jane De Gay have focused on how Woolf enlists the reader's creativity in understanding the author's intent; the reader uses "imagination to develop a sense of empathy with the writer and work" (as De Gay puts it).[8] A passage in *Orlando* goes further than this, though, to suggest that the reader independently fulfills the author's vision using his or her capacity for personal association. During a scene early in the novel in which Orlando himself is reading (the work of Sir Thomas Browne), the narrator facetiously apologizes to the reader for not saying more about Orlando's inner life. She explains why she leaves it to the reader's imagination:

> It is plain enough to those who have done a reader's part in making up from bare hints dropped here and there the whole boundary and circumference of a living person; can hear in what we only whisper a living voice; can see, often when we say nothing about it, exactly what he looked like, and know without a word to guide them precisely what he thought and felt and it is for readers such as these alone that we write.[9]

Woolf here models the constructive ability she describes an ideal reader as having: she herself builds step-by-step, through separate imaginative acts, a whole image, "a living person"—not Orlando, but an ideal reader. The breathless style, the exaggerated claims, become lyrical as the sentence culminates with the emphatic claim that "it is for readers such as these alone that we write." Woolf's repeated use of such high, at times mock-heroic rhetoric when discussing the creativity of the common reader has a slightly combative undertone, as if she is defending such readers against the academy's devaluation of them. (Her essay "How Should One Read a Book?" somewhat outlandishly ends with a vision of the Almighty on the Day of Judgment praising those who have loved reading, "not without a certain envy when he sees us coming with our books under our arms.") While Woolf proclaims (in the same essay) that a reader must have "great boldness of imagination if you are going to make use of all that the novelist—the great artist—gives you," the "great boldness" of her own writing works to promote a stance toward reading that she knew went against the literary establishment of the time.[10]

In emphasizing the reader's independence and creativity, Woolf is both responding to the literary culture of her own time and showing her orientation toward earlier literary eras. Carol Atherton, who has noted the remarkable "freedom which [Woolf] was prepared to grant the reader's imagination" interprets Woolf's "individualistic" model of reading and the reader persona Woolf often assumes in her literary critical writings within the institutional context of her time. Atherton argues that Woolf's emphatic validation of this outsider's mode of reading was an antiauthoritarian response to Oxbridge and all it represents and, specifically, to the consolidation of literary studies into an academic discipline. She describes Woolf's model of reading as belonging to an earlier, private sphere of aesthetic experience and having much in common "with a tradition of aesthetic criticism that stretches back to Pater in its resistance to academic norms."[11] That Woolf's version of literary reading looks backward should not be surprising, as we have become increasingly knowledge-able about Woolf's deep involvement with the Victorian past, despite her claims to reject it. The past two decades have brought significant acknowledgment of what Steve Ellis calls Woolf's "powerful nostalgia for various elements of Victorian culture," her "pervasive preoccupation with the relationship between Victorian and modern culture," which coexists with her formal experimentation.[12] In fact, Wolfgang Iser describes modern texts as simply making deliberate the process of "filling in the gaps left by the text itself," a process that he claims is "more or less unconscious" in reading so-called traditional texts.[13] Thus, while Woolf's descriptions of literary reading as "making up from bare hints dropped here and there" sound quintessentially modernist, they are also continuous with nineteenth-century writers who recognize the personal and imaginative nature of inevitably "filling in the gaps left by the text."

Woolf herself viewed reading practices as both historically determined and as having histories. Brenda Silver, who edited the publication of Woolf's last, unfinished essay, "The Reader," refers to a note in Woolf's diary for March 8, 1941, in which Woolf imagines this essay organized around different historical readers: "Suppose I selected one dominant figure in every age and wrote round and about." Silver suggests Woolf follows this plan in the unfinished essay, which begins with a specific person, Lady Anne Clifford, and "builds around her an image of the reader in the beginning of the 17th century." Known for making bold claims about the history of subjectivity (e.g., "on or about December 1910 human nature changed"), Woolf asserts in this essay that the reader, as a fixture in an author's mind, "comes into existence sometime at the end of the sixteenth century." This reader specifically first appears, she claims, in Burton's *The Anatomy of Melancholy*, "for it is there that we find the writer completely conscious of his relation with the reader."[14] For her Burton is the first writer to be aware that solitary reading is a new form of aesthetic experience, in which the solitary reader—unlike a spectator at a play—has the ability to stop, to go back, and to reflect independently on what is read:

> He can pause; he can ponder; he can compare; he can draw back from the page and see behind it a man sitting alone in the centre of the labyrinth of words in a college room thinking of suicide. He can gratify many different moods. He can read directly what is on the page, or, drawing aside, can read what is not written. There is a long drawn continuity in the book that the play has not. It gives a different pace to the mind. We are in a world where nothing is concluded.[15]

These are, hauntingly, the last words of the essay, which was still in fragments when Woolf died by suicide. The passage, however, is not despairing but emphasizes limitless possibility, with its list of the multiple mental acts the reader can perform, the "many" moods in which he can read, and the unboundedness of reading "directly what is on the page, or, drawing aside" to read "what is not written." The short clauses piled on top of one another convey a mind darting from one possibility to another, exercising a newfound mental freedom and inspiration that comes into being through reading.

One key difference between Woolf and her Victorian predecessors is that she portrays the reader's imagination as free to indulge without bounds. Woolf's appreciation of the psychological theories that had emerged by her time are evident in her portrayal of imagination as belonging to an only partly conscious mind. Kate Flint says it can be "hard to tell where, for Woolf, intelligent reading stops and day-dreaming, or the exercise of the imagination, takes over."[16] In "How Should One Read a Book?" Woolf says explicitly that the aim of reading can be "to refresh and exercise our own creative powers," and models step-by-step a reader turning from a book to daydream. The bucolic landscape in the passage seems to belong in a nineteenth-century realist novel, not a modernist stream of consciousness:

> Is there not an open window on the right hand of the bookcase? How delightful to stop reading and look out! How stimulating the scene is, in its unconsciousness, its irrelevance, its perpetual movement—the colts galloping round the field, *the woman filling her pail at the well*, the donkey throwing back his head and emitting his long, acrid moan. The greater part of any library is nothing but the record of such fleeting moments in the lives of men, women, and donkeys. . . . None of this has any value; it is negligible in the extreme; yet how absorbing it is now and again to go through the rubbishheaps and find rings and scissors and *broken noses buried in the huge past* and try to piece them together while the colt gallops round the field, the woman fills her pail at the well, and the donkey brays.[17]

Whether consciously or not, Woolf echoes George Eliot's manifesto about realistic representation in *Adam Bede*. Woolf imagines looking out to an everyday rural scene in which a woman fills a pail at the well and then turning back to the library where she finds "broken noses buried in the huge past." Eliot describes an old woman scraping carrots and writes of a world of ordinary neighbors, in which one "can neither straighten their noses, nor brighten their wit" (222). Indeed, the reader looking out the window at life could be

Dorothea Brooke in her boudoir, looking out after a night of private suffering and seeing figures moving in a field and feeling "the largeness of the world" (846). But where Eliot's scenes solicit sympathy for others outside of one's self, outside the window, Woolf focuses on the reader's own pleasure: it is "absorbing" and "delightful" to piece together and construct stories out of what one either sees or reads, stories that dissolve the separation between inside and outside the window, between the world and the book. Her scene differs from Eliot's in being comic rather than morally instructive, for Woolfian reading is ultimately, proudly, about oneself, not about sympathizing with others. She writes, "We may stress the value of sympathy; we may try to sink our identity as we read. But we know that we cannot sympathise wholly or immerse ourselves wholly; there is always a demon in us who whispers, 'I hate, I love,' and we cannot silence him."[18] For Victorian critics, remaining aware of how a work stimulates one's own self-awareness, and not becoming wholly immersed in identification with a fictional character, could be an analytical, artistically sensitive mode of reading literature. Overidentification, too completely "sink[ing] our identity as we read," was the problem Victorian literary commentators associated with allegedly mindless readers of popular fiction, not the assertion of subjectivity.[19] Woolf's full embrace of this imaginative, subjective mode of reading in which "I hate, I love" models how to take seriously reading practices that have long been valued outside the academy and have recently taken deeper root within its classrooms.

A Prehistory of Relatability

Disowning or devaluing the individual reader's experience because of its variable subjectivity, affect, and imagination has remained the normative perspective of literary studies for a century. Victorian studies especially spent many years, beginning in the 1980s, dominated by a Foucauldian logic that denied the potential for novels to stimulate individual imagining. However, as our critical influences have shifted, the common reader's stock has risen. Rachel Sagner Buurma and Laura Heffernan note how the practices of a naive, surface-oriented "common" reader have become "mascot, muse, or model for critics who have become impatient with what they see as the routinized protocols of professional reading in English."[20] Buurma and Heffernan have been questioning how the history of the discipline continues to be told as a succession of marquee critics at elite universities, excluding other ways that literature is experienced even within academia—such as in the classroom, where they note common reading practices have thrived.[21] Their focus, however, is on the teacher-scholar in the early to mid-twentieth century. There is work yet to be done toward taking seriously the reading practices of twenty-first-century students, who have their own role to play in the discipline. Doing so enables us to see today's students as part of a long tradition of readers who may appear idle but in fact make us aware of how wide a range of seemingly unlikely reading practices may engage with and enhance a reader's appreciation of literary artistry.

As we know, critics have been separating and labeling reading practices as belonging to different audiences since at least the Victorian period, repeating social hierarchies as they do so. Recent scholarship about the discipline of literary studies has continued to distinguish hierarchically between critical, professional, objective readers and uncritical, amateurish, subjective readers. In fact, these differences have been reinforced by efforts to distinguish different modes of interpretation based on how much objectivity they achieve.[22] Thus, when Michael Warner uses the term "uncritical" to describe students' reading, he is suggesting their reading is different not just in degree but in kind from the professional critic's practice. His use of "uncritical" also confirms that we only have negations, and not a nuanced critical vocabulary, with which to talk about how students read "in all the ways they aren't supposed to."[23] Although "the self-conception of the discipline seems perversely antagonistic to all the ways our students actually read," he notes, "it has worked quite well—at least throughout the twentieth century—to legitimate the profession."[24] Buurma and Heffernan similarly describe the twenty-first-century common reader as "defined largely by her undisciplinary and undisciplined reading practices."[25] Yet the ways students "actually" read belong to our discipline's orbit too.

The term students are known for using to describe their relationship to literature, "relatable," is often seen as an idle way to fill a space that could otherwise be used for critical exertion. Full disclosure: I detested the word "relatable" until I realized that I was writing a prehistory of it as a popular reading practice. Laura Salisbury describes the contemporary meaning of "relatable" as "a short-cut in critical thinking that privileges a strong, undefined feeling of relation in the present over the reflective, temporally extended close work that criticism understands texts to be inviting and yielding."[26] Salisbury sees relatability as a vague, "undefined feeling" incompatible with, and winning out "over," literary critical practice. Although the rise of the term in classroom discussion is fairly new, a historical perspective shows us that readers of fiction, in particular, have long been criticized for their seeming lack of mental effort. In a *New Yorker* article from 2014, "The Scourge of Relatability," Rebecca Mead describes, from a lay perspective, how the word reflects a "circumscribed" aesthetic experience: "To reject any work because we feel that it does not reflect us in a shape that we can easily recognize—because it does not exempt us from the active exercise of imagination or the effortful summoning of empathy—is our own failure. It's a failure that has been dispiritingly sanctioned by the rise of 'relatable.'"[27] What Mead calls out is not just the solipsism that relatability is often charged with but the laziness of it: she suggests that students are drawn to what is familiar because this makes for an easier, more comfortable aesthetic experience. As we know, novelists have been pushing back against readers choosing comfort since at least the early nineteenth century. The dynamic of readers seeking ease and realist authors finding ways to create an uncomfortable, even painful reading experience has a long history in the novel genre. From a student's perspective, what we have missed about reading for relatability is how such a personalized approach to literature, which consists of identifying unique connections and forming bridges between one's own experiences and fictional ones, highlights students' active mental agency rather than the passivity imposed on and ascribed to today's screened-out students.

Some academic critics have been showing how relatability can be a pedagogical tool for highlighting the relationality intrinsic to reading literature. Though the object of analysis may shift from the work itself to its effect on the student's mind, finding relatability can be a means of paying close attention, of close reading. Brian Glavey describes a classroom experience of students finding a Frank O'Hara poem relatable and worrying that they were "not directed toward a reading of the details of the Coke poem, mobilizing instead a generalizable mood that the poem makes available."[28] Glavey moves beyond this original disappointment, past judging relatability as a facile aesthetic response dominated by generality and the projection of normativity, to understanding how this response leads the way to seeing relatability, relationality, and sociability as connected and at the heart of O'Hara's poetics. Arguing for the pedagogical value of choosing to teach books based on their relatability, rather than their representativeness, Stefanie Stiles suggests that students' "relatability approach" has much in common with other popular scholarly approaches. Affect theory and cognitive science–based approaches to literature also "share an interest in what works *do*, how they are processed as information and understood by human beings in various social contexts, not reaching some objective consensus on what works *are*."[29]

This was, in fact, one of I. A. Richards's innovations: to be interested in the psychology of poetry reading. In *Practical Criticism* he writes:

The personal situation of the reader inevitably (and within limits rightly) affects his reading, and many more are drawn to poetry in quest of some reflection of their latest emotional crisis than would admit it. . . . Though it has been fashionable—in deference to sundry confused doctrines of "pure art" and "impersonal aesthetic emotions"—to deplore such a state of affairs, there is really no occasion. For a comparison of the feelings active in a poem with some personal feeling *still* present in the reader's lively recollection does give a standard, a test for reality. The dangers are that the recollected feelings may overwhelm and distort the poem. . . . It exists perhaps to control and order such feelings and *to bring them into relation with other things*, not merely to arouse them.[30]

Richards's frank, colloquial style of writing reminds me of D. A. Miller acknowledging "the open secret everyone knows and no one wants to: the immense amount of daydreaming that accompanies the ordinary reading of a novel," with which this book began. Richards, too, acknowledges the "inevitabl[e]" presence of the personal, which is "still" present despite the critic's efforts to denounce and suppress it, for the personal has a serious role to play in literary critique: instigating new relations with what is outside the self. That goal is not so different from George Eliot's aim for readers of her novels to develop new sympathy for their fellow mortals. What Richards, like Eliot, condemns is easy, ready-made, or stock responses (part of the title of his chapter on "Irrelevant Associations and Stock Responses"), the ease of responding with "just what we happen to have already in our minds": "Even the best poetry, if we read into it just what we happen to have already in our minds, and do not use it as a means for reorganizing ourselves, does less good than harm."[31] In suggesting how the ever-present reader's subjectivity may be put to the productive use of understanding a work of literature at an artistic level, Richards seems to echo both earlier Victorian critics and his contemporary, Woolf. As we have seen Woolf write, "We may stress the value of sympathy; we may try to sink our identity as we read. But we know that we cannot sympathise wholly or immerse ourselves wholly; there is always a demon in us who whispers, 'I hate, I love,' and we cannot silence him." The novel reader's independent imagination has long been demonized, but, hiding in plain sight, has also been a significant tradition of writers who recognize and reckon with the inevitable presence of another imagination.

NOTES

Introduction: Imagining Readers

1. D. A. Miller, *Novel and the Police*, 215.

2. Barthes, "Writing Reading," 29; and Stevenson, "Gossip on Romance," 142.

3. Woolf, *Orlando*, 73.

4. Eliot, *Middlemarch*, 510. All subsequent references are cited by page number in the text.

5. Eliot, *Adam Bede*, 221–22. All subsequent references are cited by page number in the text.

6. On how readers also establish identificatory relationships with novels, see Laura Green, *Literary Identification*; Maria Palacios Knox, *Victorian Women and Wayward Reading*; and Rita Felski, "Identifying with Characters."

7. In *Novel Relations*, Alicia Mireles Christoff challenges the presumed self-containment of Victorian fiction and the field's "firm divides between characters, narrators, readers, and authors rather than theorizing their interrelation" (2). She likens novel reading to the psychoanalyst W. R. Bion's concept of O, "the powerful but ineffable reality of the in-the-moment meeting of two (or more) people" (5).

8. Dickens, *Little Dorrit*, 250. All subsequent references are cited by page number in the text.

9. Timothy Gao shows how, in the late eighteenth and early nineteenth centuries, observers and biographers began to recognize in children's play "a specific activity with an imaginative or psychological component . . . alternatively described through the idioms of daydream, invention, make-believe, or castle-building." While he argues compellingly that this "virtualising capacity" develops concurrently with the novel form, his focus is on how nineteenth-century novels model the imaginative practice of constructing "artificial realities," as opposed to how readers' imaginative play contributes to an authored construction (*Virtual Play*, 15–16).

10. Coleridge, *Biographia Literaria*, 48.

11. See Kate Flint, *The Woman Reader*; Richard de Ritter, *Imagining Women Readers*; Joe Bray, *Female Reader in the English Novel*; and Christina Lupton, *Knowing Books*.

12. Q. D. Leavis, *Fiction and the Reading Public*, 164.

13. Of the numerous histories of the discipline, I am particularly indebted to Deidre Lynch, *Loving Literature*; Carol Atherton, *Defining Literary Criticism*; and Gerald Graff, *Professing Literature*.

14. Marcus and Best, "Surface Reading," 17.

15. Stewart, *Dear Reader*, 21.

16. For instance, Elaine Auyoung's *When Fiction Feels Real* employs research on reading and cognition to show how nineteenth-century realist authors use particular narrative techniques

in order to enhance their novels' verisimilitude in the reader's mind. See also Andrew Elfenbein, *Gist of Reading*; Kay Young, *Imagining Minds*; and Lisa Zunshine, *Why We Read Fiction*.

17. Nicholas Dames, John Plotz, Leah Price, Stephen Arata, and Elisha Cohn have shown in varied ways how Victorians understood novel reading as involving gradations and fluctuations between absorption and detachment. See Dames, *Physiology of the Novel*; Plotz, *Semi-Detached*; Price, *How to Do Things with Books*; Cohn, *Still Life*; and Arata, "On Not Paying Attention." Natalie Phillips similarly discusses eighteenth-century novelists who were drawn to think about the reader's distractible mind in *Distraction: Problems of Attention*.

18. Jackson, *Romantic Readers*, 251.

19. Nicholas Abercrombie and Brian Longhurst discuss a relatively fluid continuum from consumer to "petty producer." They note that consumers "are involved in textual production through talk, which can often create alternative texts, even if these are fleeting and not written down." "Fans and Enthusiasts," 171.

20. George Henry Lewes to George Eliot, January 1872, in *George Eliot Letters*, vol. 5, 243.

21. Plotz, "No Future?," 25. More than establishing a genre, Barthes posits that this "trajectory of choices and alternatives which gives narration the appearance of a huge traffic-control center, furnished with a referential (and not merely discursive) temporality" helps to impart the "reality effect" to narrative. "Reality Effect," 143.

22. Catherine Gallagher's *Telling It Like It Wasn't* focuses on how alternate history narratives, which proliferated in the late twentieth century, use counterfactual thinking to unsettle the "inert givenness" of the actual world and make comparative judgments about its justice (15).

23. Andrew Miller, *Burdens of Perfection* and *On Not Being Someone Else*.

24. For example, Michael Tondre has shown how new models of mathematical probability influenced Victorian novelists to think about "alternatives to the actual"—alternate lives, narratives, and plots—that offer valuable possibilities other than Victorian "norms." *Physics of Possibility*, 2. See also Tina Choi, *Victorian Contingencies* and "Natural History's Hypothetical Moments"; Carra Glatt, *Narrative and Its Nonevents*; James Buzard, "Item of Mortality"; and Jonathan Farina, "'Dickens's As If.'"

25. See, for example, Warhol, "'What Might Have Been Is Not What Is.'"

26. On novelists' use of perceptual cues, see Auyoung, *When Fiction Feels Real*.

27. Jenkins, "Textual Poachers," 26.

28. Knox is a notable exception in arguing that, contrary to prevailing rhetoric about passive or quixotic reading habits, "both fictional and real Victorian women readers exercised identification as a flexible capacity," one that "could and did unite women in imaginative affiliations that they translated into creative, political, and professional action." *Victorian Women and Wayward Reading*, 3–4.

29. See, especially, Kelly Mays, "The Disease of Reading and Victorian Periodicals."

30. See Linda Hughes and Michael Lund, *The Victorian Serial*.

31. Patrick Brantlinger has shown how anxieties about the emergence of a mass audience and the free circulation of novels across social boundaries (literally free, with the growth of public libraries) can be detected in several genres of fiction written for a middle-class readership. *Reading Lesson*, 193.

32. Duncan, *Scott's Shadow*, 29 (my emphasis). In addition, Michel de Certeau has described how the vast expansion of the reading public and printed material in the mid-nineteenth century made this period rife for a de-authorized, democratized approach to reading, in which "[t]he

reader takes neither the position of the author nor an author's position. He invents in texts something different from what they 'intended.'" *Practice of Everyday Life*, 169.

33. As Guinevere Griest puts it, "'Mudie' meant fiction, or more specifically, novels." *Mudie's Circulating Library*, 37.

34. Mudie's advertisement, *The Reader*, July 30, 1864.

35. As Caroline Levine has argued in *The Serious Pleasures of Suspense*, realist authors trained readers to fill these pauses with speculations, rather than conclusions, to suspend judgment and develop skeptical habits of mind that they carried back into their lives.

36. Trollope, "On English Prose Fiction," 108 (my emphasis).

37. Lynch, *Loving Literature*, 8. See also Andrew Piper, *Dreaming in Books*.

38. Alexander Main to George Eliot, September 29, 1872, in *Letters from Alexander Main*.

39. George Eliot to Mrs. Bray, December 22, 1873, in *George Eliot Letters*, vol. 5, 471.

40. Thomas Hardy, "The Profitable Reading of Fiction," 279.

41. Stevenson, "Gossip on Romance," 142.

42. [Cleghorn?,] "Writings of Charles Dickens," 190.

43. "British Novelists," 21.

44. Collins, "Unknown Public," 222.

45. "Recent Works of Fiction," 87.

46. For further discussion, see Gettelman, "'Those Who Idle Over Novels.' "

47. This phenomenon is both related to and distinct from Audrey Jaffe's insight that "realist ideology and individual fantasy have to overlap in order for realist dreams to come true." Jaffe highlights conventions that structure "the individual fantasies, dreams, and daydreams of the novel's characters" rather than the extratextual daydreams of novel readers. *Victorian Novel Dreams of the Real*, 5.

48. As George Levine has suggested, realist fiction is defined by its "attempt to use language to get beyond language, to discover some nonverbal truth out there." *Realistic Imagination*, 6.

49. Eliot, "Natural History of German Life," 54.

50. Woolf, *Orlando*, 73.

51. In 2009 the *Oxford English Dictionary* added a new definition of "relatable" as that "with which one can identify or empathize." Rebecca Mead defines the contemporary use of relatable as "describ[ing] a character or a situation in which an ordinary person might see himself reflected." "Scourge of 'Relatability.'"

Chapter 1. Jane Austen's Other Endings

1. Austen, *Sense and Sensibility*, 379. All subsequent references are cited by page number in the text.

2. Tondre examines how alternate lives, narratives, and plots within Victorian fiction point toward the cultural influence of new models of mathematical probability. See also Carra Glatt, *Narrative and Its Nonevents*.

3. Morson, *Narrative and Freedom*, 117–18.

4. Austen, *Emma*, 431. All subsequent references are cited by page number in the text.

5. Austen's knowledge of and engagement with the contemporary culture of "fashionable" novels is well known. See Barbara Benedict, "Sensibility by the Numbers"; Marilyn Butler, *Jane Austen*; and Olivia Murphy, *Jane Austen the Reader*.

6. Spacks, *Privacy*, 10.

7. Richter, "Reception of the Gothic Novel," 123.

8. St Clair, *Reading Nation*, 284. Novel reading became so tied to eroticism that, as William Warner argues, language suggesting that an eroticized play of mind results from reading fiction can be found even within novels that defend the genre, such as Eliza Haywood's *Love in Excess*. Warner, *Licensing Entertainment*, 116.

9. Du Bose, *Accomplish'd Woman* (1753), 17, quoted in Brown, "Novel Instruction," 31.

10. St Clair, *Reading Nation*, 283. St Clair cites the work of Hannah More as well as an advice book by Emma Parker, *Important Trifles: Chiefly Appropriate to Females on their Entrance into Society* (1817), as examples.

11. Flint makes a similar argument about nineteenth-century women readers of sensation fiction in *The Woman Reader*, 274–93.

12. Warner, *Licensing Entertainment*, 145.

13. Ibid., 126

14. Samuel Johnson, *Rambler*, no. 4; also quoted in Poovey, *Proper Lady and the Woman Writer*, 182.

15. Klancher, *Making of English Reading Audiences*, 33 (emphasis in original).

16. Lynch, *Loving Literature*, 183; 12.

17. Galperin, "Austen's Earliest Readers," 103. Galperin claims that "the irresistible similitude of Austen's representations" and the "absence of any specific judgment or position to which her representations apparently lead" encouraged in Austen's earliest readers a sense of "independen[ce] of narrative authority" (108).

18. [Whately,] Review, 89–90.

19. Johnson, *Rambler*, no. 4.

20. Hunter, *Before Novels*, 91.

21. Phillips, *Distraction: Problems of Attention*.

22. Lupton, "Contingency, Codex, and the Eighteenth-Century Novel," 1175.

23. Piper, *Dreaming in Books*.

24. Lynch, *Economy of Character*, 126; 213.

25. Jackson, *Marginalia*, 297.

26. Piper, *Dreaming*, 3.

27. Wordsworth, *Lyrical Ballads*, 46.

28. Perkins, "Romantic Reading as Revery," 184; 191.

29. [Whately,] Review, 88.

30. [Scott,] *Emma*, 63.

31. Piper, *Dreaming*, 3; and [Scott,] *Emma*, 60.

32. Brooks, *Reading for the Plot*, 19.

33. [Scott,] *Emma*, 63.

34. A Google Ngram graph shows a sharp spike in usage of the phrase "pleasure reading" between 1920 and 1930. https://books.google.com/ngrams/graph?content=pleasure+reading&year_start=1800&year_end=2000&corpus=15&smoothing=3&share=&direct_url=t1%3B%2Cpleasure%20reading%3B%2Cc0.

35. Some of the richest recent work on Austen has focused on the reception history of her novels, including Deidre Lynch, *Janeites*; Claudia Johnson, *Jane Austen's Cults and Cultures*; Devoney Looser, *Making of Jane Austen*; and Katie Halsey, *Jane Austen and Her Readers*.

36. Spacks, *Privacy*, 30.

37. Pinch, *Strange Fits of Passion*, 139.

38. Halsey, *Jane Austen and Her Readers*, 95.

39. *Jane Austen's Letters*, 343.

40. Lynch, *Loving Literature*, 186.

41. Austen-Leigh, *Memoir of Jane Austen*, 376.

42. Halsey, *Jane Austen and Her Readers*, 28; 38.

43. Simons, "Jane Austen and Popular Culture," 472.

44. Beer, *Romance*, 1.

45. Southam, *Jane Austen's Literary Manuscripts*, 85; 81.

46. *Jane Austen's Letters*, 289.

47. Austen, *Northanger Abbey*, 232.

48. Austen treats conventions of popular literature playfully: Marilyn Butler has shown how she observes but also subtly rewrites conventions she would have known from her reading of popular stage comedies and fiction written in the 1780s and 1790s. *Jane Austen*, 33. See also Jan Fergus's *Jane Austen and the Didactic Novel* for her discussion of how Austen's first three novels "exploit and expose" literary conventions (39).

49. Jane Austen's Fiction Manuscripts, online at https://janeausten.ac.uk/edition/ms/OpinionsHeadNote.html.

50. Brodie, "Jane Austen and the Common Reader," 55–56.

51. "Opinions of *Mansfield Park* and *Emma*," 436. All subsequent references are cited by page number in the text.

52. Milbanke wrote this to her mother on May 1, 1813. Malcolm Elwin, *Lord Byron's Wife* (1962), 159, quoted in Southam, *Jane Austen: The Critical Heritage*, 8 (emphasis in original).

53. *Jane Austen's Letters*, 301.

54. Gallagher, "Rise of Fictionality," 341–42.

55. Review of *Life and Adventures*, 109.

56. [Lewes,] "Novels of Jane Austen," 155.

57. George Henry Lewes, Journal, February 9, 1859, quoted in Haight, *George Eliot: A Biography*, 273.

58. Letter, December 20, 1814, *Life of Mary Russell Mitford*, edited by A. G. L'Estrange (1870), quoted in Southam, *Jane Austen: The Critical Heritage*, 54.

59. Kreisel, "Where Does the Pleasure Come From?," 221.

60. Austen, *Mansfield Park*, 470. All subsequent references are cited by page number in the text.

61. Lupton, "Contingency," 1177.

62. See Andrew Miller, *Burdens of Perfection*.

63. Brooks, *Reading for the Plot*, 29; 23.

64. Jesse Molesworth has suggested that the former type of reader was served by the many eighteenth-century novels with single-character plot lines. Though several eighteenth-century novelists were moving away from the unitary, "dialectical narrative of simple causes," we as readers of a novel like *Roxana* "experience discomfort, perhaps even dread, . . . in witnessing the Newtonian universe of reversible causes and effects crumble into a universe of irreversibility and chance mutation—a transition from homogeny to abundance." "'A Dreadful Course of Calamities,'" 505.

65. Austen, *Persuasion*, 100. All subsequent references are cited by page number in the text.

66. Gallagher, "Telling It Like It Wasn't," 17.

67. Jane Austen to Cassandra Austen, March 5, 1814 (her emphasis), in Southam, *Jane Austen: The Critical Heritage*, 52.

68. Park Honan, *Jane Austen: Her Life* (1987), 343, quoted in Yeazell, *Fictions of Modesty*, 143.

69. Austen, *Pride and Prejudice*, 245; 373.

70. Peter Graham, noting that readers commonly resist and resent Fanny's ultimate marriage to Edmund, suggests they are responding to how persistently the novel entertains the prospect of Fanny and Edmund each marrying one of the Crawfords. See "Falling for the Crawfords," 867–91.

71. Yeazell, *Fictions of Modesty*, 155.

72. See Halsey, *Jane Austen and Her Readers*.

73. Rozema, *Mansfield Park*.

74. Gallagher, "Telling It Like It Wasn't," 12.

75. Galperin, *History of Missed Opportunities*, 76.

76. Austen, *Northanger Abbey*, 77.

77. Trollope, *Autobiography*, 220.

78. See Mary Favret, *War at a Distance*; and Emily Rohrbach, *Modernity's Mist*.

79. Greiner, "Art of Knowing Your Own Nothingness," 906.

80. *Jane Austen's Letters*, 291

81. Ibid., 292.

82. Tanner, *Jane Austen*, 211.

83. See chapter 4 of Rohrbach, *Modernity's Mist*.

84. D. A. Miller, *Jane Austen, or The Secret of Style*, 56; Deresciewicz, *Jane Austen and the Romantic Poets*, 128. As Favret argues, some of this discomfiture was not only personal: Austen was, after all, writing at a historical moment when "what is daily taking place all around *Persuasion*, prior to 1814 and afterward, is not at all peaceful." *War at a Distance*, 162–63.

85. Favret, *War at a Distance*, 163; 170–71.

86. Maria Edgeworth to Mrs. Ruxton, February 21, 1818, quoted in Southam, *Jane Austen: The Critical Heritage*, 17.

87. Claudia Johnson, *Jane Austen's Cults and Cultures*, 22–23. Pinch also describes the sensory nature of the way the outside world is present to the characters in the novel—often through noise, as well as how the renewed courtship between Anne and Wentworth "takes place through physical contact." *Strange Fits of Passion*, 149; 153.

88. Lynch, *Economy of Character*, 218.

89. Rohrbach notes that Anne's and Wentworth's nonlinguistic ways of communicating has been interpreted numerous times, beginning with Alistair Duckworth. *Modernity's Mist*, 117.

90. Rohrbach similarly notices Austen's "mixing the moment of triumph with the anticipatory sadness of its eventual loss or lessening" in the novel. Ibid., 115.

91. Deresciewicz, *Jane Austen and the Romantic Poets*, 35; 81; 39.

92. Wordsworth, *Lyrical Ballads*, 106.

93. Francis O'Gorman talks about the "cauterized possibilities," the alternative outcomes that Eliot makes present in *The Mill on the Floss*, so that she "presses her reader to imagine it as different." "'A Long Deep Sob,'" 260–61.

94. Eliot, *Mill on the Floss*, 490.

95. Review of *Mill on the Floss*, 119.

96. George Eliot to John Blackwood, July 9, 1860, in *George Eliot Letters*, vol. 3, 317–18.

Chapter 2. *Little Dorrit's* Complaint

1. Dickens, *Bleak House*, 256. All subsequent references are cited by page number in the text.

2. John Butt and Kathleen Tillotson note how even Dickens's working notes "show the measure of control which Dickens exercised" in each serial number. *Dickens at Work*, 33–34. On his control over the serial form, see also Nicola Bradbury, "Dickens and the Form of the Novel," 152–66. On Dickens's relationship with the reading public, see Malcolm Andrews, *Charles Dickens and His Performing Selves* and Collins, *Public Readings*.

3. Andrew Miller, "'A Case of Metaphysics,'" 791.

4. Forster, *Life of Charles Dickens*, vol. 2, 182. Victorian reviewer Mowbray Morris wrote in an 1882 *Fortnightly Review* article of "an imagination of such astonishing fertility . . . not to be surpassed outside the works of Shakespeare" ("Charles Dickens," 603); Barbara Hardy's 2008 monograph *Dickens and Creativity* takes as its subject his "teeming imagination and energy" (17). Garrett Stewart also offers an explanation in *Dickens and the Trials of Imagination* of why Dickens is so often compared to Shakespeare: his novels are not only driven by, but take as their subject, "the energies of an adventurous and versatile imagination" (xv).

5. Measuring the sizes of his various audiences, Dickens writes in the preface to *Little Dorrit*: "In the Preface to *Bleak House* I remarked that I had never had so many readers. In the Preface to its next successor, *Little Dorrit*, I have still to repeat the same words" (6). Some critics, such as Carolyn W. de la L. Oulton, see his claims of an emotional connection with his readers as couched in individualized terms. But this connection is imagined as happening in unison with "so many readers" at once (as he says in the preface to *Little Dorrit*).

6. Sarah Winter's work on the psychology of reading Dickens identifies reading as an experience of collective imagination, memory, and consciousness. See *Pleasures of Memory*.

7. Helen Small suggests that Dickens's reading tours brought what was otherwise an abstraction of the reading public together into a concrete public body, so that, "normally an invisible constituency, on these occasions the fiction reading public was to a significant degree made visible to itself as a collectivity." "A Pulse of 124," 266.

8. See Tyson Stolte, *Dickens and Victorian Psychology*.

9. Forster, *Life of Charles Dickens*, vol. 1, 97.

10. The first English edition to feature Doré's illustrations was *The History of Don Quixote*. Thanks to Leah Price for pointing out this engraving.

11. Dickens, *David Copperfield*, 66. All subsequent references are cited by page number in the text.

12. Louise Henson argues that for Dickens, "the ghost story was an important focus of inquiry into the mysteries of the mind." "'In the Natural Course of Physical Things,'" 115.

13. Lewes, "Dickens in Relation to Criticism," 152.

14. Dickens's fiction has been read as innovative in understanding how the mind functions at an unconscious level. Catherine Bernard and Jill Matus both note respectively that in his perceptions about dreams and how trauma affects the mind, he comes to similar conclusions as Freud,

whom he predates. See Bernard, "Dickens and Victorian Dream Theory"; and Matus, "Trauma, Memory, and Railway Disaster." On Dickens and less conscious states of mind, see also Kaplan, *Dickens and Mesmerism*; and Winter, *Mesmerized: Powers of Mind*, especially 320–31.

15. Athena Vrettos, discussing Dickens's use of habit "as a mode of characterization," argues for his respect for "the overwhelming power of habit to shape both body and mind." "Dickens and the Psychology of Repetition," 419; 410.

16. Dames, *Amnesiac Selves*, 139. See also Rick Rylance, *Victorian Psychology and British Culture*.

17. Dames, *Amnesiac Selves*, 139.

18. John Stuart Mill, *Autobiography*, 123.

19. Rylance, *Victorian Psychology and British Culture*, 55.

20. Dickens, "A Preliminary Word."

21. Harry Stone describes how, for Dickens, fairy stories and fantasy did the "beneficent work of nurturing man's birthright of feeling and fancy." *Dickens and the Invisible World*, 4–5.

22. Dickens, *Hard Times*, 89.

23. Ibid., 90.

24. In *A Tale of Two Cities* (1859), Dr. Manette is first seen absorbed in his similarly compulsive shoemaking, whose tools, Mr. Lorry later suggests, are a "reminder of his sufferings" in prison. Though he does not return, aloud, to his experience in prison, Miss Pross and Mr. Lorry discuss the likelihood that "he thinks of it much." Dickens, *A Tale of Two Cities*, 79; 82.

25. Matus has noted elsewhere in Dickens's fiction his apprehension of "the hallmark of trauma . . . unbidden repetition and return." "Trauma, Memory, and Railway Disaster," 429.

26. Forster, *Life of Charles Dickens*, vol. 1, 23.

27. Dickens, "Discovery of a Treasure Near Cheapside," 448; 443.

28. Review of *Our Mutual Friend*, 455.

29. Forster, *Life of Charles Dickens*, vol. 2, 126.

30. Forster, *Life of Charles Dickens*, vol. 1, 295; 274.

31. Forster, *Life of Charles Dickens*, vol. 2, 189; 422.

32. Review of *Little Dorrit*, 364. [Bagehot,] "Charles Dickens," 391.

33. Forster, *Life of Charles Dickens*, vol. 2, 182. Forster, *Life of Charles Dickens*, vol. 1, 111.

34. Charles Dickens to Leigh Hunt, May 4, 1855, in *Letters of Charles Dickens*, vol. 7, 608.

35. Kaplan, *Dickens: A Biography*, 335.

36. Forster, *Life of Charles Dickens*, vol. 1, 382.

37. Quoted in Kaplan, *Dickens: A Biography*, 340–41.

38. Forster, *Life of Charles Dickens*, vol. 2, 194.

39. *Letters of Charles Dickens*, vol. 7, 135.

40. Forster, *Life of Charles Dickens*, vol. 2, 20–21.

41. Forster, *Life of Charles Dickens*, vol. 1, 295–96.

42. Forster, *Life of Charles Dickens*, vol. 2, 31.

43. Levine, *Serious Pleasures of Suspense*, 9. In writing about the word "seriality" for a special issue about keywords in Victorian studies, Lauren Goodlad uses affirming language to describe "communities" "sharing" during serial publication, as "the sync between narrative time and the lived time of audiences which they accentuate, invites communities of conversation around shared temporal, affective, and aesthetic experience." "Seriality," 871.

44. Eliot, *Daniel Deronda*, 621. All subsequent references are cited by page number in the text.

45. Garrett, *Victorian Multiplot Novel*, 2. Garrett underscores the negative nature of the reader's experience: "To multiply plots is to *divide* the fictional world, to *disrupt* the continuity of each line in order to shift from one to the other, to *disperse* the reader's attention" (ibid.; my emphases).

46. Dickens, *Pickwick Papers*, 722; xxxiv. These comments, quoted from the 1837 preface, are reiterated in the preface to the cheap edition published in 1847.

47. Forster, *Life of Charles Dickens*, vol. 2, 114 (my emphasis).

48. As one Victorian reviewer wrote of *Our Mutual Friend*, "The chief characters even of his earliest books dwell in the mind with extraordinary tenacity, sometimes quite apart from the plot wherein they figure, which may be utterly forgotten" (455). George Orwell's well-known assessment is more caustic: "At any moment some scene or character, which may come from some book you cannot even remember the name of, is liable to drop into your mind. . . . Dickens is obviously a writer whose parts are greater than his wholes. He is all fragments, all details— rotten architecture, but wonderful gargoyles." See Orwell, "Charles Dickens."

49. Butt and Tillotson, *Dickens at Work*, 16; Ford, *Dickens and His Readers*, 50.

50. Ford describes the main development in Dickens's art over time as "an increasingly contrived suspense" and an "increased concern with plot," both as a means of "attempting to unify his novels." Ford claims that in Dickens's letters and prefaces, "the two aspects of fiction most often discussed by him are probability and unity," the two areas for which he was also most criticized. *Dickens and His Readers*, 122–23.

51. Dickens, *Our Mutual Friend*, 798.

52. Review of *Bleak House*, *Bentley's Miscellany*, 288.

53. Ibid., 289.

54. [Brimley,] Review of *Bleak House*, 283.

55. Hughes and Lund, *Victorian Serial*, 8.

56. Review of *Our Mutual Friend*, 456 (my emphasis). Dickens's reviewers complain that a meaningful story never does emerge, or does so hastily, in "a slurring over of required explanations." Review of *Bleak House*, *Bentley's Miscellany*, 288.

57. Bradbury, "Form of the Novel," 164. Dickens, *Our Mutual Friend*, 798.

58. Dickens, *Our Mutual Friend*, 798.

59. Plotz, *Semi-Detached*, 46–47.

60. Forster, *Life of Charles Dickens*, vol. 1, 289 (emphasis in original).

61. Oulton, *Dickens and the Myth of the Reader*, 176.

62. Grossman, *Charles Dickens's Networks*, online edition, https://doi.org/10.1093/acprof:osobl/9780199682164.003.0003.

63. Garrett, *Victorian Multi-Plot Novel*, 45.

64. Ibid., 74–75.

65. Brooks, *Reading for the Plot*, 141.

66. Charles Dickens to John Forster, August 19, 1855, in *Letters*, vol. 7, 692–93.

67. Hilary Schor writes that "in *Little Dorrit* fantasy seems dangerous, story-telling either pathetic compensation or lethal self-delusion." Except for Amy it is two-sided: "story-telling is part of maintaining the fiction of a family . . . but it is also part of envisioning a place for herself in society." "Novels of the 1850s," 70–71.

68. Brooks, *Reading for the Plot*, 125.

69. Garrett, *Victorian Multi-Plot Novel*, 59–60; 49.

70. J. Hillis Miller, "Introduction."

71. Anderson, "Thinking with Character," 166.

72. Cohn, *Still Life*.

Chapter 3. Reading Ahead in *Adam Bede*

1. *George Eliot Letters*, vol. 3, 17.

2. Haight, *Selections from George Eliot's Letters*, 204.

3. David Kurnick makes a related argument about *Romola*, suggesting that Eliot portrays reading in the novel as a state of dreamy detachment and Romola herself as a distanced, distracted reader of her own life. See "Abstraction and the Subject of Novel Reading," 490–96.

4. Letter quoted in Martin, *George Eliot's Serial Fiction*, 235 (my emphasis).

5. See Sally Shuttleworth, *George Eliot and Nineteenth-Century Science*; Shuttleworth, "Fairy Tale or Science?"; Betty Kusher, "Dreams, Reveries, and the Continuity of Consciousness"; and Rylance, *Victorian Psychology and British Culture*.

6. Levine, *Realistic Imagination*, 9.

7. My focus on readers wishing for conventional romance plots looks especially narrow next to Alicia Mireles Christoff's explication of the nuanced forms that wishing takes in Eliot's work. Christoff brings the theories of British psychoanalyst Wilfred Bion to bear on Eliot's idea expressed in *The Mill on the Floss* (as Philip Waken says), that "we can never give up wishing and longing while we are thoroughly alive." While her argument deserves reading rather than condensing into summary, her aim is to explicate in both Eliot's novel and Bion's thinking "a belief in wishing and acts like it . . . to not only overspill containers of self, psyche, and given social position, but also, crucially, to make contact with something beyond them" (82). See *Novel Relations*, especially chapter 2, "Wishfulness," 46–107.

8. Andrew Stauffer connects the history of sentimental reading with students today, "who often want literature to be relatable, to refer to their own emotional experiences." He shows how Felicia Hemans's poem "The Image in Lava" (written in 1827) models a form of "sympathetic reading" that makes an image from the past "refer to her own biography and feelings." *Book Traces*, 27.

9. See chapter 1 of Hilary Havens, *Revising the Eighteenth-Century Novel*.

10. In Britain, the novel was published in eight installments between December 1871 and December 1872; American readers had to wait fourteen months for the ending, from December 1871 to February 1873.

11. Hughes and Lund, *Victorian Serial*, 10.

12. Ibid., 8.

13. *The Examiner*, March 4, 1876, 265, quoted in Hughes and Lund, *Victorian Serial*, 157.

14. Brooks, *Reading for the Plot*, 35.

15. *The Examiner*, March 4, 1876, quoted in Martin, *George Eliot's Serial Fiction*, 245.

16. James, *Nation*, February 24, 1876, 363. Eliot refers to "the Nightmare of the Serial" in reference to deciding against such a format for *The Mill on the Floss* (Martin cites the phrase but does not offer a source; *George Eliot's Serial Fiction*, 3). For a related argument that suspense, when

generated by a realist narrative, could be salutary in teaching readers to suspend judgment, to value "uncertainty rather than closure and complacency," see Levine, *Serious Pleasures of Suspense*, 2. Levine makes a persuasive case that in *Adam Bede*, "The Lifted Veil," and *Romola*, Eliot proves suspicious of and begins "to unravel the claims of suspense" (15), though she is chiefly interested in Eliot's concerns about "the implications of suspenseful plotting for ethics and feminine subjectivity" (127).

17. George Eliot to John Blackwood, April 18, 1876, in Haight, *Selections from George Eliot's Letters*, 471.

18. Martin, *George Eliot's Serial Fiction*, 260–61. Late in her career, Eliot actually chose the serial form. Along with Lewes, she was keenly interested in marketing her work, not only for commercial gain but also, Donald Gray suggests, for the wide moral influence her popularity offered. "George Eliot and Her Publishers," 195; 199.

19. Price, *Anthology and the Rise of the Novel*, 135. See also John Picker, "George Eliot and the Sequel Question."

20. *Gwendolen: A Sequel*, 5 (my emphasis).

21. George Eliot to Alexander Main, November 14, 1872, in *George Eliot Letters*, vol. 5, 325.

22. See chapter 3 of Price, *Anthology and the Rise of the Novel*, 105–56.

23. Mead sums up Main's letters by emphasizing the reciprocal uplifting, sustaining effect Eliot's work had on Main and her letters had on him: "Eliot must also have been moved by Main's frequent assurances that her work was achieving the elevated moral effect he had intended." *My Life in Middlemarch*, 237.

24. Alexander Main to George Eliot, August 7 and 31, 1871, in *Letters from Alexander Main*.

25. George Henry Lewes to John Blackwood, September 29, 1871, in *George Eliot Letters*, vol. 5, 193.

26. Main to Eliot, March 26, 1872, in *Letters from Alexander Main* (emphasis in original).

27. Main to Eliot, December 2, 1871, in *Letters from Alexander Main* (emphasis in original).

28. Eliot to Main, November 14, 1872, in *George Eliot Letters*, vol. 5, 324.

29. Eliot to Main, March 29, 1872, in Haight, *Selections from George Eliot's Letters*, 401.

30. Main to Eliot, January 31, 1872, in *Letters from Alexander Main*.

31. Main to Eliot, September 29, 1872, in *Letters from Alexander Main*.

32. Ibid.

33. Gillian Beer, "The Reader's Wager," 111.

34. Eliot, *Mill on the Floss*, 267.

35. Caroline Levine argues that, "Eliot's characters are relentlessly forward-looking: they anticipate, fear, calculate, plot, compete, presume, forewarn, speculate, hypothesize, dread, hope, desire, and wonder." "Surprising Realism," 73. See also Adela Pinch, "*The Mill on the Floss* and *The Lifted Veil*."

36. Lewes to Blackwood, November 25, 1872, quoted in Martin, *George Eliot's Serial Fiction*, 210.

37. Broome, Review of *Middlemarch*, 111.

38. See Cohn, *Still Life*.

39. This is not to contest Eliot's interest in memory as a broader narrative resource. As Steven Marcus writes, "It is true to say that [Eliot] was almost unable to set pen to paper on a work of fiction without invoking or repairing to the historical past." "Literature and Social Theory," 187. Alexander Welsh, in *George Eliot and Blackmail*, makes further convincing the centrality of the

past in Eliot's work. On the other hand, Nicholas Dames, in *Amnesiac Selves*, offers an intriguing account of memory lapse in *Romola* and the general absence of passages about memory in Victorian fiction.

40. Eliot, *The Lifted Veil*, 37.

41. Eliot, "Silly Novels by Lady Novelists," 454.

42. Stewart, in *Dear Reader*, discusses more broadly the recurrence of "embedded analogues" in Victorian fiction: scenes that depict an extrapolated version of the experience one might have in reading, grafted onto another activity, so that the author can engage the real reader without disrupting his act of imagining the scene at hand.

43. Jaffe, *Vanishing Points*, 5–6.

44. To be clear, this is not a judgment about the quality of this work, like Elaine Auyong's excellent *When Fiction Feels Real*.

45. Eliot, "History of Adam Bede," in Eliot, *Adam Bede*, 585.

46. Ibid., 587 (emphasis in original).

47. Gray, "George Eliot and Her Publishers," 187.

48. Bodenheimer, *Real Life of Mary Ann Evans*, 55.

49. Harvey, *Art of George Eliot*, 70.

50. Bodenheimer, *Real Life of Mary Ann Evans*, 50–52.

51. Scarry suggests that the awareness that the author is in fact instructing the reader to perform a series of imaginative acts is usually "suppressed"; this suppression is part of what allows the literary work to replicate the "given" quality of actual perception, and what makes willed imagining under "authorial direction" more vivid than unassisted, volitional daydreaming. See *Dreaming by the Book*, 33; 30–31.

52. Eliot, *Leaves from a Notebook*, 445.

53. Christoff, *Novel Relations*, 178.

54. Eliot to Charles Ritter, February 11, 1873, in Holmstrom and Lerner, *George Eliot and Her Readers*, 121 (my emphasis).

55. George Eliot to Mrs. Bray, December 22, 1873, in *George Eliot Letters*, vol. 5, 471.

56. Eliot, "Natural History of German Life," 51.

57. See Ashton, *G. H. Lewes: A Life*.

58. Haight, *George Eliot: A Biography*, 270.

59. Dallas, *Gay Science*, vol. 1, 196. All subsequent references are cited by page number in the text.

60. See Taylor and Shuttleworth, *Embodied Selves*, 95–96.

61. Carpenter, *Principles of Mental Physiology*, 586–87; 591.

62. See Greiner, *Sympathetic Realism*.

63. Sully, *Outlines of Psychology*, 326.

64. Bain, *The Senses and the Intellect*, 641–42.

65. Edward S. Reed argues that this proliferation occurred in part because theories of the unconscious provided a middle ground in the growing debate between materialist and spiritualist accounts of the mind. *From Soul to Mind*, 19.

66. See Sally Shuttleworth, "The Language of Science and Psychology in George Eliot's *Daniel Deronda*."

67. [Dallas,] Review of *Adam Bede*, 81–82.

68. Lewes, *Problems of Life and Mind, First Series*, vol. 2, 140. On Lewes's view that several sensations occur at once, and how this view proves characteristic of Victorian psychology, see Reed, *From Soul to Mind*, chapter 4.

69. Haight, *Selections from George Eliot's Letters*, 217.

70. Maudsley, *Physiology of Mind*, 324.

71. [Mozley], Review of *Adam Bede*, 87.

72. George Eliot to Sara Sophia Hennell, February 9, 1849, in *George Eliot Letters*, vol. 1, 277.

73. [Mozley,] Review of *Adam Bede*, 87.

74. Mead, *My Life in Middlemarch*, 243.

75. John Blackwood to George Eliot, July 29, 1872, in *George Eliot Letters*, vol. 5, 293.

76. George Henry Lewes, Journal, February 9, 1859, quoted in Haight, *George Eliot: A Biography*, 273.

77. Uglow, *George Eliot*, 107 (my emphasis).

78. Langan, *Romantic Vagrancy*, 242.

79. Kathryn Hughes, in *George Eliot: The Last Victorian*, suggests that to Eliot he was "her beloved Jean Jacques Rousseau" (89). For an account of the connections between Eliot and Rousseau, including the *Rêveries*, and particularly in "The Lifted Veil," see chapter 3 of Neil Hertz, *George Eliot's Pulse*.

80. Harvey refers to the fact that critics have frequently observed "something like personal animus in George Eliot's attitude to Hetty" and the novelist's seemingly "unjustified hostility" toward her. *Art of George Eliot*, 86–87. Neil Hertz has also written incisively of the "violence, explicit or dissimulated, visited upon certain characters in George Eliot's novels," Hetty in particular. *George Eliot's Pulse*, 138.

81. Andrew Miller, "'Wasting the Invincible Energy.'"

82. "Incapacity is a requirement of our encounter with characters; it is something like a transcendental condition of reading," Andrew Miller writes about reading Jane Austen. Moments in which characters appear helpless, he suggests, magnify the reader's sympathy with them, by mirroring the reader's constant experience of feeling constrained in the desire to help them. See "Perfectly Helpless," 69–70. Gillian Beer suggests this predicament is keenly felt in reading *Daniel Deronda*: "Watching and playing, without being able to redeem, describes the reader's predicaments in that particular novel" ("Reader's Wager," 109).

Chapter 4. *Middlemarch's* Negations

1. Trollope, *Autobiography*, 224–25.

2. Scarry describes how passing a transparent, gauzy substance over a solid one results in an image that more closely resembles the actual perception of solidity. See *Dreaming by the Book*, 10–30.

3. See, especially, Horn, *Natural History of Negation*.

4. Milton is particularly known for his use of negative similes, as Michele Martinez helpfully reminded me.

5. Orwell, "Politics and the English Language."

6. Gallagher, *Telling It Like It Wasn't*, 1 (my emphasis). See also Andrew Miller, *Burdens of Perfection* and *On Not Being Someone Else*.

7. John Picker describes unauthorized sequels published soon after *Daniel Deronda* as "critical attacks" on Eliot's novel; he argues that "with Eliot, and especially with *Deronda*, the sequel is a reproach." "George Eliot and the Sequel Question," 363. On theories of fan complaints, see Lesley Goodman, "Fandom, Fictional Theory."

8. Barbara Hardy, *Novels of George Eliot*, 136. Andrew Miller says of Hardy's observations in this passage that Eliot's "realism, on this picture, requires generous attention to what does not happen." *Burdens of Perfection*, 197.

9. Some recent scholarship that has begun to move in this direction uses the digital humanities to probe syntax and style. In *Everyday Words*, Jonathan Farina analyzes the frequency with which particular authors use characteristic phrases, work that "models how technologically savvy data mining might serve interpretive ends without reducing literary scholarship to data and graphs" (xix). See also Allison, *Reductive Reading*.

10. Gillian Beer identifies the evolutionary resonance of the "emphasis upon plurality, rather than upon singleness . . . crucial to the developing argument of *Middlemarch*" (*Darwin's Plots*, 143).

11. Barbara Hardy, *Novels of George Eliot*, 143.

12. See, in particular, Allison, *Reductive Reading*, and Melissa Raines, *George Eliot's Grammar of Being*.

13. Horn, *Natural History of Negation*, 168.

14. For discussions of the varied ways and reasons different novelists achieve this sense of plotlessness, narrative suspension, or stillness, see Amanpal Garcha, *From Sketch to Novel*; Cohn, *Still Life*; and Maia McAleavey, "Anti-Individualism in the Victorian Family Chronicle."

15. Clare Carlisle argues for a philosophical underpinning to Eliot's use of formal patterns that make expansion and interconnectedness part of the reading experience. Carlisle describes the affinity between Eliot and Spinoza, whose *Ethics* she translated just before she began writing fiction, in how both writers use repetition and establish "relations and associations between 'images'" in order "to form and reform the reader's mind." "George Eliot and Spinoza," 607.

16. See chapter 2, "Constructing the Reader," in Bodenheimer, *Real Life of Mary Ann Evans*.

17. In *When Fiction Feels Real*, Auyoung suggests that the aim of Eliot's narratorial intrusion in this passage is to push readers "to pursue a deeper level of comprehension, in which they do not merely read for the plot but undertake the effortful process of forming uncommonly vivid and accurate impressions of the fictional world" (83).

18. J. Hillis Miller, *Reading for Our Time*, 107, and "Narrative and History," 467.

19. Horn, *Natural History of Negation*, 171.

20. Beer, "What's Not in *Middlemarch*," 15.

21. See Lisa Zunshine, *Why We Read Fiction*, 47–54.

22. Eliot, *Leaves from a Note-book*, 446.

23. Ibid.

24. *George Eliot Letters*, vol. 5, 353.

25. Ibid., 294.

26. Rosemary Ashton discussed the importance of the word "half" in *Middlemarch* during her plenary lecture at "George Eliot 2019: An International Bicentenary Conference."

27. See Isobel Armstrong, "George Eliot, Hegel, and *Middlemarch*."

28. Eliot, "Natural History of German Life," 51–52 (emphasis in original).

29. Ibid., 69.

30. As Daniel Wright argues, "If vagueness is real, Eliot suggests, and if we cannot get away from it either as a property of language or as a property of feeling, desire, and thought, we must learn how to make use of it, or how to understand it as strengthening, rather than disintegrating, our ethical lives." "George Eliot's Vagueness," 641.

31. George Eliot to Sara Sophia Hennell, June 14, 1858, in *George Eliot Letters*, vol. 2, 464–65 (emphasis in original).

32. George Eliot to R. H. Hutton, August 8, 1863, in *George Eliot Letters*, vol. 4, 97.

33. Eliot, "Leaves from a Note-book," 446.

34. [Eliot,] "Belles Lettres," 306.

35. Ibid., 307.

36. See, in particular, Ruth Yeazell's *Art of the Everyday*.

37. Eliot, *Impressions of Theophrastus Such*, 12.

38. George Eliot to John Blackwood, November 1, 1873, in *George Eliot Letters*, vol. 5, 458–59.

39. James Benson writes that Eliot "resents the way in which contemporary reviewers fragment the unity of her fiction, though she understands the lack of critical categories that would enable them to perceive and describe the kind of unity she feels her novels possess. It is her firm conviction that sympathy is the prerequisite of responsible criticism. Only if a critic is receptive will it be possible for him to transcend the fragmentary approach." "'Sympathetic Criticism,'" 429.

40. *George Eliot Letters*, vol. 5, 373; quoted in Benson, "Sympathetic Criticism," 434.

41. *George Eliot Letters*, vol. 5, 324.

42. David Kurnick describes the "critical consensus" that *Middlemarch* is almost punitive in denying its characters the all-important breadth of vision of its narrator. "Troublingly for an author whose highest value is the sympathetic imagination," he writes, "Eliot seems incapable of conceiving of characters who might be capable of conceiving of something like *Middlemarch*." "An Erotics of Detachment," 583–84.

43. Caroline Levine, "Surprising Realism," 67.

44. George Eliot to Alexander Main, November 14, 1872, in *George Eliot Letters*, vol. 5, 324 (my emphasis).

45. Sierra Eckert, "The Way We Quote Now," 226.

46. Barbara Hardy, *Novels of George Eliot*, 144.

47. Eliot, "Leaves from a Note-book," 445.

48. Alexander Main to George Eliot, December 2, 1871, in *Letters from Alexander Main* (emphasis in original).

Chapter 5. *Daniel Deronda* and Us

1. One exception is Carolyn Burdett's "Sympathy-Antipathy in *Daniel Deronda*," where she shows how sympathy in *Daniel Deronda* is transfigured into antipathy, which is equally "at the foundation of being human" and gives the novel "the affective coloring of aversion and repugnance."

2. Audrey Jaffe argues that Eliot "rejects, or at least severely qualifies, the intersubjective ideal her novels have come to represent" in *Daniel Deronda* in *Scenes of Sympathy*, 131.

3. This exchange of disgust echoes how Sara Ahmed describes hate as more than an individual emotion, but rather as part of an "economy of hate," in which "hate does not *reside* in a given subject or object. . . . It circulates between signifiers in relationships of difference and displacement." *Cultural Politics of Emotion*, 44.

4. Neil Hertz sees a mirroring of affect between Eliot's fraught relationship to her own writing and the distraught emotional patterns within her novels. Hertz finely explains the pattern of violence Eliot visits on some characters as an allegorical expression of the author's guilty, ambivalent relationship to her writing, "hinting at some initiating 'crime' that is both like writing and like what writing must redeem." *George Eliot's Pulse*, 10.

5. George Eliot to Harriet Beecher Stowe, October 29, 1876, in *George Eliot Letters*, vol. 6, 301–2.

6. Barbara Hardy, *Particularities*, 190.

7. Eliot to Stowe, October 29, 1876, in *George Eliot Letters*, vol. 6, 301–2.

8. Helen Small argues that Eliot's lifelong affinity with the philosophies of Cynicism served as a reality check on Eliot's being "tempted to press idealism upon others (as she so nearly was in *Daniel Deronda*)" and informed her focus on "what is practicable in this world, given what we know about human nature." "George Eliot and the Cosmopolitan Cynic," 102–3. For influential work on Eliot's cosmopolitanism, see Amanda Anderson, *The Powers of Distance*, 119–46; David Kurnick, "Unspeakable George Eliot"; and Thomas Albrecht, "The Balance of Separateness and Communication."

9. Christoff, *Novel Relations*, 199.

10. One exception is Greiner's *Sympathetic Realism*, which (as Greiner says of Eliot) seeks "to disentangle sympathy, identification, and knowledge" (125). Greiner revisits Adam Smith's "nineteenth-century afterlife" (9) to show how sympathy undergirds the period's literature as a mode of thought, not feeling. Christoff has also illuminated other affects in Eliot's work, such as the weariness and enervation that represents *Middlemarch*'s "dominant affective tone." *Novel Relations*, 154. *Daniel Deronda* is dominated by a more active, outward-facing cluster of negative affects: repulsion, repugnance, and disgust.

11. Eliot is not mentioned in Zachary Samalin's otherwise excellent *The Masses Are Revolting*.

12. Armstrong, "George Eliot, Spinoza, and the Emotions," 301.

13. George Eliot to Charles Bray, July 5, 1859, in *George Eliot Letters*, vol. 3, 111 (my emphasis).

14. See Armstrong, "George Eliot, Spinoza, and the Emotions," for an illuminating discussion of how "imaging and the imagination are at the core of all affective experience" (299–300). Armstrong does not discuss the affect generated by novel reading, which is my extrapolation.

15. Armstrong, *Novel Politics*, 169.

16. George Eliot, Diary, April 12, 1876, in Harris and Johnston, *Journals of George Eliot*, 145 (emphasis in original).

17. Picciotto, "Deronda the Jew," 409.

18. Francillon, "George Eliot's First Romance," 382.

19. Saintsbury, Review of *Daniel Deronda*, 374–75.

20. Lewes wrote to Blackwood that he "sometimes shared her doubts on whether people would sufficiently sympathize with that element in the story. Though I have reflected that [as] she formerly contrived to make one love Methodists, there was no reason why she should not conquer the prejudice against the Jews." Quoted in Martin, "Contemporary Critics and Judaism," 91.

21. George Eliot to Sara Sophia Hennell, in *George Eliot Letters*, vol. 4, 49.

22. George Eliot, Diary, December 1, 1876; Harris and Johnston, *Journals of George Eliot*, 146. The *Westminster Review* also referred to "a great deal of hostile criticism" toward the novel; quoted in Martin, "Contemporary Critics," 91.

23. Review of *Daniel Deronda*, *Saturday Review*, 377.

24. On readers' excessive emotional responses to fiction, see Lesley Goodman, "Rebellious Identification."

25. Adela Pinch suggests that the slim thread of Gwendolen's and Daniel's continually thinking of each other (and Eliot's quantifying how much each thinks of the other) suggestively becomes "the action that holds together the two plots." *Thinking about Other People*, 151.

26. Leavis, "Gwendolen Harleth," *London Review of Books*.

27. Claudia Johnson, "F. R. Leavis: The 'Great Tradition,'" 227. Although Leavis's cleaving of Deronda and Gwendolen's stories is well known, Johnson offers a more nuanced reading of how including the novel at all "in *The Great Tradition* is thus a radical move, for with or without the Jewish 'parts' of Mordecai or Daniel, Eliot's novel is still about Jews in England" (223).

28. Felski helpfully breaks the broad category of "identification" into strands that include alignment, allegiance, recognition, empathy, and (the closest strand to the phenomenon I focus on) irritation situations. See "Identifying with Characters." For an overview of the resurgent interest in character, see the introduction to Anderson, Felski, and Moi, *Character: Three Inquiries*.

29. See Christopher Lane, *Hatred and Civility*. Sarah Allison also argues that Eliot examines this social dynamic in other novels as a result of correcting self-centered vision, writing that "a major philosophical problem in *Middlemarch* is how to see others clearly, but without contempt." "Discerning Syntax: George Eliot's Relative Clauses," 1294.

30. Robson, "50 Eskimo Words for Snow."

31. Smith, *Theory of Moral Sentiments*, 10.

32. Keen, *Empathy and the Novel*, xii; 41.

33. Smith, *Theory of Moral Sentiments*, 11.

34. See Sianne Ngai, *Ugly Feelings*, 332–54.

35. See, in particular, Rachel Ablow, *The Marriage of Minds*; Deidre Lynch, *Loving Literature*; Andrew Miller, *Burdens of Perfection*; and Christoff, *Novel Relations*.

36. Lynch, *Loving Literature*, 14.

37. On negative affect in the novel, see Burdett, "Sympathy-Antipathy"; Hertz, *George Eliot's Pulse*; and Armstrong, *Novel Politics*, 162–73.

38. Green, "'I Recognized Myself in Her,'" 57.

39. Armstrong has suggested that a Hegelian process of mutual self-recognition, in which one sees oneself clearly by seeing the other, unfolds between couples in *Middlemarch*; she calls it "a highly unstable process, prone to asymmetry, one-sidedness, and reversal" and "potentially dysfunctional." See "George Eliot, Hegel, and *Middlemarch*."

40. Jaffe, *Scenes of Sympathy*, 121–57.

41. Muñoz, *Disidentifications*, 161.

42. Anna Henchman has discussed this language Eliot uses of the mind having a fleshly "sore" and being "maimed" as not just metaphorical but as Eliot's way of representing inner character as a living tissue that can be made sore or that can be healed. "Mollusk Minds."

43. Anna Clark has described how sympathetic identification in the novel is not idealized but acts capriciously and occurs as the result of "spontaneous emotional connections." "Expectation and 'Fellow-Feeling,'" 823.

44. Freud, "Repression," 570–71.

45. Felski, "Identifying with Characters," 104.

46. Armstrong describes this image as "a shut off part of [Gwendolen's] self as outcast from which she flees." *Novel Politics*, 173.

47. Rebecca Mitchell argues that some dissociation, a lack of complete likeness, is crucial to realist art, which "does not make empathy possible by teaching readers what it is like to be another person" but "by teaching us that the alienation that exists between the self and the other cannot be fully overcome." That "inalterable alterity" makes possible instead an "ethical engagement" with the other. *Victorian Lessons in Empathy and Difference*, x.

48. Ngai suggests that ugly feelings offer occasions for examining a sense of powerlessness that extends beyond the individual, to the work of art itself in the modern world. She calls this "bourgeois art's increasingly resigned and pessimistic understanding of its own relationship to political action." *Ugly Feelings*, 3.

49. Barbara Hardy, *Novels of George Eliot*, 156.

50. Ibid., 163; Barbara Hardy, *Particularities*, 90.

51. Barbara Hardy notes that Eliot increasingly relies on imagery, miniature narratives, and other "indirect methods rather than . . . the open generalization in her own voice which is blatant and unashamed." *Novels of George Eliot*, 215.

52. Review of *Daniel Deronda*, *Nation*, 400.

53. [Leslie Stephen,] Obituary of George Eliot, 468.

54. "Daniel is the character whose consciousness coincides most closely with that of the narrator," Cynthia Chase writes in an influential essay on the novel. "Decomposition of the Elephants," 218.

55. Eliot to Stowe, October 29, 1876, in *George Eliot Letters*, vol. 6, 301–2.

56. An engraving of *The Chess-Players* was published in the *Saturday Magazine* in 1837; Clemence Schultze describes the image as well known to mid-nineteenth-century English audiences and Retzsch as popular in England for his illustrations of *Faust* and Shakespeare.

57. Francillon, Review of *Daniel Deronda*, 385.

58. Janice Radway calls the practice of sympathetic identification "the most common shared trait of fiction in English that reaches a wide audience"; quoted in Keen, *Empathy*, x.

59. In *An Autobiography*, Trollope insisted that Lily Dale's refusal to marry John Eames endeared her to readers: "It was because she could not get over her troubles that they loved her" (179).

60. Oliphant, "Novels," 276.

61. Trollope, *The Small House*, 135.

Afterword. The Reader's Part from Virginia Woolf to Relatability

1. One exception is Emily Sun's theorizing about the common reader in the contexts of Romantic England and Republican China. See *On the Horizon of World Literature*.

2. Victorian reviews of new fiction in periodicals depended on long excerpts from novels in order to "produce in the reader of the critical piece, even if only momentarily, the kind of

entranced attention characteristic of the novel as a whole." This practice disappeared in the late nineteenth century, Dames says, reflecting a new "discomfort with reading experience as a worthwhile datum." Dames, "On the Protocols of Victorian Citation," 328–29; 330. For further discussion of literary criticism's "disowning of reading," see *Physiology of the Novel*, 33.

3. Booth, *Rhetoric of Fiction*, 122; 120. See also Lynch, *Loving Literature*; Rachel Sagner Buurma and Laura Heffernan, *The Teaching Archive*; and Elaine Freedgood, *Worlds Enough*.

4. Woolf, *Orlando*, 73; 229–30.

5. See Jonathan Kramnick, "Criticism and Truth"; and Michael Warner, "Uncritical Reading."

6. Flint, "Reading Uncommonly," 191–92.

7. Woolf, *Common Reader: First Series*, 1.

8. De Gay, *Virginia Woolf's Novels*, 4. For further discussion of Woolf's views on reading, see pages 4–12.

9. Woolf, *Orlando*, 73.

10. Woolf, "How Should One Read a Book?," in *Second Common Reader*, 270; 260–61 (my emphasis).

11. Atherton, *Defining Literary Criticism*, 188; 106; 110.

12. Ellis, *Virginia Woolf and the Victorians*, 1; 6. Woolf returned again and again over the course of her career to the immediate past, as Jane Marcus, De Gay, Emily Blair, Marion Dell, and others have argued to different ends. Most recently, her portrayal of this past has been nuanced by Mary Jean Corbett, who shows Woolf's engagement with her late Victorian context even as she claimed to reject all of the Victorian past. See *Behind the Times*.

13. Iser, "The Reading Process," 959.

14. Silver, "'Anon' and 'The Reader,'" 425; 428; 429.

15. Ibid., 429.

16. Flint, "Reading Uncommonly," 191.

17. Woolf, "How Should One Read a Book?," in *Second Common Reader*, 263–64 (my emphasis).

18. Ibid., 268.

19. "Purely affective" reading, Ann Cvetkovich has argued, was the real target of antisensation novel rhetoric (*Mixed Feelings*, 21).

20. Buurma and Heffernan, "Common Reader and the Archival Classroom," 114.

21. Buurma and Heffernan, *Teaching Archive*, 3.

22. See Emre, *Paraliterary*; and Warner, "Uncritical Reading."

23. Warner, "Uncritical Reading," 13.

24. Ibid., 14.

25. Buurma and Heffernan, "Common Reader and the Archival Classroom," 113.

26. Salisbury, "Relatable," 1156–57. Brian Glavey quotes Salisbury in discussing the relatability of a Frank O'Hara poem. "Having a Coke with You," 997.

27. Mead, "Scourge of Relatability."

28. Glavey, "Having a Coke with You," 999.

29. Stiles, "From 'Representative' to Relatable," 495 (emphasis in original).

30. Richards, *Practical Criticism*, 227 (my emphasis).

31. Ibid., 238.

BIBLIOGRAPHY

Abercrombie, Nicholas, and Brian Longhurst. "Fans and Enthusiasts." In *The Fan Fiction Studies Reader*, edited by Karen Hellekson and Kristina Busse, 159–76. Iowa City: University of Iowa Press, 2014.

Ablow, Rachel, ed. *The Feeling of Reading: Affective Experience and Victorian Literature*. Ann Arbor: University of Michigan Press, 2010.

———. *The Marriage of Minds: Reading Sympathy in the Victorian Marriage Plot*. Stanford, CA: Stanford University Press, 2007.

———. "Victorian Feeling and the Victorian Novel." *Literature Compass Online* 4, no. 1 (2007): 298–316.

Ahmed, Sara. *The Cultural Politics of Emotion*. Edinburgh: Edinburgh University Press, 2014.

Albrecht, Thomas. "The Balance of Separateness and Communication: Cosmopolitan Ethics in George Eliot's *Daniel Deronda*." *ELH* 79, no. 2 (2012): 389–416.

Allen, Christie. "The Browsing Victorian Reader." *Victorian Literature and Culture* 46, no. 1 (2018): 1–21.

Allison, Sarah. "Discerning Syntax: George Eliot's Relative Clauses." *ELH* 81, no. 4 (2014): 1275–97.

———. *Reductive Reading: A Syntax of Victorian Moralizing*. Baltimore, MD: Johns Hopkins University Press, 2018.

Altick, Richard. *The English Common Reader: A Social History of the Mass Reading Public, 1800–1900*. Chicago: University of Chicago Press, 1957.

Anderson, Amanda. "George Eliot and the Jewish Question." *Yale Journal of Criticism* 10, no. 1 (1997): 39–61.

———. *The Powers of Distance: Cosmopolitanism and the Cultivation of Detachment*. Princeton, NJ: Princeton University Press, 2001.

———. "Thinking with Character." In Anderson, Felski, and Moi, *Character: Three Inquiries*, 127–77.

———. "Trollope's Modernity." *ELH* 74, no. 3 (2007): 509–34.

Anderson, Amanda, Rita Felski, and Toril Moi. *Character: Three Inquiries in Literary Studies*. Chicago: University of Chicago Press, 2019.

Anderson, Amanda, and Harry Shaw, eds. *A Companion to George Eliot*. Hoboken, NJ: John Wiley & Sons, 2013.

Anderson, Ronald. "George Eliot Provoked: John Blackwood and Chapter 17 of *Adam Bede*." *Modern Philology* 71 (1973–74): 39–47.

Andrews, Malcolm. *Charles Dickens and His Performing Selves: Dickens and the Public Readings.* Oxford: Oxford University Press, 2008.

Arata, Stephen. "The Impersonal Intimacy of Marius the Epicurean." In Ablow, *Feeling of Reading,* 131–56.

———. "On Not Paying Attention." *Victorian Studies* 46 (2004): 193–205.

———. "Stevenson, Morris, and the Value of Idleness." In *Robert Louis Stevenson: Writer of Boundaries,* edited by Richard Ambrosini and Richard Dury, 3–12. Madison: University of Wisconsin Press, 2006.

Armstrong, Isobel. "George Eliot, Hegel, and *Middlemarch.*" *19: Interdisciplinary Studies in the Long Nineteenth Century* (29).

———. "George Eliot, Spinoza, and the Emotions." In Anderson and Shaw, *A Companion to George Eliot,* 294–307.

———. *Novel Politics: Democratic Imaginations in Nineteenth-Century Fiction.* Oxford: Oxford University Press, 2016.

Arnold, Matthew. *Culture and Anarchy.* Cambridge: Cambridge University Press, 1971.

[Arnold, Thomas.] "Recent Novel Writing." *Macmillan's* 13 (1866): 202–9.

Ashton, Rosemary. "George Eliot and the Difficulty of Coming to Conclusions." Plenary lecture at "George Eliot 2019: An International Bicentenary Conference," University of Leicester, July 2019.

———. *G. H. Lewes: A Life.* Oxford: Oxford University Press, 1991.

Atherton, Carol. *Defining Literary Criticism: Scholarship, Authority, and the Possession of Literary Knowledge, 1880–2002.* London: Palgrave, 2005.

Austen, Jane. *Emma.* Edited by R. W. Chapman. 3rd ed. Oxford: Oxford University Press, 1952.

———. *Mansfield Park.* Edited by R. W. Chapman. 3rd ed. Oxford: Oxford University Press, 1948.

———. *Minor Works.* Edited by R. W. Chapman. 3rd ed. Oxford: Oxford University Press, 1958.

———. *Northanger Abbey.* Edited by R. W. Chapman. 3rd ed. Oxford: Oxford University Press, 1954.

———. *Persuasion.* Edited by R. W. Chapman. 3rd ed. Oxford: Oxford University Press, 1954.

———. *Pride and Prejudice.* Edited by James Kinsley. Oxford: Oxford University Press, 2004.

———. *Sense and Sensibility.* Edited by R. W. Chapman. 3rd ed. Oxford: Oxford University Press, 1953.

Austen-Leigh, J. E. *A Memoir of Jane Austen.* In *Persuasion,* by Jane Austen, 271–391. Harmondsworth, UK: Penguin, 1985.

[Austin, Alfred.] "The Vice of Reading." *Temple Bar Magazine* 42 (1874): 251–57.

Auyoung, Elaine. *When Fiction Feels Real: Representation and the Reading Mind.* Oxford: Oxford University Press, 2018.

Bachelard, Gaston. *The Poetics of Reverie: Childhood, Language, and the Cosmos.* Translated by David Russell. Boston: Beacon Press, 1971.

———. *The Poetics of Space.* Translated by Maria Jolas. Boston: Beacon Press, 1994.

[Bagehot, Walter.] "Charles Dickens." *National Review* (October 1858): 458–86. In Collins, *Dickens: The Critical Heritage,* 390–401.

Bain, Alexander. *The Emotions and the Will.* London: John W. Parker, 1859.

———. *The Senses and the Intellect.* 4th ed. New York: Appleton, 1894.

Barnett, George L. *Nineteenth-Century British Novelists on the Novel.* New York: Meredith, 1971.

Barthes, Roland. "The Reality Effect." In *The Rustle of Language,* translated by Richard Howard, 141–48. Berkeley: University of California Press, 1989.

———. "Writing Reading." In *Rustle of Language*, 29–32.

Beer, Gillian. *Darwin's Plots: Evolutionary Narrative in Darwin, George Eliot, and Nineteenth-Century Fiction*. London: Routledge, 1983.

———. "The Reader as Author." *Authorship* 3, no. 1 (2014). http://www.authorship.ugent.be.

———. "The Reader's Wager: Lots, Sorts, Futures." *Essays in Criticism* 40, no. 2 (1990): 99–123.

———. *The Romance*. London: Methuen, 1970.

———. "What's Not in *Middlemarch*." In *Middlemarch in the Twenty-First Century*, edited by Karen Chase, 15–36. Oxford: Oxford University Press, 2006.

"Belles Lettres." *Westminster Review* 30 (1866): 268–80.

Benedict, Barbara. "Sensibility by the Numbers: Austen's Work as Regency Popular Fiction." In Lynch, *Janeites*, 63–86.

Benson, James. "'Sympathetic Criticism': GE's Response to Contemporary Reviewing." *Nineteenth-Century Fiction* 29, no. 4 (1975): 428–40.

Bernard, Catherine. "Dickens and Victorian Dream Theory." In *Victorian Science and Victorian Values*, edited by James Paradis and Thomas Postlewait, 197–216. New York: New York Academy of Sciences, 1981.

Bewes, Timothy. "Reading with the Grain: A New World in Literary Criticism." *differences: A Journal of Feminist Cultural Studies* 21, no. 3 (2010): 1–33.

Bodenheimer, Rosemarie. *Knowing Dickens*. Ithaca, NY: Cornell University Press, 2010.

———. *The Real Life of Mary Ann Evans*. Ithaca, NY: Cornell University Press, 1994.

"Books and Their Uses." *Macmillan's* 1 (1859): 110–13.

Booth, Wayne. *The Rhetoric of Fiction*. 2nd ed. Chicago: University of Chicago Press, 1983.

Bourdieu, Pierre. *Distinction: A Social Critique of the Judgement of Taste*. Translated by Richard Nice. Cambridge, MA: Harvard University Press, 1984.

Bradbury, Nicola. "Dickens and the Form of the Novel." In *The Cambridge Companion to Charles Dickens*, edited by John Jordan, 152–66. Cambridge: Cambridge University Press, 2001.

Bradley, Matthew, and Juliet John, eds. *Reading and the Victorians*. Farnham, Surrey: Ashgate, 2015.

Brake, Laurel. *Subjugated Knowledges: Journalism, Gender, and Literature in the Nineteenth Century*. Basingstoke, Hampshire: Macmillan, 1994.

Brantlinger, Patrick. *The Reading Lesson: The Threat of Mass Literacy in Nineteenth-Century British Fiction*. Bloomington: Indiana University Press, 1998.

Bray, Joe. *The Female Reader in the English Novel: From Burney to Austen*. Abingdon-on-Thames, Oxfordshire, England: Routledge, 2008.

Brewer, David. *The Afterlife of Character, 1726–1825*. Philadelphia: University of Pennsylvania Press, 2005.

[Brimley, George.] Review of *Bleak House*. *Spectator*, September 24, 1853, 923–25. In Collins, *Dickens: The Critical Heritage*, 283–86.

"British Novelists—Richardson, Miss Austen, Scott." *Fraser's Magazine* 61 (1860): 20–38.

Brocklebank, Lisa. "Psychic Reading." *Victorian Studies* 48 (2006): 233–39.

Brodie, Laura Fairchild. "Jane Austen and the Common Reader: 'Opinions of *Mansfield Park*,' 'Opinions of *Emma*,' and the Janeite Phenomenon." *Texas Studies in Literature and Language* 37, no. 1 (1995): 54–71.

Bronstein, Michaela. "How Not to Re-Read Novels: The Critical Value of First Reading." *Journal of Modern Literature* 39, no. 3 (2016): 76–94.

Brontë, Charlotte. *Jane Eyre*. Edited by Margaret Smith. Oxford: Clarendon Press, 1969.

Brooks, Peter. *Reading for the Plot: Design and Intention in Narrative*. 1984. Cambridge, MA: Harvard University Press, 1992.

Broome, Frederick Napier. Review of *Middlemarch*. *The Times*, March 7, 1873. In *George Eliot and Her Readers: A Selection of Contemporary Reviews*, edited by John Holmstrom and Laurence Lerner. Oxford: Bodley Head, 1966.

Burdett, Carolyn. "Sympathy-Antipathy in Daniel Deronda." *19: Interdisciplinary Studies in the Long Nineteenth Century* (29).

Butler, Marilyn. *Jane Austen*. Oxford: Oxford University Press, 2007.

Butt, John, and Kathleen Tillotson. *Dickens at Work*. Fair Lawn, NJ: Essential Books, 1958.

Buurma, Rachel Sagner, and Laura Heffernan. "The Common Reader and the Archival Classroom: Disciplinary History for the Twenty-First Century." *New Literary History* 43, no. 18 (2012): 113–35.

———. *The Teaching Archive: A New History for Literary Study*. Chicago: University of Chicago Press, 2021.

Buzard, James. "Item of Mortality: Lives Led and Unled in *Oliver Twist*." *ELH* 81, no. 4 (2014): 1225–51.

Carlisle, Clare. "George Eliot and Spinoza: Philosophical Formations." *Victorian Studies* 62 (2020): 590–615.

Carlisle, Janice. "*Little Dorrit*: Necessary Fictions." *Studies in the Novel* 7 (1975): 195–214.

———. *The Sense of an Audience: Dickens, Thackeray, and George Eliot at Mid-Century*. Brighton, Sussex: Harvester Press, 1982.

Carpenter, William. *Principles of Mental Physiology*. 1874. New York, 1887.

Carroll, David, ed. *George Eliot: The Critical Heritage*. London: Routledge, 1971.

Castle, Terry. *The Female Thermometer: Eighteenth-Century Culture and the Invention of the Uncanny*. Oxford: Oxford University Press, 1995.

Cervantes, Miguel de. *The History of Don Quixote*. Edited by J. W. Clark. Illustrated by Gustave Doré. London: Cassell, Petter, and Galpin, 1864–67.

Chartier, Roger. "Labourers and Voyagers: From the Text to the Reader." In *The Book History Reader*, edited by David Finkelstein and Alistair McCleery, 47–58. London: Routledge, 2002.

———. *The Order of Books*. Translated by Lydia Cochrane. Stanford, CA: Stanford University Press, 1994.

Chase, Cynthia. "The Decomposition of the Elephants: Double-Reading *Daniel Deronda*." *PMLA* 93, no. 2 (1978): 215–27.

Choi, Tina. "Natural History's Hypothetical Moments: Narratives of Contingency in Victorian Culture." *Victorian Studies* 51 (2009): 273–95.

———. *Victorian Contingencies: Experiments in Literature, Science and Play*. Stanford, CA: Stanford University Press, 2021.

Christoff, Alicia Mireles. *Novel Relations: Victorian Fiction and British Psychoanalysis*. Princeton, NJ: Princeton University Press, 2019.

Clark, Anna E. "Expectation and 'Fellow-Feeling' in George Eliot's *Daniel Deronda*." *English Studies* 97, no. 8 (2016): 821–36.

[Cleghorn, Thomas?] "Writings of Charles Dickens." *North British Review*, May 1845, 65–87. In Collins, *Dickens: The Critical Heritage*, 186–91.

Cohn, Dorrit. *Transparent Minds: Narrative Modes for Presenting Consciousness in Fiction*. Princeton, NJ: Princeton University Press, 1978.

Cohn, Elisha. *Still Life: Suspended Development in the Victorian Novel*. Oxford: Oxford University Press, 2015.

Colclough, Stephen. *Consuming Texts: Readers and Reading Communities, 1695–1870*. London: Palgrave, 2007.

Coleridge, Samuel Taylor. *Biographia Literaria*. Edited by W. Jackson Bate and James Engell. Princeton, NJ: Princeton University Press, 1983.

Collins, Philip, ed. *Dickens: The Critical Heritage*. London: Routledge, 1971.

———. *The Public Readings*. Edited by Philip Collins. Oxford: Oxford University Press, 1975.

Collins, Wilkie. "The Unknown Public." *Household Words*, August 21, 1858, 217–22.

Corbett, Mary Jean. *Behind the Times: Virginia Woolf in Late-Victorian Contexts*. Ithaca, NY: Cornell University Press, 2020.

Cvetkovich, Ann. *Mixed Feelings: Feminism, Mass Culture, and Victorian Sensationalism*. New Brunswick, NJ: Rutgers University Press, 1992.

Dallas, Eneas Sweetland. *The Gay Science*. 2 vols. 1866. New York: Garland, 1986.

[Dallas, E. S.] Review of *Adam Bede*. *The Times*, April 12, 1859, 5. In Carroll, *George Eliot: The Critical Heritage*, 77–84.

Dames, Nicholas. *Amnesiac Selves: Nostalgia, Forgetting, and British Fiction, 1810–1870*. Oxford: Oxford University Press, 2001.

———. "The Clinical Novel: Phrenology and *Villette*." *Novel* 29, no. 3 (1996): 367–90.

———. "On Hegel, History, and Reading as if for Life: Response." *Victorian Studies* 53 (2011): 437–44.

———. "On Not Close Reading: The Prolonged Excerpt as Victorian Critical Protocol." In Ablow, *Feeling of Reading*, 11–26.

———. "On the Protocols of Victorian Citation." *Novel* 42, no. 2 (2009): 326–331.

———. *The Physiology of the Novel: Reading, Neural Science, and the Form of Victorian Fiction*. Oxford: Oxford University Press, 2007.

———. "Reverie, Sensation, Effect: Novelistic Attention and Stendhal's *De l'amour*." *Narrative* 10 (2002): 47–68.

———. "Wave-Theories and Affective Physiologies: The Cognitive Strain in Victorian Novel Theories." *Victorian Studies* 46 (2004): 206–16.

———. "'The Withering of the Individual': Psychology in the Victorian Novel." In O'Gorman, *A Concise Companion*, 91–112.

Darnton, Robert. "First Steps Towards a History of Reading." In *The Kiss of Lamourette: Reflections in Cultural History*, 154–87. New York: W. W. Norton, 1990.

Daston, Lorraine, and Peter Galison. *Objectivity*. New York: Zone Books, 2010.

David, Deirdre. *Intellectual Women and Victorian Patriarchy: Harriet Martineau, Elizabeth Barrett Browning, George Eliot*. Ithaca, NY: Cornell University Press, 1987.

Deane, Bradley. *The Making of the Victorian Novelist: Anxieties of Authorship in the Mass Market*. London: Routledge, 2003.

De Certeau, Michel. *The Practice of Everyday Life*. Translated by Steven Rendall. Berkeley: University of California Press, 1988.

De Gay, Jane. *Virginia Woolf's Novels and the Literary Past*. Edinburgh: Edinburgh University Press, 2006.

Deresciewicz, William. *Jane Austen and the Romantic Poets*. New York: Columbia University Press, 2004.

De Ritter, Richard. *Imagining Women Readers, 1789–1820: Well-Regulated Minds*. Manchester, UK: Manchester University Press, 2014.

[Dicey, A. V.] Review of *Daniel Deronda*. *Nation*, October 19, 1876, 245–46. In Carroll, *George Eliot: The Critical Heritage*, 399–404.

Dickens, Charles. *Bleak House*. Edited by Norman Page. Harmondsworth, UK: Penguin, 1971.

———. *David Copperfield*. Edited by Jeremy Tambling. Harmondsworth, UK: Penguin, 2004.

———. "Discovery of a Treasure Near Cheapside." *Household Words*, November 13, 1852. In *Charles Dickens's Uncollected Writings from "Household Words," 1850–1859*, edited by Harry Stone, vol. 2, 443–54. Bloomington: Indiana University Press, 1968.

———. *Dombey and Son*. Edited by Alan Horsman. Oxford: Oxford University Press, 1999.

———. *Great Expectations*. Edited by Angus Calder. Harmondsworth, UK: Penguin, 1985.

———. *Hard Times*. Edited by David Craig. Harmondsworth, UK: Penguin, 1985.

———. *The Letters of Charles Dickens*. Edited by Graham Storey, Kathleen Tillotson, and Angus Easson. 12 vols. Oxford: Clarendon Press, 1965.

———. *Little Dorrit*. Edited by Stephen Wall and Helen Small. Harmondsworth, UK: Penguin, 1998.

———. "Lying Awake." *Household Words*, October 30, 1852. In *Reprinted Pieces and the Lazy Tour of Two Idle Apprentices*, 183–89. New York, 1896.

———. *The Mystery of Edwin Drood*. Edited by David Paroissien. Harmondsworth, UK: Penguin, 2002.

———. *Oliver Twist*. Edited by Peter Fairclough. Harmondsworth, UK: Penguin, 1966.

———. *Our Mutual Friend*. Edited by Adrian Poole. Harmondsworth, UK: Penguin, 1997.

———. *The Pickwick Papers*. Edited by James Kinsley. Oxford: Oxford University Press, 2008.

———. "A Preliminary Word." *Household Words*, March 30, 1850.

———. *A Tale of Two Cities* and *The Mystery of Edwin Drood*. New York: Macmillan, 1896.

Du Bosc, Jacques. *The Accomplished Woman*. London: J. Watts, 1753. In *Novel Instruction: Reading, Pedagogy, and the Ideal of Innocence in Eighteenth-Century British Fiction* by Tamar Brown. Harvard, PhD dissertation, 2006.

Duncan, Ian. *Scott's Shadow: The Novel in Romantic Edinburgh*. Princeton, NJ: Princeton University Press, 2007.

Eckert, Sierra. "The Way We Quote Now." Paper presented at the North American Victorian Studies Association Conference, Columbus, Ohio, November 2019.

Eigner, Edwin, and George Worth, eds. *Victorian Criticism of the Novel*. Cambridge: Cambridge University Press, 1985.

Elfenbein, Andrew. "Cognitive Science and the History of Reading." *PMLA* 121 (2006): 484–502.

———. *The Gist of Reading*. Stanford, CA: Stanford University Press, 2018.

Eliot, George. *Adam Bede*. Edited by Stephen Gill. Harmondsworth, UK: Penguin, 1985.

———. "Belles Lettres." *Westminster Review* 67 (January 1857): 306–26.

———. *Daniel Deronda*. Edited by Terence Cave. Harmondsworth, UK: Penguin, 1995.

———. *Essays*. Boston: Dana Estes, n.d.

———. *The George Eliot Letters*. Edited by Gordon Haight. 9 vols. New Haven: Yale University Press, 1954–78.

———. *Impressions of Theophrastus Such*. Edited by Nancy Henry. Iowa City: University of Iowa Press, 1994.

———. *Leaves from a Note-book*. In *The Essays of George Eliot*, edited by Thomas Pinney, 437–51. New York: Columbia University Press, 1963.

———. *The Lifted Veil*. Harmondsworth, UK: Penguin, 1995.

———. *Middlemarch*. Edited by W. J. Harvey. Harmondsworth, UK: Penguin, 1985.

———. *The Mill on the Floss*. Edited by Gordon Haight. Boston: Houghton Mifflin, 1961.

———. "The Natural History of German Life." *Westminster Review* 64 (July 1856): 51–79.

———. Review of *Aurora Leigh*. *Westminster and Foreign Quarterly Review* 11 (January 1857).

———. "Silly Novels by Lady Novelists." *Westminster Review* 66 (October 1856): 442–61.

Ellis, Steve. *Virginia Woolf and the Victorians*. Cambridge: Cambridge University Press, 2007.

Emre, Merve. *Paraliterary: The Making of Bad Readers in Postwar America*. Chicago: University of Chicago Press, 2017.

Farina, Jonathan. "'Dickens's As If': Analogy and Victorian Virtual Reality." *Victorian Studies* 53 (2011): 427–36.

———. *Everyday Words and the Character of Prose in Nineteenth-Century Britain*. Cambridge: Cambridge University Press, 2019.

Favret, Mary. *War at a Distance: Romanticism and the Making of Modern Wartime*. Princeton, NJ: Princeton University Press, 2010.

Felski, Rita. "Identifying with Characters." In Anderson, Felski, and Moi, *Character: Three Inquiries*, 77–126.

Fergus, Jan. *Jane Austen and the Didactic Novel*. New York: Barnes and Noble, 1983.

Ferris, Ina. *The Achievement of Literary Authority: Gender, History, and the Waverley Novels*. Ithaca, NY: Cornell University Press, 1991.

Flint, Kate. "Reading Uncommonly: Virginia Woolf and the Practice of Reading." *Yearbook of English Studies* 26 (1996): 187–98.

———. "Traveling Readers." In Ablow, *Feeling of Reading*, 27–46.

———. "The Victorian Novel and Its Readers." In *The Cambridge Companion to the Victorian Novel*, edited by Deirdre David, 17–36. Cambridge: Cambridge University Press, 2001.

———. *The Woman Reader, 1837–1914*. Oxford: Oxford University Press, 1993.

———. "Women, Men, and the Reading of *Vanity Fair*." In Raven, Small, and Tadmor, *The Practice and Representation of Reading in England*, 246–62.

Ford, George. *Dickens and His Readers*. Princeton, NJ: Princeton University Press, 1955.

Forster, John. *The Life of Charles Dickens*. 2 vols. London: Dent, 1969.

Foucault, Michel. *Discipline and Punish: The Birth of the Prison*. Translated by Alan Sheridan. New York: Vintage, 1995.

Francillon, R. E. "George Eliot's First Romance." *Gentleman's Magazine* (October 1876): 411–27. In Carroll, *George Eliot: The Critical Heritage*, 382–98.

Freedgood, Elaine. *Worlds Enough: The Invention of Realism in the Victorian Novel*. Princeton, NJ: Princeton University Press, 2019.

Freud, Sigmund. "Creative Writers and Day-Dreaming." In *The Standard Edition of the Complete Psychological Works of Sigmund Freud*, edited by James Strachey, vol. 9, 141–53. London: Hogarth Press, 1959.

———. "Repression." In *The Freud Reader*, edited by Peter Gay. New York: W. W. Norton, 1989.

Fried, Michael. *Absorption and Theatricality: Painting and Beholder in the Age of Diderot.* Chicago: University of Chicago Press, 1988.

Gallagher, Catherine. "The Rise of Fictionality." In *The Novel*, edited by Franco Moretti, vol. 1, 336–63. Princeton, NJ: Princeton University Press, 2006.

———. "Telling It Like It Wasn't." *Pacific Coast Philology* 45 (2010): 12–25.

———. *Telling It Like It Wasn't: The Counterfactual Imagination in History and Fiction.* Chicago: University of Chicago Press, 2018.

Galperin, William. "Austen's Earliest Readers and the Rise of the Janeites." In Lynch, *Janeites*, 87–114.

———. *The History of Missed Opportunities: British Romanticism and the Emergence of the Everyday.* Stanford, CA: Stanford University Press, 2017.

Gao, Timothy. *Virtual Play and the Victorian Novel: The Ethics and Aesthetics of Fictional Experience.* Cambridge: Cambridge University Press, 2021.

Garcha, Amanpal. *From Sketch to Novel: The Development of Victorian Fiction.* Cambridge: Cambridge University Press, 2009.

Garrett, Peter. *The Victorian Multiplot Novel: Studies in Dialogic Form.* New Haven, CT: Yale University Press, 1980.

Gettelman, Debra. "The Psychology of Reading and the Victorian Novel." *Literature Compass* 9, no. 2 (2012): 199–212.

———. "'Those Who Idle Over Novels': Victorian Critics and Post-Romantic Readers." In *A Return to the Common Reader: Print Culture and the Novel, 1850–1900*, edited by Beth Palmer and Adelene Buckland, 55–68. Farnham, Surrey, England: Ashgate, 2011.

Gillooly, Eileen, and Deirdre David, eds. *Contemporary Dickens.* Columbus: Ohio State University Press, 2009.

Glatt, Carra. *Narrative and Its Nonevents: The Unwritten Plots that Shaped Victorian Realism.* Charlottesville: University Press of Virginia, 2022.

Glavey, Brian. "Having a Coke with You Is Even More Fun Than Ideology Critique." *PMLA* 134, no. 5 (2019): 996–1011.

Goodlad, Lauren. "Seriality." *Victorian Literature and Culture* 46, no. 3–4 (2018): 869–72.

Goodman, Lesley. "Fandom, Fictional Theory, and the Death of the Author." *Journal of Popular Culture* 48 (2015): 662–76.

———. "Rebellious Identification, or, How I Learned to Stop Worrying and Love Arabella." *Narrative* 18, no. 2 (2010): 163–78.

Graff, Gerald. *Professing Literature: An Institutional History.* 1987. Chicago: University of Chicago Press, 2007.

Graham, Kenneth. *English Criticism of the Novel, 1865–1900.* Oxford: Clarendon Press, 1965.

Graham, Peter W. "Falling for the Crawfords: Character, Contingency, and Narrative." *ELH* 77 (2010): 867–91.

Gray, Donald. "George Eliot and Her Publishers." In *The Cambridge Companion to George Eliot*, edited by George Levine, 181–201. Cambridge: Cambridge University Press, 2001.

Green, Laura. "'I Recognized Myself in Her': Identifying with the Reader in George Eliot's *The Mill on the Floss* and Simone de Beauvoir's *Memoirs of a Dutiful Daughter*." *Tulsa Studies in Women's Literature* 24, no. 1 (2005): 57–79.

———. *Literary Identification from Charlotte Brontë to Tsitsi Dangarembga*. Columbus: Ohio State University Press, 2012.

Greiner, Rae. "The Art of Knowing Your Own Nothingness." *ELH* 77 (2010): 893–914.

———. *Sympathetic Realism in Nineteenth-Century British Fiction*. Baltimore, MD: Johns Hopkins University Press, 2013.

Griest, Guinevere. *Mudie's Circulating Library and the Victorian Novel*. Bloomington: Indiana University Press, 1970.

Grossman, Jonathan. *Charles Dickens's Networks: Public Transport and the Novel*. Oxford: Oxford University Press, 2013.

Gwendolen: A Sequel to George Eliot's "Daniel Deronda." Boston: Ira Bradley, 1878.

Haight, Gordon. *George Eliot: A Biography*. 1968. Harmondsworth, UK: Penguin, 1985.

———, ed. *The George Eliot Letters*. 9 vols. New Haven, CT: Yale University Press, 1954–78.

———, ed. *Selections from George Eliot's Letters*. New Haven, CT: Yale University Press, 1985.

Halsey, Katie. *Jane Austen and Her Readers, 1786–1945*. New York: Anthem Press, 2012.

Hammond, Mary. *Reading, Publishing and the Formation of Literary Taste in England, 1880–1914*. Aldershot, England: Ashgate, 2006.

Hardy, Barbara. *Dickens and Creativity*. London: Continuum, 2008.

———. *The Novels of George Eliot: A Study in Form*. London: Athlone Press, 1959.

———. *Particularities: Readings in George Eliot*. Columbus: Ohio University Press, 1982.

Hardy, Thomas. "The Profitable Reading of Fiction." 1888. In *Nineteenth-Century British Novelists on the Novel*, edited by George L. Barnett, 276–88. New York: Meredith, 1971.

Harris, Margaret, and Judith Johnston, eds. *The Journals of George Eliot*. Cambridge: Cambridge University Press, 1998.

Harvey, W. J. *The Art of George Eliot*. London: Chatto and Windus, 1969.

Havens, Hilary. *Revising the Eighteenth-Century Novel: Authorship from Manuscript to Print*. Cambridge: Cambridge University Press, 2019.

Hearnshaw, Leslie. *A Short History of British Psychology, 1840–1940*. London: Methuen, 1964.

Henchman, Anna. "Mollusk Minds." A paper presented at the North American Victorian Studies Association Annual Conference, Columbus, Ohio, October 2019.

Henson, Louise. "'In the Natural Course of Physical Things': Ghosts and Science in Dickens's *All the Year Round*." In *Culture and Science in the Nineteenth-Century Media*, edited by Louise Henson et al., 113–23. Aldershot, England: Ashgate, 2004.

Hertz, Neil. *George Eliot's Pulse*. Stanford, CA: Stanford University Press, 2003.

Higbie, Robert. *Dickens and Imagination*. Gainesville: University of Florida Press, 1998.

Holmstrom, John, and Laurence Lerner, eds. *George Eliot and Her Readers: A Selection of Contemporary Reviews*. Oxford: Bodley Head, 1966.

Horn, Laurence. *A Natural History of Negation*. 1989. Stanford, CA: Center for the Study of Language and Information, 2001.

Hughes, Kathryn. *George Eliot: The Last Victorian*. New York: Farrar, Straus and Giroux, 1998.

Hughes, Linda, and Michael Lund. *The Victorian Serial*. Charlottesville: University Press of Virginia, 1991.

Hunter, J. Paul. *Before Novels: The Cultural Contexts of Eighteenth-Century English Fiction*. New York: W. W. Norton, 1990.

Iser, Wolfgang. *The Implied Reader: Patterns of Communication in Prose Fiction from Bunyan to Beckett*. Baltimore, MD: Johns Hopkins University Press, 1974.

———. "The Reading Process: A Phenomenological Approach." In *The Critical Tradition*, edited by David Richter, 956–68. New York: Bedford Books, 1998.

Jackson, Heather. *Marginalia: Readers Writing in Books*. New Haven, CT: Yale University Press, 2002.

———. *Romantic Readers: The Evidence of Marginalia*. New Haven, CT: Yale University Press, 2005.

Jaffe, Audrey. *Scenes of Sympathy: Identity and Representation in Victorian Fiction*. Ithaca, NY: Cornell University Press, 2000.

———. *Vanishing Points: Dickens, Narrative, and the Subject of Omniscience*. Berkeley: University of California Press, 1991.

———. *The Victorian Novel Dreams of the Real: Conventions and Ideology*. Oxford: Oxford University Press, 2016.

James, Henry. "Daniel Deronda: A Conversation." 1876. In *The Critical Muse: Selected Literary Criticism*, edited by Roger Gard, 104–22. Harmondsworth, UK: Penguin, 1987.

———. *The Portrait of a Lady*. Harmondsworth, UK: Penguin, 1984.

James, William. *The Principles of Psychology*. Vol. 1. New York: Dover, 1950.

Jenkins, Henry. "Textual Poachers." In *Fan Fiction Studies Reader*, edited by Karen Hellekson and Kristina Busse, 26–43. Iowa City: University of Iowa Press, 2014.

Johnson, Claudia. "F. R. Leavis: The 'Great Tradition' of the English Novel and the Jewish Part." *Nineteenth-Century Literature* 56, no. 2 (2001): 198–227.

———. *Jane Austen's Cults and Cultures*. Chicago: University of Chicago Press, 2012.

Johnson, Samuel. *The Yale Edition of the Works of Samuel Johnson: The Rambler*. Edited by W. J. Bate and Albrecht B. Strauss. 14 vols. New Haven, CT: Yale University Press, 1969.

Jordan, John, and Robert Patten, eds. *Literature in the Marketplace: Nineteenth-Century British Publishing and Reading Practices*. Cambridge: Cambridge University Press, 1995.

Kaplan, Fred. *Dickens: A Biography*. 1988. Baltimore, MD: Johns Hopkins University Press, 1998.

———. *Dickens and Mesmerism: The Hidden Springs of Fiction*. Princeton, NJ: Princeton University Press, 1975.

Kearns, Michael. *Metaphors of Mind in Fiction and Psychology*. Lexington: University Press of Kentucky, 1987.

Keen, Suzanne. *Empathy and the Novel*. Oxford: Oxford University Press, 2007.

Klancher, Jon. *The Making of English Reading Audiences, 1790–1832*. Madison: University of Wisconsin Press, 1987.

Knox, Maria Palacios. *Victorian Women and Wayward Reading: Crises of Identification*. Cambridge: Cambridge University Press, 2020.

Kramnick, Jonathan. "Criticism and Truth." *Critical Inquiry* 47, no. 2 (2021): 218–40.

Kreisel, Deanna. "Where Does the Pleasure Come From? The Marriage Plot and Its Discontents in Jane Austen's *Emma*." *Persuasions: The Jane Austen Journal* 29 (2007): 217–27.

Kurnick, David. "Abstraction and the Subject of Novel Reading: Drifting through *Romola*." *Novel: A Forum on Fiction* 42, no. 3 (2009): 490–96.

———. "An Erotics of Detachment: *Middlemarch* and Novel-Reading as Critical Practice." *ELH* 74, no. 3 (2007): 583–608.

———. "Unspeakable George Eliot." *Victorian Literature and Culture* 38, no. 2 (2010): 489–509.

Kusher, Betty. "Dreams, Reveries, and the Continuity of Consciousness in Three Nineteenth-Century Novelists." *Journal of Evolutionary Psychology* 15 (1994): 112–28.

Lane, Christopher. *Hatred and Civility: The Antisocial Life in Victorian England.* New York: Columbia University Press, 2004.

Langan, Celeste. *Romantic Vagrancy: Wordsworth and the Simulation of Freedom.* Cambridge: Cambridge University Press, 1995.

Leavis, F. R. "Gwendolen Harleth." *London Review of Books*, January 21, 1982.

Leavis, Q. D. *Fiction and the Reading Public.* 1932. London: Chatto and Windus, 1965.

Le Faye, Deirdre, ed. *Jane Austen's Letters.* Oxford: Oxford University Press, 1995.

Levine, Caroline. *The Serious Pleasures of Suspense: Victorian Realism and Narrative Doubt.* Charlottesville: University Press of Virginia, 2003.

———. "Surprising Realism." In Anderson and Shaw, *A Companion to George Eliot*, 62–75.

Levine, George. *The Realistic Imagination: English Fiction from "Frankenstein" to "Lady Chatterley."* Chicago: University of Chicago Press, 1981.

Lewes, G. H. "Consciousness and Unconsciousness." *Mind* 2 (1877): 156–67.

———. "Dickens in Relation to Criticism." *Fortnightly Review* 17, 1872.

———. *First Series: The Foundations of a Creed; Problems of Life and Mind.* Vol. 2. London: Trubner, 1875.

———. "The Novels of Jane Austen." *Blackwood's Edinburgh Magazine* (July 1859): 99–113. In Southam, *Jane Austen: The Critical Heritage*, 148–66.

———. *The Physiology of Common Life.* 2 vols. New York: D. Appleton, 1860.

Lonoff, Sue. *Wilkie Collins and His Victorian Readers.* New York: AMS Press, 1982.

Looser, Devoney. *The Making of Jane Austen.* Baltimore, MD: Johns Hopkins University Press, 2017.

Lupton, Christina. "Contingency, Codex, and the Eighteenth-Century Novel." *ELH* 81, no. 4 (2014): 1173–92.

———. *Knowing Books: The Consciousness of Mediation in Eighteenth-Century Britain.* Philadelphia: University of Pennsylvania Press, 2011.

Lynch, Deidre. *The Economy of Character: Novels, Market Culture, and the Business of Inner Meaning.* Chicago: University of Chicago Press, 1998.

———. *Janeites: Austen's Disciples and Devotees.* Edited by Deidre Lynch. Princeton, NJ: Princeton University Press, 2000.

———. *Loving Literature: A Cultural History.* Chicago: University of Chicago Press, 2015.

Machor, James. "Introduction: Readers/Texts/Contexts." In *Readers in History: Nineteenth-Century American Literature and the Contexts of Response*, edited by James Machor, vii–xxix. Baltimore, MD: Johns Hopkins University Press, 1993.

MacNish, Robert. *The Philosophy of Sleep.* New York: D. Appleton, 1834.

Main, Alexander. *Letters from Alexander Main, 1871–1876.* Edinburgh: National Library of Scotland.

[Mansel, Henry.] "Sensation Novels." *Quarterly Review* 113 (1863): 482–514.

Marcus, Sharon, and Stephen Best. "Surface Reading: An Introduction." *Representations* 108, no. 1 (2009): 1–21.

Marcus, Steven. *Representations: Essays on Literature and Society*. New York: Random House, 1974.

Martin, Carol. "Contemporary Critics and Judaism in *Daniel Deronda*." *Victorian Periodicals Review* 21, no. 3 (1988): 90–107.

———. *George Eliot's Serial Fiction*. Columbus: Ohio State University Press, 1994.

Matus, Jill. *Shock, Memory and the Unconscious in Victorian Fiction*. Cambridge: Cambridge University Press, 2009.

———. "Trauma, Memory, and Railway Disaster: The Dickensian Connection." *Victorian Studies* 43 (2001): 413–36.

———. "Victorian Framings of the Mind: Recent Work on Mid-Nineteenth Century Theories of the Unconscious, Memory, and Emotion." *Literature Compass Online* 4, no. 4 (2007): 1257–76.

Maudsley, Henry. *The Physiology of Mind*. 1867. New York: D. Appleton, 1878.

Maunder, Andrew, ed. *Varieties of Women's Sensation Fiction: 1855–1890*. Vol. 1, *Sensationalism and the Sensation Debate*. London: Pickering, 2004.

Mays, Kelly. "The Disease of Reading and Victorian Periodicals." In *Literature in the Marketplace: Nineteenth-Century British Publishing and Reading Practices*, edited by John Jordan and Robert Patten, 165–94. Cambridge: Cambridge University Press, 1995.

McAleavey, Maia. "Anti-Individualism in the Victorian Family Chronicle." *NOVEL: A Forum on Fiction* 53, no. 2 (2020): 213–34.

Mead, Rebecca. *My Life in Middlemarch*. New York: Crown, 2014.

———. "The Scourge of 'Relatability.'" *New Yorker*, August 1, 2014.

Mill, John Stuart. *Autobiography*. Harmondsworth, UK: Penguin, 1989.

Miller, Andrew H. *The Burdens of Perfection: On Ethics and Reading in Nineteenth-Century British Literature*. Ithaca, NY: Cornell University Press, 2008.

———. "'A Case of Metaphysics': Counterfactuals, *Great Expectations*, Realism." *ELH* 79, no. 3 (2012): 773–96.

———. *On Not Being Someone Else: Tales of Our Unled Lives*. Cambridge, MA: Harvard University Press, 2020.

———. "Perfectly Helpless." *Modern Language Quarterly* 63 (2002): 65–88.

———. "Wasting the Invincible Energy of Young Years." Paper presented at the Mahindra Humanities Center, Cambridge, Massachusetts, April 2003.

Miller, D. A. *Jane Austen, or The Secret of Style*. Princeton, NJ: Princeton University Press, 2003.

———. *Narrative and Its Discontents: Problems of Closure in the Traditional Novel*. Princeton, NJ: Princeton University Press, 1981.

———. *The Novel and the Police*. Berkeley: University of California Press, 1988.

Miller, J. Hillis. *Black Holes*. Stanford, CA: Stanford University Press, 1999.

———. Introduction to *Bleak House* by Charles Dickens. Harmondsworth, UK: Penguin, 1971.

———. "Narrative and History." *ELH* 41, no. 3 (1974): 455–73.

———. *Reading for Our Time: "Adam Bede" and "Middlemarch" Revisited*. Edinburgh: Edinburgh University Press, 2012.

Mitchell, Rebecca. *Victorian Lessons in Empathy and Difference*. Columbus: Ohio State University Press, 2011.

Molesworth, Jesse. "'A Dreadful Course of Calamities': *Roxana's* Ending Reconsidered." *ELH* 74, no. 2 (2007): 493–508.

Morris, Mowbray. "Charles Dickens." *Fortnightly Review*, December 1, 1882, 762–79. In Collins, *Dickens: The Critical Heritage*, 599–611.

Morson, Gary Saul. *Narrative and Freedom: The Shadows of Time*. New Haven, CT: Yale University Press, 1994.

[Mozley, Anne.] Review of *Adam Bede*. *Bentley's Quarterly Review*, July 1859, 433–56. In Carroll, *George Eliot: The Critical Heritage*, 86–103.

Muñoz, José Esteban. *Disidentifications: Queers of Color and the Performance of Politics*. Minneapolis: University of Minnesota Press, 1999.

Murphy, Olivia. *Jane Austen the Reader: The Artist as Critic*. London: Palgrave, 2013.

Nayder, Lillian. *Unequal Partners: Charles Dickens, Wilkie Collins, and Victorian Authorship*. Ithaca, NY: Cornell University Press, 2002.

Nell, Victor. *Lost in a Book: The Psychology of Reading for Pleasure*. New Haven, CT: Yale University Press, 1988.

Newlyn, Lucy. *Reading, Writing, and Romanticism: The Anxiety of Reception*. Oxford: Oxford University Press, 2000.

Ngai, Sianne. *Ugly Feelings*. Cambridge, MA: Harvard University Press, 2005.

Norquay, Glenda. *Robert Louis Stevenson and Theories of Reading: The Reader as Vagabond*. Manchester, UK: Manchester University Press, 2007.

Northcote, Stafford Henry (Earl of Iddesleigh). *The Pleasures, the Dangers, and the Uses of Desultory Reading*. West Kensington, London: Kegan Paul, Trench, 1885.

"Novels, Past and Present." *Saturday Review*, April 14, 1866, 438–40.

Nunokawa, Jeff. "Eros and Isolation: The Antisocial George Eliot." *ELH* 69 (2002): 835–60.

———. "Speechless in Austen." *differences* 16 (2005): 1–36.

O'Gorman, Francis, ed. *A Concise Companion to the Victorian Novel*. Malden, MA: Blackwell, 2005.

———. "'A Long Deep Sob of that Mysterious Wondrous Happiness that Is One with Pain': Emotion in the Victorian Novel." In O'Gorman, *Concise Companion*, 253–70.

Oliphant, Margaret. "Novels." *Blackwood's Edinburgh Magazine* 102 (1867): 257–80.

———. "Sensation Novels." *Blackwood's Edinburgh Magazine* 91 (1862): 564–84.

Olmsted, John Charles, ed. *A Victorian Art of Fiction: Essays on the Novel in British Periodicals, 1830–1850*. New York: Garland, 1979.

"Opinions of *Mansfield Park* and *Emma*." In *The Works of Jane Austen*. Vol. 6, *Minor Works*, edited by R. W. Chapman, 431–39. Oxford: Oxford University Press, 1954.

Orwell, George. "Charles Dickens." 1940. In *Dickens, Dali, and Others*. San Diego, CA: Harcourt, 1973.

———. "Politics and the English Language." *Horizon*, April 1946.

Oulton, Carolyn W. de la L. *Dickens and the Myth of the Reader*. London: Routledge, 2017.

Oxford English Dictionary. Paperback. 7th edition. Oxford: Oxford University Press, 2013.

Palmer, Beth, and Adelene Buckland, eds. *A Return to the Common Reader: Print Culture and the Novel, 1850–1900*. Farnham, Surrey: Ashgate, 2011.

Patten, Robert. *Charles Dickens and His Publishers.* Oxford: Clarendon Press, 1978.

Pearson, Jacqueline. *Women's Reading in Britain, 1750–1835.* Cambridge: Cambridge University Press, 1999.

Pennington, Sarah. *A Mother's Advice to Her Absent Daughters.* New York: Garland, 1986. Quoted in *Novel Instruction: Reading, Pedagogy, and the Ideal of Innocence in Eighteenth-Century British Fiction* by Tamar Brown. Harvard University, PhD dissertation, 2006.

Perkins, David. "Romantic Reading as Revery." *European Romantic Review* 4 (1994): 183–99.

Phillips, Natalie. *Distraction: Problems of Attention in Eighteenth-Century Literature.* Baltimore, MD: Johns Hopkins University Press, 2016.

Picciotto, James. "Deronda the Jew." *Gentleman's Magazine,* November 1876, 593–603. In Carroll, *George Eliot: The Critical Heritage,* 406–17.

Picker, John. "George Eliot and the Sequel Question." *New Literary History* 37 (2006): 361–88.

Pinch, Adela. "*The Mill on the Floss* and *The Lifted Veil*: Prediction, Prevention, Protection." In Anderson and Shaw, *A Companion to George Eliot,* 117–28.

———. *Strange Fits of Passion: Epistemologies of Emotion, Hume to Austen.* Stanford, CA: Stanford University Press, 1996.

———. *Thinking about Other People in Nineteenth-Century British Writing.* Cambridge: Cambridge University Press, 2010.

Piper, Andrew. *Dreaming in Books: The Making of the Bibliographic Imagination in the Romantic Age.* Chicago: University of Chicago Press, 2009.

Plotz, John. "Mediated Involvement: John Stuart Mill's Antisocial Sociability." In Ablow, *Feeling of Reading,* 69–92.

———. "No Future? The Novel's Pasts." *Novel: A Forum on Fiction* 44, no. 1 (2011): 23–26.

———. *Semi-Detached: The Aesthetics of Virtual Experience since Dickens.* Princeton, NJ: Princeton University Press, 2018.

Poovey, Mary. *The Proper Lady and the Woman Writer: Ideology as Style in the Works of Mary Wollstonecraft, Mary Shelley, and Jane Austen.* Chicago: University of Chicago Press, 1984.

Price, Leah. *The Anthology and the Rise of the Novel.* Cambridge: Cambridge University Press, 2000.

———. *How to Do Things with Books in Victorian Britain.* Princeton, NJ: Princeton University Press, 2012.

———. "Reader's Block: Response." *Victorian Studies* 46 (2004): 231–42.

———. "Reader's Block: Trollope and the Book as Prop." In Ablow, *Feeling of Reading,* 47–68.

———. "Reading: The State of the Discipline." *Book History* 7 (2004): 303–20.

Radway, Janice. *A Feeling for Books: The Book of the Month Club, Literary Taste, and Middle-Class Desire.* Chapel Hill: University of North Carolina Press, 1997.

———. "Reading Is Not Eating: Mass-Produced Literature and the Theoretical, Methodological, and Political Consequences of a Metaphor." *Book Research Quarterly* 2, no. 3 (1986): 7–29.

———. *Reading the Romance: Women, Patriarchy, and Popular Culture.* Chapel Hill: University of North Carolina Press, 1984.

Raines, Melissa. *George Eliot's Grammar of Being.* London: Anthem, 2011.

Raven, James. "The Anonymous Novel in Britain and Ireland, 1750–1830." In *The Faces of Anonymity: Anonymous and Pseudonymous Publications from the Sixteenth to the Twentieth Century*, edited by Robert J. Griffin, 141–66. London: Palgrave, 2003.

Raven, James, Helen Small, and Naomi Tadmor, eds. *The Practice and Representation of Reading in England*. Cambridge: Cambridge University Press, 1996.

"Reading as a Means of Culture." *Sharpe's London Magazine* 31, no. 46 (1867): 316–23.

"Recent Works of Fiction." *Prospective Review* 9 (April 30, 1853): 222–47. In Eigner and Worth, *Victorian Criticism*, 84–92.

Reed, Edward S. *From Soul to Mind: The Emergence of Psychology from Erasmus Darwin to William James*. New Haven, CT: Yale University Press, 1997.

Review of *Bleak House. Bentley's Miscellany*, October 1853, 372–74. In Collins, *Dickens: The Critical Heritage*, 287–89.

Review of *Daniel Deronda. Saturday Review*, September 16, 1876, 356–58. In Carroll, *George Eliot: The Critical Heritage*, 376–81.

Review of *Life and Adventures of Peter Wilkins. Retrospective Review* (1823): 131–35. In Southam, *Jane Austen: The Critical Heritage*, 107–11.

Review of *Little Dorrit. Leader*, June 27, 1857, 616–17. In Collins, *Dickens: The Critical Heritage*, 362–65.

Review of *The Mill on the Floss. Saturday Review*, April 14, 1860, 470–71. In Carroll, *George Eliot: The Critical Heritage*, 114–19.

Review of *Our Mutual Friend. London Review*, October 28, 1865, 467–68. In Collins, *Dickens: The Critical Heritage*, 454–58.

Richards, I. A. *Practical Criticism: A Study of Literary Judgment.* 1929. New York: Harcourt, Brace, 2021.

Richardson, Alan. *British Romanticism and the Science of the Mind*. Cambridge: Cambridge University Press, 2001.

Richter, David. "The Reception of the Gothic Novel in the 1790s." In *The Idea of the Novel in the Eighteenth Century*, edited by Robert Uphaus, 117–37. East Lansing, MI: Colleagues Press, 1988.

Robson, David. "There Really Are 50 Eskimo Words for Snow." *Washington Post*, January 13, 2014.

Rohrbach, Emily. *Modernity's Mist: British Romanticism and the Poetics of Anticipation*. New York: Fordham University Press, 2016.

Rose, Jonathan. *The Intellectual Life of the British Working Classes*. New Haven, CT: Yale University Press, 2001.

Rozema, Patricia. *Mansfield Park*. Miramax, 1999.

Rubery, Matthew. *The Novelty of Newspapers: Victorian Fiction after the Invention of the News*. Oxford: Oxford University Press, 2009.

Ryan, Judith. *The Vanishing Subject: Early Psychology and Literary Modernism*. Chicago: University of Chicago Press, 1991.

Ryan, Vanessa. *Thinking without Thinking in the Victorian Novel*. Baltimore, MD: Johns Hopkins University Press, 2012.

Rylance, Rick. *Victorian Psychology and British Culture, 1850–1880*. Oxford: Oxford University Press, 2000.

Saintsbury, George. Review of *Daniel Deronda*. *Academy*, September 9, 1876, 253–54. In Carroll, *George Eliot: The Critical Heritage*, 374–55.

Salisbury, Laura. "Relatable." *Textual Practice* 30, no. 7 (2016): 1156–57.

Samalin, Zachary. *The Masses Are Revolting: Victorian Culture and the Political Aesthetics of Disgust*. Ithaca, NY: Cornell University Press, 2021.

Scarry, Elaine. *Dreaming by the Book*. New York: Farrar, Straus and Giroux, 1999.

Schor, Hilary. "Novels of the 1850s: *Hard Times, Little Dorrit*, and *A Tale of Two Cities*." In *The Cambridge Companion to Charles Dickens*, edited by John Jordan, 64–77. Cambridge: Cambridge University Press, 2001.

Schultze, Clemence. "More than Meets the Eye: Moritz Retzsch and *The Chess-Players*." *Journal (Charlotte M. Yonge Fellowship)* 10 (2011): 102–12.

[Scott, Walter.] Review of *Emma*. *Quarterly Review*, October 1815, 188–201. In Southam, *Jane Austen: The Critical Heritage*, 58–69.

Seafield, Frank, ed. *The Literature and Curiosities of Dreams: A Commonplace Book*. Vol. 1. London: Chapman and Hall, 1865.

Shuttleworth, Sally. "Fairy Tale or Science? Physiological Psychology in *Silas Marner*." In *Languages of Nature: Critical Essays on Science and Literature*, edited by L. J. Jordanova, 244–87. New Brunswick, NJ: Rutgers University Press, 1986.

———. *George Eliot and Nineteenth-Century Science: The Make-Believe of a Beginning*. Cambridge: Cambridge University Press, 1984.

———. "Language of Science and Psychology in George Eliot's *Daniel Deronda*." In *Victorian Science and Victorian Values: Literary Perspectives*, edited by James Paradis and Thomas Postlewait, 269–98. New Brunswick, NJ: Rutgers University Press, 1985.

Silver, Brenda R. "'Anon' and 'The Reader': Virginia Woolf's Last Essays." *Twentieth Century Literature* 25, no. 3–4 (1979): 356–441.

Simons, Judy. "Jane Austen and Popular Culture." In *A Companion to Jane Austen*, edited by Claudia Johnson and Clara Tuite, 467–77. Chichester, UK: Wiley-Blackwell, 2009.

Small, Helen. "George Eliot and the Cosmopolitan Cynic." *Victorian Studies* 55, no. 1 (2012): 85–105.

———. "A Pulse of 124: Charles Dickens and a Pathology of the Mid-Victorian Reading Public." In Raven, Small, and Tadmor, *The Practice and Representation of Reading in England*, 263–90.

Smith, Adam. *The Theory of Moral Sentiments*. Edited by D. D. Raphael and A. L. Macfie. Oxford: Clarendon Press, 1976.

Smith, Roger. "The Physiology of the Will: Mind, Body, and Psychology in the Periodical Literature, 1855–1875." In *Science Serialized: Representations of the Sciences in Nineteenth-Century Periodicals*, edited by Sally Shuttleworth and Geoffrey Cantor, 81–110. Cambridge, MA: MIT Press, 2004.

Southam, Brian, ed. *Jane Austen: The Critical Heritage*. London: Routledge, 1968.

———. *Jane Austen's Literary Manuscripts: A Study of the Novelist's Development through the Surviving Papers*. London: Athlone Press, 2001.

Spacks, Patricia Meyer. *Privacy: Concealing the Eighteenth-Century Self*. Chicago: University of Chicago Press, 2003.

Stang, Richard. *The Theory of the Novel in England, 1850–1870*. New York: Columbia University Press, 1959.

Stauffer, Andrew. *Book Traces: Nineteenth-Century Readers and the Future of the Library*. Philadelphia: University of Pennsylvania Press, 2021.

St Clair, William. *The Reading Nation in the Romantic Period*. Cambridge: Cambridge University Press, 2004.

[Stephen, Leslie.] Obituary of George Eliot. *Cornhill Magazine*, February 1881, 152–68. In Carroll, *George Eliot: The Critical Heritage*, 464–84.

Stevenson, Robert Louis. "A Gossip on Romance." In *The Works of Robert Louis Stevenson: South Seas Edition*. Vol. 13. New York: Scribner's, 1925.

Stewart, Dugald. *Elements of the Philosophy of the Human Mind*. 1792. Boston: W. H. Dennet, 1866.

Stewart, Garrett. *Dear Reader: The Conscripted Audience in Nineteenth-Century British Fiction*. Baltimore, MD: Johns Hopkins University Press, 1996.

———. *Dickens and the Trials of Imagination*. Cambridge, MA: Harvard University Press, 1974.

Stiles, Stefanie. "From 'Representative' to Relatable: Constructing Pedagogical Canons Based on Student Ethical Engagement." *Pedagogy: Critical Approaches to Teaching Literature, Language, Composition, and Culture* 13, no. 3 (2013): 487–503.

Stolte, Tyson. *Dickens and Victorian Psychology: Introspection, First-Person Narration, and the Mind*. Oxford: Oxford University Press, 2022.

Stone, Harry. *Dickens and the Invisible World: Fairy Tales, Fantasy, and Novel-Making*. Bloomington: Indiana University Press, 1979.

Stonehouse, J. H., ed. *Catalogue of the Library of Charles Dickens from Gadshill*. London: Piccadilly Fountain Press, 1935.

Sully, James. *My Life and Friends: A Psychologist's Memories*. London: T. Fisher Unwin, 1918.

———. *Outlines of Psychology*. London: Longman, 1885.

———. *Sensation and Intuition: Studies in Psychology and Aesthetics*. London, 1880.

Sun, Emily. *On the Horizon of World Literature: Forms of Modernity in Romantic England and Republican China*. New York: Fordham University Press, 2021.

Sutherland, John. *Victorian Fiction: Writers, Publishers, Readers*. Basingstoke, Hampshire: Macmillan, 1995.

Tadmor, Naomi. "'In the Even My Wife Read to Me': Women, Reading, and Household Life in the Eighteenth Century." In Raven, Small, and Tadmor, *The Practice and Representation of Reading in England*, 162–74

Tanner, Tony. *Jane Austen*. Cambridge, MA: Harvard University Press, 1986.

Taylor, Jenny Bourne. *In the Secret Theatre of Home: Wilkie Collins, Sensation Narrative, and Nineteenth-Century Psychology*. London: Routledge, 1988.

———. "Obscure Recesses: Locating the Victorian Unconscious." In *Writing and Victorianism*, edited by J. B. Bullen, 137–79. London: Longman, 1997.

Taylor, Jenny Bourne, and Sally Shuttleworth, eds. *Embodied Selves: An Anthology of Psychological Texts, 1830–1900*. Oxford: Clarendon Press, 1998.

Thomas, Ronald. *Dreams of Authority: Freud and the Fictions of the Unconscious*. Ithaca, NY: Cornell University Press, 1990.

Thompson, Andrew. *George Eliot and Italy: Literary, Cultural and Political Influences from Dante to the Risorgimento*. Basingstoke, Hampshire: Macmillan, 1998.

Tondre, Michael. *The Physics of Possibility: Victorian Fiction, Science, and Gender*. Charlottesville: University of Virginia Press, 2018.

Trilling, Lionel. Introduction to *Little Dorrit*, by Charles Dickens. Oxford: Oxford University Press, 1953. Reprint in *Charles Dickens: A Critical Anthology*, edited by Stephen Wall, 363–75. Harmondsworth, UK: Penguin, 1970.

Trollope, Anthony. *An Autobiography*. Edited by Michael Sadleir and Frederick Page. Oxford: Oxford University Press, 1999.

———. *Barchester Towers*. Edited by Michael Sadleir and Frederick Page. Oxford: Oxford University Press, 1998.

———. "On English Prose Fiction as a Rational Amusement." In *Four Lectures*, edited by Morris Parrish, 94–124. London: Constable, 1938.

———. *The Small House at Allington*. Edited by Julian Thompson. Harmondsworth, UK: Penguin, 1991.

Uglow, Jennifer. *George Eliot*. London: Virago, 1987.

Vincent, David. *Literacy and Popular Culture: England, 1750–1914*. Cambridge: Cambridge University Press, 1989.

Vrettos, Athena. "Dickens and the Psychology of Repetition." *Victorian Studies* 42 (1999/2000): 399–426.

Wall, Stephen, ed. *Charles Dickens: A Critical Anthology*. Harmondsworth, UK: Penguin, 1970.

Warhol, Robyn. "'What Might Have Been Is Not What Is': Dickens's Narrative Refusals." *Dickens Studies Annual* 41, no. 1 (2010): 45–59.

Warner, Michael. "Uncritical Reading." In *Polemic: Critical or Uncritical*, edited by Jane Gallop, 13–38. New York: Routledge, 2004.

Warner, William. *Licensing Entertainment: The Elevation of Novel Reading in Britain, 1684–1750*. Berkeley: University of California Press, 1998.

Welsh, Alexander. *George Eliot and Blackmail*. Cambridge, MA: Harvard University Press, 1985.

[Whately, Richard.] Review of *Northanger Abbey* and *Persuasion*. *Quarterly Review*, January 1821, 352–76. In Southam, *Jane Austen: The Critical Heritage*, 87–105.

Whyte, Lancelot Law. *The Unconscious before Freud*. London: Tavistock, 1960.

Winter, Alison. *Mesmerized: Powers of Mind in Victorian Britain*. Chicago: University of Chicago Press, 1998.

Winter, Sarah. *The Pleasures of Memory: Learning to Read with Charles Dickens*. New York: Fordham University Press, 2011.

Woolf, Virginia. *The Common Reader: First Series*. Annotated edition. San Diego, CA: Harcourt, 1984.

———. "How Should One Read a Book?" In *The Second Common Reader*, annotated edition, 258–70. San Diego, CA: Harcourt, 1986.

———. *Orlando*. San Diego, CA: Harcourt, 1996.

———. *The Second Common Reader*. Annotated edition. San Diego, CA: Harcourt, 1986.

Wordsworth, William, and Samuel Taylor Coleridge. *Lyrical Ballads: 1798 and 1802*. Edited by Fiona Stafford. Oxford: Oxford University Press, 2013.

Wright, Daniel. "George Eliot's Vagueness." *Victorian Studies* 56, no. 4 (2014): 625–48.

Wynne, Deborah. *The Sensation Novel and the Victorian Family Magazine*. London: Palgrave, 2001.

Yeazell, Ruth. *Art of the Everyday: Dutch Painting and the Realist Novel.* Princeton, NJ: Princeton University Press, 2009.

———. *Fictions of Modesty: Women and Courtship in the English Novel.* Chicago: University of Chicago Press, 1991.

Young, Kay. *Imagining Minds: The Neuro-Aesthetics of Austen, Eliot, and Hardy.* Columbus: Ohio State University Press, 2010.

Zunshine, Lisa. *Why We Read Fiction: Theory of Mind and the Novel.* Columbus: Ohio State University Press, 2006.

INDEX

A NOTE ON THE TYPE

This book has been composed in Arno, an Old-style serif typeface in the classic Venetian tradition, designed by Robert Slimbach at Adobe.

Printed in the USA
CPSIA information can be obtained
at www.ICGtesting.com
JSHW020750030724
65820JS00002B/8